The Presence of the Dead in Our Lives

The Presence of the Dead in Our Lives

Edited by

Nate Hinerman and Julia Apollonia Glahn

Amsterdam - New York, NY 2012

The paper on which this book is printed meets the requirements of "ISO 9706:1994, Information and documentation - Paper for documents - Requirements for permanence".

ISBN: 978-90-420-3577-5
E-Book ISBN: 978-94-012-0852-9
©Editions Rodopi B.V., Amsterdam - New York, NY 2012
Printed in the Netherlands

Table of Contents

Introduction
The Presence of the Dead in Our Lives   vii
Nate Hinerman and Julia Apollonia Glahn

Part 1   Death, Presence, and the Self

Pragmatic Immortality and the Insignificance of My Own
Death   3
Peter Caws

On the Notion of Presence and its Importance for a Concept
of Dignity of the Dead   15
Julia Apollonia Glahn

The Deathless Self: Death and Immortality in the
Discourse of Vedanta   37
Dhruv Raj Nagar

Sites that Cope, Cure and Commemorate: Weblogs
of Terminally Ill   55
Marga Altena and Nothando Ngwenya

Survivor's Guilt in Caretakers of Cancer   77
*Shulamith Kreitler, Frida Barak, Yasmin Alkalay,
and Nava Siegelman-Danieli*

Part 2   Death, Presence, and Ritual

The Haunt/Demons and The Complex of Noon   101
Tolulope Onabolu

Planning a Funeral: The Encounter between Bereaved
and Officiant   117
Glenys Caswell

Living with the Dead: Cremating and Reburying the
Dead in a Megalopolis   139
Marcel Reyes-Cortez

Heroic Death and Selective Memory: The US's WWII
Memorial and the USSR's Monument to the Heroic
Defenders of Leningrad   165
Susan M. Behuniak

Preserving the Dead in the Lives of the Living   185
Nate Hinerman

Introduction: The Presence of the Dead in Our Lives

Nate Hinerman and Julia Apollonia Glahn

We are all survivors. Even if we have not experienced the death of someone close, we are survivors of losses that occur in our lives because of changes and endings. In its most humble ambition, this text surveys the strata of such experiences, to see whether by sharing such stories we can understand our own respective experiences of loss and those of others a little better. Yet, this book is not intended to be a guidebook per se for enduring the terrain of grief, nor one that promises 'strategies' as such for coping with death. Instead, the research design of this volume involves an inter-disciplinary appreciation for how various cultural phenomena reflect the knowledge and system of meanings that guide individual and cultural responses to mortality. As a result, this volume emerges more like a series of ethnographies rather than as an example of self-help literature, or as something more methodologically philosophical.

Included here is a selection of articles from authors representing a wide array of disciplines, all of whom participated in the 6th global conference entitled, 'Making Sense of: Dying and Death,' sponsored by Inter-Disciplinary.Net in 2008 in Salzburg, Austria. This conference centred its attention on the following theme: how does the presence of the dead take life in the hearts and minds of the living? At the very core of this idea stands the assumption that even when individuals die, they can indeed remain 'present.' But how? This volume provides a series of articles that address this very question. The guiding presumption here is that although every life will end, one's narrative can indeed continue. Of course, the very essence of mourning presumes that by integrating the deceased in one's life narrative, the dead can survive in some meaningful way. Such an existence may take a variety of forms, and be sponsored by myriad acts of commemoration and recollection. Dutifully engraving a name on a tombstone, passing a decedent's name on within a family, and honouring the decedent's will are common ways one's presence is commemorated and respected. However, survivors can meaningfully recollect the deceased in other ways, perhaps by adopting the decedent's principles and virtues, or even by modelling certain traits and habits.

Hence, the continued 'presence' of the dead is constituted by the very practices and activities we engaged in while they were alive. As a result, interacting with the deceased is, for some, at least analogous to relationships enjoyed *prior to* the death. Language takes this fascinating phenomenon into account. The words we often use when referring to the dead are almost always applicable to living persons as well. Such expressions help to frame the experience of loss while making it easier to orient oneself to the loss. This becomes even more obvious when we study common euphemisms used to describe a person's death: 'eternal slumber,' the 'fallen soldier,' 'crossed the river,' 'hung up their hats,' 'passed onward.' All of these descriptions contain images of life, and include action verbs for tasks done by the living.

Whatever silhouette of the deceased that is mirrored and fashioned in the hearts of others, such manifestations demonstrate the continuity of the decedent's life and story in those who are alive. There are infinite ways that the 'presence' of the dead can be realised and lived. This volume aims to explore how.

In the first section, 'Death, Presence, and the Self,' **Peter Caws** begins by approaching philosophically the prospects of human immortality. In his approach, human beings are considered to be more than mere biological entities; they are in fact transcendental subjects. As such, humans do not have empirical knowledge about their own death. All anticipations of mortality must necessarily come then from the 'outside' (i.e., from those still living). 'This situation satisfies the Aristotelian definition of infinity,' Caws concludes, which, as lived subjectivity, is 'equivalent to immortality.' Caws, however, does not assume that human beings are *practically* immortal. Yet, since we do not 'live' our own ends, perhaps 'death,' as an assigned label, may matter less than otherwise presumed.

Julia Apollonia Glahn expands the basic concept of human dignity beyond that routinely assigned to individuals, and emphasises the social moment of human dignity which manifests itself through personal interactions. By interacting with others in certain fundamental ways, human beings create a realm in which the *conditions* for human dignity arise. Glahn shows how one can ascribe dignity to all human beings, regardless of their mental or physical capacities or stage of development, and then shows how one can ascribe dignity to dead human beings (i.e., corpses). Glahn focuses on how dead bodies maintain an immaterial presence, and she makes a compelling case for why the dead retain *human* dignity, and as such, are still very much subjects for whom dignity should be bestowed.

Dhruv Raj Nagar analyses the concepts of immortality ('preservation') and dignity from a different point of view. Using wisdom found in the *Upanishads*, Nagar elaborates ancient Indian philosophical ideas to amplify contemporary understandings of death. At the centre of Nagar's vision is the notion that, 'the self … is immortal and does not perish at the time of death.' Nagar goes on to argue that, paradoxically, by becoming aware of death in 'the midst of life and activity,' we can live a fuller, more engaged life. Nagar's article expands how this is possible.

Marga Altena and **Nothando Ngwenya** present cutting-edge research regarding how the terminally ill can use weblogs to express their attitudes and emotions about dying, and to find companionship in the process. The findings here support the conclusion that weblogs provide an innovative tool to experience, reflect on, and discover affect; they also provide practical ways to plan for death (e.g., funeral preparations). Weblogs can also *mediate* the complex sets of inter-relations between the dying and their family/friends, and give the latter ways to express their grief and locate coping strategies during the weblog encounters. Such logs provide an on-going means for remembrance, and can even function as an on-line archive.

The concluding paper from this section focuses on the psychological phenomenon of *survivors guilt* . **Shulamith Kreitler, Frida Barak, Yasmin Alkalay**, and **Nava Siegelman-Danieli** describe this phenomenon and explain its correlates, functions and consequences. Furthermore, they present findings of an important study on caregivers of cancer patients. Their results support the claim that survivor's guilt is indeed a distinct form of remorse. This article explores the taproots of this affective experience, and what might be done to address it, both before and after a death.

In the second section of this book, 'Death, Presence, and Ritual,' the focus shifts to practical contexts for acknowledging the presence of the dead. In the first article, **Tolulope Onabolu** elaborates how the transformation of the soul in dying can be understood as an 'awakening.' Through an ingenious use of art and architecture, Tolulope weaves historical locations into a larger, more ephemeral landscape that emerges in 'the Haunt of the Magicians,' 'the Noon Complex,' and 'Lequeu's Gothic House.' The article concludes by considering how dying and death can give rise to experiences of 'passage.'

Glenys Caswell's article explores encounters between bereaved persons and funerary officiants in Scotland. Although only a minority of the population self-identifies as 'religious,' most funeral ceremonies still take place in a church, where services are conducted by a minister. Caswell describes how when certain funerary traditions fade, culture must discover/uncover alternative ways to remember the dead, which include developing meaningful and appropriate ceremonies to honour those deceased. Caswell invokes Norbert Elias' game model to identify and describe six different games that might emerge during the funeral planning process, and she presents ideas for how each can be practically addressed.

Marcel Reyes-Cortez utilises his expertise in photography to discuss very distinctive ways to keep the dead present for the living. Marcel describes how Mexico City, as one the world's largest megalopolises, deals with its increasing number of dead bodies. Marcel argues that even though cremation offers a feasible solution to dispose of the dead, it is still met with considerable resistance among many religious residents in Mexico. As a result, Marcel elaborates latent *cultural tools* that can enable the bereaved to maintain the dead as active participants in the lives and spirituality of the living.

Next, **Susan M. Behuniak**'s article explores how dead soldiers can be memorialised, and she compares and contrasts two World War II memorials, one in the United States and the other in Russia. Besides honouring the fallen soldiers, both memorials seek to impart a certain political rhetoric: dying for one's country in war is a heroic death, one worthy of the personal sacrifice. The politicised agenda of these memorials asks observers not only to enter a shared 'collective' memory of past events as told within a political system (e.g., a democratic narrative, a communist narrative, etc.), but these encounters also epitomise how 'memorials represent a complex nexus between politics, trauma, collective memory, and public art.'

In the final article of this volume, **Nate Hinerman** examines how one might use grief archives to study and validate experiences of grief and mourning. Using such archives provides a vehicle to share stories that promote individual and collective meaning-making. Moreover, they enable people to establish an alternative but no less meaningful relationship to the deceased. By writing and thus reflecting on their experiences with the dead, survivors keep the deceased a present part of their life. Furthermore, it enables individuals to '(re-)orient and (re-)frame their own histories/identities with the deceased within the context of a larger societal matrix.'

Finally, every death tells a story. The basic idea of this volume is that sharing these stories can provide emotional relief and promote a search for meaning for those who are grieving. These articles provide a panoply of alternatives for gathering support during times of loss. The authors here showcase how individuals and communities can revise, reform, and continue relationships with the deceased over time. The bonds sustained through memories and linking objects serve as 'threads of connectedness' to those deceased, whose deaths are grieved and remembered. The authors here also point out how such attachments form complex (and sometimes problematic) lineages through which individuals preserve, (re-)orient and (re-)frame their own histories/identities within the larger society.

As a closing word, the editors are privileged to be of service to this fascinating project of collaborative interdisciplinary research and would like to acknowledge those who made this volume possible: Daniel Riha, whose crucial leadership and hard work brought this volume to publication; Rob Fisher, whose vision as Network Leader of Inter-Disciplinary.Net continues to inspire us, and without whom none of this would have been possible; and Jessamine and Cana Quinn, who proved as patient with my time on this project as they do with my humour, and simply offered, 'no comment.'

Part 1

Death, Presence, and the Self

Pragmatic Immortality and the Insignificance of My Own Death

Peter Caws

Abstract
The human being who lives and dies, seen not as a biological entity but as a centre of experience and feeling, is a transcendental subject in the Husserlian sense, essentially temporal in its structure (though essentially timeless in its situation), essentially situated over against a world. 'Transcendental' means that the subject is not an object in its own world but is presupposed by the experienced unity of that world. The transcendental subject in time remembers past states and anticipates future ones, but can know neither its beginning nor its end. The one event of which the subject cannot have empirical knowledge is its own death. It can accept the prediction that its embodiment will cease, but this is to cast itself in the role of another, as seen from outside. It cannot anticipate its own cessation from within - at every moment into which it can imaginatively enter there will always be another moment to come. This situation satisfies the Aristotelian definition of infinity.[1] Infinity of lived subjectivity is equivalent to immortality. Put aphoristically and paradoxically, 'until the moment of death, everyone is immortal.' The point is not so much to make another argument for rising above a preoccupation with death, after the fashion of Spinoza or Wittgenstein, as to draw attention to the possibility of living an effective or pragmatic immortality, not being touched by death at all, suspending all attention to it, like a permanent phenomenological bracketing. But even if we accept and anticipate death it still matters less than most people think (and fear). My own sudden and painless death cannot possibly matter to me. And even pain can be borne. (My death can of course matter to others.) If life is animation, metabolism, endurance through time, death is nothing more or less than the suspension of these things, not temporarily as happens in sleep, for example, but definitively - and yet, to repeat, the subject cannot know that it is definitive. It does not live its own end.

Key Words: Death, immortality, infinity, pragmatic, transcendental subject.

*****

Preface

Diogenes of Oenoanda (2nd century CE) left a legacy to his fellow townspeople in the form of excerpts from the doctrines of Epicurus, carved into a wall in a public place.[2] Four of the principal maxims were:

> God is not feared
> Death is not felt
> Good is easily grasped
> Evil is easily overcome.

Subscription to these claims would clearly go some way to producing the *ataraxia*, or untroubled state, that the Epicureans valued. It is a state that is still desirable today. For the purposes of this communication I concentrate on the first two, since they are connected in the popular mind: death is feared, because God's judgment is feared, but also because death is associated with pain. 'Not felt' is *anaístheton*, which can mean without sensation but also with indifference; this can apply to death but also to what is taken to follow death.

To begin with the former: I remember being struck in a book I read as an adolescent, a great Antarctic adventure story by Apsley Cherry-Garrard called *The Worst Journey in the World*, with a passing remark as he is recounting one of the nearly fatal episodes of the journey: 'men do not fear death, they fear the pain of dying.'[3] This seemed to me, when I thought about it, to be obviously true, perhaps especially because I had been taught to fear both death and God and had come to regard both threats with a kind of native skepticism. When, later on, I discovered Diogenes (in Gilbert Murray's elegant little book on Greek religion), I recognised him at once as an ally. If death is not felt, and God not feared, I am free to direct my life to higher objectives than craven avoidance or propitiation.

Putting aside the oxymoronic concept of the survival of death, I concluded that my own death could not really matter much *to me*. If it were sudden, quick, unexpected, and painless, it would not matter at all. That is what I mean by 'insignificance' in my title. My death could matter to others, and the anticipation of it could matter, temporarily, to me. But my subsequent thinking about death has led me to even more radical conclusions. I sometimes amuse and sometimes perplex my students by telling them, quite matter-of-factly, that I am not going to die. Dying, I say, is just not the sort of thing I do - it would be quite out of character, and I have no intention of starting now. I cannot envisage making a true assertion using the first person active singular of that particular verb.

Does that mean I think I am going to live for ever? Well in a sense, yes (making sense of this sense is partly what this communication is about), but in another, of course not. I do not deny that some years from now (their number depending on luck, prudence, and the state of the art of medicine) this body will be absent in its present form from the earthly scene. It will be present as distributed in other forms, but they will not be me. The question is whether between now and then something called 'my dying' will take place. But nothing can be 'mine' except in relation to me, so that even my eventual absence can be properly spoken of only from the point of view of my present presence - in the event it will not be *my* absence. Similarly for my dying - if I decline to do it, will it have taken place?

Eventually, someone might insist, I will certainly be dead. But there is that troubling first person: *I* will be - but if the time ever comes, *I* will not be, anything or anywhere. This is the force of that other and more familiar saying of Epicurus, in his letter to Menoeceus, as recorded by Diogenes Laertius:

> Death, therefore, the most awful of evils, is nothing to us, seeing that, when we are, death is not come, and, when death is come, we are not. It is nothing, then, either to the living or to the dead, for with the living it is not and the dead exist no longer.[4]

It is possible to envisage *someone else's* use of the first person active singular of the verb 'to die,' but even then only by literary device. Two classic cases come to mind, out of many, no doubt; one is of playing dead, one of being dead. In Shakespeare's *A Midsummer Night's Dream* Bottom, the weaver, as Pyramus, shattered by the death of Thisbe, decides to join her: 'Thus die I, thus, thus, thus. Now am I dead ... .'[5]

There are many comic examples of this sort, in some of which the dead actor gets up to reassure the audience that it is, after all, only a play. The second case is early science fiction, in Edgar Allen Poe's 'The Facts in the Case of M. Valdemar.' The narrator wishes to try mesmerism (i.e., hypnotism) *in articulo mortis*, and succeeds in this with his friend, M. Valdemar, who is on the point of death. On being asked at intervals whether he is asleep (hypnotic subjects can apparently understand and respond to such questions) M. Valdemar gives a succession of answers that Poe builds to a point of horror:

> 'Yes;- asleep now. Do not wake me! - let me die so!'
> 'No pain - I am dying!'
> 'Yes; still asleep - dying,'
> and finally, in a hollow voice that seemed to "reach our ears ... from a vast distance, or from some deep cavern within the earth":
> 'Yes; - no; - I *have been* sleeping - and now - now - *I am dead*'.[6]

The whole apparatus of the story has been devoted to rendering this last remark plausible, and Poe can stand in here for generations of writers

who have explored similar themes, the most notable among them perhaps
Bram Stoker and his imitators with their tales of the Undead.

All this is fiction. Such imaginations apart, there seems to be a
problem about being dead, as seen from the point of view of the speaking
subject. Hoping for life on the other side of death does not really change
things, because that will, after all, be life, not death. Plato encourages us to
practice death metaphorically - as the separation of the soul from the body -
but this is not real death, not death as the end of existence. Socrates confronts
his own bodily death quite cheerfully, and seeks to reassure his disciples:

> I can't persuade Crito that I am this Socrates here who is
> talking to you and marshaling all the arguments. He thinks
> that I am the one who he will see presently lying dead ... .[7]

Socrates is not quite sure whether, after his bodily death, he will be
nowhere or elsewhere; at his trial he explains that one of two things must be
the case - an endless sleep without dreams, or a journey to another place,
where he will meet the good judges.[8] Going to sleep is clearly not really
dying - even the resurrection miracles in the Gospels involve sleep, on the
part of Lazarus and the daughter of Jairus, rather than real death. Still this
option is suggestive: according to Socrates, time in dreamless sleep will be
like a single night, and if one went to bed the night before exactly as on all
the other nights, in the assured expectation of waking up the next morning,
how could one distinguish between the last day and all the others? One might
have lived as fully on that day as on any day, physical weakness apart
perhaps. I note here that for Aristotle a quantity is infinite if, no matter how
much one takes away from it, some is always left - and if what is left remains
only in the mode of anticipation, does that change the situation so much?

The sleep analogy can be reinforced by a technological one, that of
the turning off (or putting into 'sleep mode') of a computer. I may turn a
computer off and never turn it on again; sometimes I cannot turn it on again,
in which case I may say of it that it died. But from the computer's point of
view, if I am allowed a bit of anthropomorphism (something I have explored
elsewhere),[9] is there an obvious difference between the two cases? Life, we
might say, is animation and metabolism, death the suspension of these things
- if it really is death, their definitive and not merely temporary suspension.
The program is no longer running, and cannot be re-started. What happened
to it? Children sometimes ask: what happens to the light, when it goes out?
We have to explain that that is not a well-formed question: there is no longer
a light for anything to happen to. To revert to Aristotelian infinity, one does
not just keep taking away and seeing what is left, the whole thing is gone, at
one swoop - and we with it, so that we cannot know it did not go on for ever.

A less extreme form of this puzzle might be put like this: when we are asleep but not dreaming, where are we exactly?

Taking a journey is not dying either, even less so. If 'death' were really, convincingly, understood as a change rather than as an ending, if it marked a stage in a history of which only a part (perhaps a minor or preliminary part) was called 'life,' or if there were two or more successive lives separated by one or more deaths, the first death would lose, for most people, most of its seriousness. There would remain of course the fear of the unknown, the sadness of friends or lovers bereaved, the terror (for imprudent believers) of eventual judgment - but there might also remain a hope of being agreeably surprised, of being reunited, of being pardoned. Clinging to such a hope might be one way of refusing death, or of accepting it under a more comforting description: transition, metamorphosis, temporary state.

Hope, along with knowledge and moral obligation, is one of the three categories addressed by Kant's basic philosophical questions (what can I know? what ought I to do? what can I hope?). It is the most problematic because it invokes essentially an as yet inaccessible future. So hope as a component of the refusal of death occupies an anomalous position, captured well in Peirce's essay on 'The Fixation of Belief' when he says

> If it be true that death is annihilation, then the man who believes that he will certainly go straight to heaven when he dies, provided he have fulfilled certain simple observances in this life, has a cheap pleasure which will not be followed by the least disappointment.[10]

If I die in a hope that cannot be shattered, my death will, in that context at least, have no importance for me. It will make no difference.

Another way of refusing death is to refuse to think about it: this was Spinoza's strategy in the *Ethics*. 'The free man thinks of nothing less than of death, and his wisdom is a meditation, not upon death, but upon life.'[11] This can be construed in two ways, one obvious, the other less so. (a) We can take it to mean that the free man is the courageous man, who, knowing that death is certain, refuses to be preoccupied with it, having liberated himself from mundane cares. This refusal implies a prior acceptance, and rests on self-mastery, the conquest of fearful and obsessive thoughts. But it does not go deep enough for my purpose here. The second construction is much stronger: (b) The free man is liberated from death itself - it will not touch him, so he need not think of it at all.

For Spinoza this sense is possible, but in a purely cerebral fashion. Living *sub specie aeternitatis*, under the aspect of eternity - living, that is, under the dictates of reason, which operates in the same way whether its objects are past, present, or future - frees the subject from time, but it takes devotion, the cultivation of the intellectual love of God, through which the philosopher can participate in God's timelessness, in Being outside of Time. But it has also been given a much more down to earth doctrinal form, in the story of the conquest of death by the Atonement: 'O death, where is thy sting? O grave, where is thy victory?'[12] This constitutes a refusal not so much of death itself as of its power. Instead of being difficult to attain, this state is preached as simply accessible to anyone: all can face death and the idea of death in tranquil confidence. That is what has happened, in effect, throughout the centuries of Christian faith. It is one of those cases, like conversion or sin, in which a mystery of belief is doubled by a perfectly secular philosophical understanding - and vice versa.

Other philosophers have made other attempts to tame death, in some cases by embracing it - I think of Heidegger's 'Being-towards-death,' which he takes to be constitutive of the existential condition. Heidegger's problem is that he wants to characterise Dasein as a whole, which it cannot be until it is finished. But the defining character of Dasein is care, which is always ahead-of-itself, so how is he to understand the moment of completion, i.e. death? Up to that point Dasein has a constitutive 'not-yet,' because there is always something outstanding - hence Being-towards-death. But if it ever got there it would become a thing, present-at-hand, and that is not admissible. So there has to be something called 'demise' which is not death, and death has to be 'impending' rather than something that ever actually happens.

> ... [J]ust as Dasein *is* already its "not-yet," and *is* its "not-yet" constantly as long as it is, it *is* already its end too ... .
> Death is a way to be, which Dasein takes over as soon as it is.[13]

This seems to me a quite unnecessary encumbrance for the existential subject, a response to a problem that need not even arise if we are content with a less portentous conception of our own existence.

The everyday attitude of most people is to accept death as a fact of life, to think about it just enough - by making a will, or buying life insurance - but not to talk about it too much. Like taxes, it is taken to be inevitable. The evidence that I am going to die is provided for me by the deaths of other people - it seems to be forced on me, even if I rarely or never see actual corpses. There are pictures in the newspapers, there are obituaries and printed cards, and hospitals, and funerals, and cemeteries, and monuments, not to speak of more immediate cases when I myself am mourning someone whom I loved and who will never return.

All these are the deaths of *others*. Am I entitled to draw any conclusion from them about my own case? Their deaths I can experience, given the right circumstances - but mine? Wittgenstein says bluntly that 'death is not an event in life.'[14] The deaths of others count as events in my life - they have their before and after, they have their place alongside other events, other events succeed them. But the sense that we give to the term 'event' involves a certain unity and totality, it implies a closure, whereas my death, even if it *comes to me out of* some other place (which is the root sense of 'event'), cannot be packaged or confined like this. It lacks a conclusion. In the limit I can imagine something that could be called the beginning of my death, but after that point everything becomes indefinite. 'In the limit' - limits can be approached asymptotically, and do not necessarily coincide with boundaries. What if life were like that, ending with a Zeno paradox?

Clearly the death I am talking about here is not my physical death as seen from the point of view of other people, for whom it can begin and end like any other event. For them I am one among others. It is myself for myself that is in question. Where will I be when they dispose of my body? How will I have arrived there? Death is not a state that *I* can realise, voluntarily or involuntarily. What about suicide? someone may ask. One might suppose that one could always kill oneself, *se donner la mort*, as the French have it, 'give oneself death.' But the problem with suicide is not that those who kill themselves have given themselves death - on the contrary this death, which they thought was theirs, has been given to us, who are left with its consequences. To give ourselves death is less easy than we thought (though there is an interesting inversion of this case - by not committing suicide we can give ourselves life, and this can be a powerful psychological strategy).

Jacques Derrida gives a different sense to the idea of my giving myself death - I must, he says, take my death upon myself as a condition of being a self at all.

> The sameness of oneself, what remains irreplaceable in dying, doesn't become what it is - in the sense of a same that relates to self in the oneself - before encountering what relates it to its mortality understood as irreplaceability.[15]

No one can die in my place, and making myself the gift of that realisation is the only way in which I can achieve autonomy and responsibility, or put myself in the position of giving anything (including my own death, in heroic sacrifice) to anyone else. There is an obvious echo of Heidegger here. But no one can have lunch in my place either, not *my* lunch, and it seems extravagant to insist that I give myself my death as a passport to my life as an individual. That is a gift I can safely refuse without compromising in any way my capacity for giving, or even for self-sacrifice. If I were to 'go to my death' for the sake of another or others it would make no difference to the thesis of pragmatic immortality.

The situation in which I find myself in relation to my own death is reproduced in relation to my own birth. I can observe the birth of others as a daily fact, I can be present at it, it can be - if for example the birth is that of one of my own children - a central fact of my life. But I cannot know my own birth except as a story told me after the fact, and long after. There is, of course, a significant difference between the cases, in that nobody can tell me the story of my own death. But my birth cannot be an event in my life as lived by me any more than my own death can.

Everything happens as if I myself, in contrast to anything else in the world, were a being without beginning and without end. Events happen around me; time passes, but this passage belongs to it, not to me - I remain immobile at the center of my world. A megalomaniacal position, you may say. And yet a comparable position, bearing on my spatial position at a cosmic level, follows necessarily from the theory of relativity, and can be applied (as I have shown elsewhere) locally as well.[16] Why not apply the same principle to my temporal situation?

To maintain that it is other things that move around my immobility, that just now Salzburg and Austria itself took the trouble to come towards me so as to make possible my presence here, obviously involves an element of fantasy. And yet, from my original point of view on the world, that is what I was bound to think - I had to *learn* that it was I who moved against a fixed background of space and time, I had to *construct* (or have constructed for me) the system of coordinates of a world that existed before I was born, that would continue to exist after my death, and that existed elsewhere, out of the reach of my perception. This whole external world, this universe, is in a way only a part of my own personal world, at the center of which I remain in my *here* and my *now*.

It is true that I am accompanied, in the center of my world, by my own body, and that this is by no means part of an unchanging center - on the contrary, I may be (if I allow myself to be) unhappily preoccupied with the changes that are taking place in it as age does its work. Here, however, I have a choice: I can draw the line between subject and world on the far side of my body or on the near side, in the latter case assimilating the body to the other objects in my world and preserving the timelessness and changelessness of my own subjectivity. It is this that does not die.

It was Husserl who best understood the relation between the subject and its world, reversing the familiar order of container and contained so that the world was carried in the ego rather than the ego in the world.[17] Every subject lives his or her own world, a world-of-living, or *Lebenswelt*, a 'lifeworld' (the expression 'lived world' that is sometimes used misses the active sense). 'Living' could thus be understood as 'having a lifeworld.' The contrast between life and death is intelligible only from within the lifeworld, whose unity and coherence are presupposed by every human activity, including philosophy. It is the life of this world whose ending cannot be incorporated into itself, which renders it effectively boundless. This boundless character of the lifeworld is also stressed by Wittgenstein, though he does not use that term. Having remarked that death is not an event in life he continues:

> If we take eternity to mean not infinite temporal duration
> but timelessness, then eternal life belongs to those who live
> in the present. Our life has no end in just the way in which
> our visual field has no limit.[18]

The analogy is not exact - our visual field is normally limited on all sides by the materiality of seen objects. At the same time we can always push back the limits, for example by using a microscope, or by walking around objects in search of new perspectives. The visual field (and here I think of Plotinus) can be identified with the field of Being itself - if this has limits they can only be at the threshold of Nothingness, and these are limits that as we have already seen can only be approached asymptotically, and thus never reached.

According to this view, even if we think of a death long prepared, at the end of a slow illness or in extreme old age, it will always be too soon to accept it as definitive. How can I *know*, given the total absence of relevant experience, that some purely internal detour is excluded *a priori*? I think we should maintain until the very last moment the attitude of the old codger in Vermont, who, when a visitor to the village asked him condescendingly: 'So, my good man, you've lived here all your life?' replied 'Not yet I ain't!'

This 'not yet' expresses the central idea of this text. My Vermonter's 'not yet' is not, like Heidegger's, 'towards-death,' it is serenely indifferent to death - he is evidently, like me, of Spinoza's mind. Situated as I am at the immobile center of my lifeworld (immobile because it is the point of reference for all motion), able always to take refuge in the fortress of the transcendental ego, whatever may happen to the 'naively interested ego' (as Husserl describes it,[19] I remain exactly what I was at the dawn of my consciousness, and will I am convinced to continue to be that for ever. For if this being that I am one day ceases to be, it certainly will not be I who knows it. What I want to stress here is that *I am not in a position to know what I shall know*, and moreover that *no one is or could be in a position to know that*. Which is to say that in spite of the 'near-death experiences' reported by Elisabeth Kübler-Ross,[20] in spite of the long history of speculation and of doctrine on the topic, we are still in complete ignorance of what our own death will be like. It is the one thing about which it is in principle impossible for us to have any empirical knowledge. That being the case, I have no reason whatever to draw any conclusions about my own mortality. And in this light there is no reason either not to attribute to myself and to everyone else the pragmatic immortality of my title. In the absence of all definite knowledge on what the moment of death may be, nothing prevents us from living, to adapt Spinoza's formula about eternity, 'under the aspect of immortality.'

Notes

[1] Aristotle, *Physics*, Oxford University Press, Oxford, 1991, p. 207a8.

[2] Cited in G. Murray, *Five Stages of Greek Religion*, Watts, London, 1935, p. 170.

[3] A. Cherry-Garrard, *The Worst Journey in the World: Antarctic 1910-1913*, Dial Press, New York, 1930, p. 281.

[4] D. Laertius, *Lives of the Eminent Philosophers*, R. D. Hicks (trans), Vol. II, Book X, Harvard University Press, Cambridge, Massachusetts, 1931, p. 651.

[5] W. Shakespeare, *A Midsummer Night's Dream*, Yale University Press, New Haven, 2005, Act V, Scene I, Lines 295-296.

[6] E. A. Poe, 'The Facts in the Case of M. Valdemar', in *Poetry and Tales*, The Library of America, New York, 1996, pp. 840-841.

[7] Plato, *Phaedo*, Oxford University Press, Oxford, 1993, p. 115C7-10.

[8] Plato, *Apology*, Clarendon Press, Oxford, 1961, pp. 40C5-41A2.

[9] P. Caws, 'Subjectivity in the Machine', in: *Yorick's World*, P. Caws (ed), University of California Press, Los Angeles, 1993, pp. 299-317.

[10] C. S. Peirce, 'The Fixation of Belief', in *Values in a Universe of Chance: Selected Writings of Charles S. Peirce, 1839-1914*, P. P. Wiener (ed), Doubleday Anchor Books, Garden City, NY, 1958, p. 102.

[11] B. Spinoza, *Ethics*, Oxford University Press, Oxford, 2000, Part IV, Proposition LXVII.

[12] Corinthians, 15:55.

[13] M. Heidegger, *Being and Time*, J. Macquarrie and E. S. Robinson (trans), SCM Press, London, 1962, p. 289.

[14] L. Wittgenstein, *Tractatus Logico-Philosophicus*, C. K. Ogden (trans), Routledge, London, 1922, (6.4311), p. 185.

[15] J. Derrida, *The Gift of Death*, 2nd Edition, D. Wills (trans), University of Chicago Press, Chicago, 2008, p. 46.

[16] P. Caws, 'On Being in the Same Place at the Same Time', in *Yorick's World*, P. Caws (ed), op. cit.

[17] E. Husserl, *Cartesian Meditations*, D. Cairns (trans), Martinus Nijhoff, The Hague, 1960, pp. 24-26.

[18] Wittgenstein, op. cit.

[19] Husserl, op. cit., p. 35.

[20] See e.g. E. Kübler-Ross, *On Life After Death*, Celestial Arts /Ten Speed Press, Berkeley, 2008.

Bibliography

Aristotle, *Physics*. Oxford University Press, Oxford, 1991.

Caws, P., 'Subjectivity in the Machine', in *Yorick's World*. P. Caws (ed), University of California Press, Los Angeles, 1993.

Cherry-Garrard, A., *The Worst Journey in the World: Antarctic 1910-1913*. Dial Press, New York, 1930.

Derrida, J., *The Gift of Death*. 2nd Edition, D. Wills (ed), University of Chicago Press, Chicago, 2008.

Diogenes, L., *Lives of the Eminent Philosophers*. R. D. Hicks (trans), Harvard University Press, Cambridge, Massachusetts, 1931.

Heidegger, M., *Being and Time*. J. Macquarrie and E. S. Robinson (trans), SCM Press, London, 1962.

Husserl, E., *Cartesian Meditations*. D. Cairns (trans), Martinus Nijhoff, The Hague, 1960.

Kübler-Ross, E., *On Life After Death*. Celestial Arts/Ten Speed Press, Berkeley, 2008.

Murray, G., *Five Stages of Greek Religion*. Watts, London, 1935.

Paul the Apostle, *First Epistle to the Corinthians*.

Plato, *Apology*. Clarendon Press, Oxford, 1961,

——, *Phaedo*. Oxford University Press, Oxford, 1993.

Peirce, C. S., 'The Fixation of Belief', in *Values in a Universe of Chance: Selected Writings of Charles S. Peirce, 1839-1914*. P. P. Wiener (ed), Doubleday Anchor Books, Garden City, NY, 1958.

Poe, E. A., 'The Facts in the Case of M. Valdemar', in *Poetry and Tales*. The Library of America, New York, 1996.

Shakespeare, W., *A Midsummer Night's Dream*. Yale University Press, New Haven, 2005.

Spinoza, B., *Ethics*. Oxford University Press, Oxford, 2000.

Wittgenstein, L., *Tractatus Logico-Philosophicus*. C. K. Ogden (trans), Routledge, London, 1922.

Peter Caws is University Professor of Philosophy and Professor of Human Sciences at the George Washington University. His eight books and more than 150 articles include work on the philosophy of the natural sciences, on ethics and continental philosophy (Sartre, and the structuralists), and more recently on psychoanalysis and the human sciences.

On the Notion of Presence and its Importance for a Concept of Dignity of the Dead

Julia Apollonia Glahn

Abstract
Dealing with death confronts us with a cornucopia of problems. A particular - albeit long neglected - difficulty arises concerning the moral status of dead human bodies. On the one hand, we assume that what constitutes a human being - in particular human value and dignity - comes to an end with her death. On the other hand, we have strong intuitions about the duty to handle dead bodies with respect instead of violating their dignity. For example, consider the debates on organ transplantation, the plastination of human corpses for public exhibitions, and the use of human corpses as 'crash test dummies.' Thus, paradoxically, we seem to simultaneously deny and recognise the dignity of dead human bodies. However, this tension can be resolved by way of two argumentative steps. First, it behoves us to reconsider the status of dead human bodies. Second, we have to clarify our understanding of human dignity. In my paper, I argue that a human being's existence does not end with her death. In fact, dead people are still human beings. Although we usually do not treat dead humans as if they have dignity, because they do not fulfil the particular sets of criteria we associate with dignity, it turns out that dead human beings still have dignity. So, far from being without dignity, dead humans belong to a group of people who are extremely vulnerable to dignity violations. It is their material and immaterial presence that enables and forces their environment to interact with them. Through interaction a realm is constituted in which the concept of human dignity starts to make sense and where human dignity itself arises. Therefore, any concept of dignity that fails to incorporate these most vulnerable beings that are still present as human beings is highly deficient and problematic. Instead of arguing in favour of the traditional criteria of dignity, I develop a social and interactional concept of dignity. According to this approach, refusing decent and humane treatment to the dead is what Avishai Margalit called 'human-blindness,' and constitutes an instance of violation of dignity.

Key Words: Human dignity, human dignity violation, dead, death, interaction, human-blindness.

*****

1. Introduction

Although philosophy has neglected for a long time the problem of the moral status of human corpses, reality frequently teaches us otherwise. It confronts us with situations, in which we have to decide how to treat dead human bodies. Many of these situations take place in the private realm. Others, however, become a matter of special public interest. When journalists exposed that an Austrian University was using human corpses as 'crash test dummies'[1] to get more realistic testing results, the public was shocked. In many people's opinion, such a handling of dead human bodies was disrespectful and a violation of the people's human dignity.

The sentiment that a lot of people seem to share is that dead human bodies are not at the mere disposal of others,[2] but, in fact, deserve a particular treatment that respects their human dignity.

This paper explores whether our intuitive way of speaking of the dead's dignity is appropriate or rather a superficial manner of every-day-conversation that does not keep up to a profound philosophical inquiry. In order to answer the question of the dignity of the dead, it is necessary to think more clearly about the concept of human dignity in general.

2.   General Assumptions about Human Dignity

In the following section, I would like to identify four elements that seem to be inherent to any reasonable concept of human dignity. First of all, human dignity is supposed to be universal and equal. It has to be universal in the sense, that all human beings regardless of their ethnic group, nationality, or religious beliefs have human dignity and it has to be egalitarian in the sense that any human being has it to the same degree, namely all human beings have the equal moral status. When most concepts refer to the equal moral status of all human beings they implicitly assume that human beings as a species do have a higher moral status than any other living creature on earth.[3]

Second, human dignity is essentially indivisible, i.e., absolute. No one has more or less human dignity than another one; either one has it or one does not.

Third, human dignity is something one cannot voluntarily forfeit or dispose; neither can it involuntarily be taken, violated or destroyed by another human being.[4]

Fourth and finally, human dignity has to be beyond human legislation. Everything that constitutes the special status and, consequently the rights, of human beings needs to be found outside of any state or international law. Dignity is supposed to serve as a benchmark independent of the law rather than being created and established by it. Thus, human dignity can be considered conceptually anterior to the state.

Hence, human dignity contains a descriptive as well as a normative element. It is descriptive in that it is a characteristic of any human being regardless their capacities and capabilities. It is normative in that it marks the highest standard that modern societies establish as far as a moral treatment of human beings is concerned and which they try to guarantee in form of rights and duties.

3.   The Dead in Light of Various Concepts of Human Dignity
3.1   The Eliministic Position

Most contemporary concepts of human dignity agree on the four claims of human dignity discussed above. However, beyond this basic agreement they vary tremendously.

Occasionally, philosophers even argue to abandon the concept of human dignity completely, because it is too ambiguous and normatively charged.[5] Their argument goes as follows: Even contradicting positions are able to refer to the concept of human dignity as their central point; therefore, the argument is not even a real argument.[6] It is rather used as a 'knock-out argument' every time one is lacking a reasonable and profound reason for one's position. As the concept is inherently vague and 'empty' it is better to jettison it. This position is clearly provocative, nonetheless unconvincing as well. It is unconvincing to abandon a concept due to its ambiguity and vagueness, because that ignores that it is in fact due to its ambiguity and vagueness that it requires further clarification. Exactly because contradicting positions are putatively able to refer to the concept of human dignity, it is necessary to define it in a more precise and clear manner.

3.2   The Reductionist Position

Since the ancient world, and especially after the reign of fascist terror in the 20th century Europe, the idea of human dignity did not lose any of its prominence. Starting with Cicero[7] and the Stoa.[8] to Augustinus,[9] Kant[10] and Hegel,[11] numerous philosophers tried to justify the special moral status of human beings. The period of Enlightenment paved the way to the realm of politics until, with the experiences of the 20th century terror at back, the idea of human dignity now presides the Charter of the United Nations[12] as well as the German constitution.

One of the reductionist positions[13] explains human dignity by arguing for equating human rights with human dignity. Everyone who has human rights has human dignity and vice versa.[14] A variation of this approach assumes human dignity as the explanatory primacy of any human right.[15] Thus, human beings have human rights because they have human dignity. There is no doubt about the internal connection between human rights and human dignity, and yet, this approach is not convincing either. In fact, it is only relocating the crucial question without answering it. Instead of asking what human dignity is, we now have to ask what human rights are. Moreover, this approach is violating the criterion of human dignity being anterior to the state as human rights are clearly defined by state and international laws.

3.3   Capabilities Position

The majority of human dignity concepts, however, refer to certain human capacities and capabilities. Human dignity is tied to the capacity for reason or autonomy,[16] self-consciousness, morality[17] or free will.[18]

This approach looks appealing: if a uniquely human capacity that no other living creature shares can be found, this could indeed be the justification to ascribe a special moral status to human beings. Nonetheless, this strategy fails. Be it the capacity for reason, autonomy or self-consciousness or less traditional traits like the capability of dialogical speech, creativity or a sense of fine arts, humour or (scientific) curiosity. Whatever single or set of capacities and capabilities are invoked, they all are confronted with numerous questions that, at the end of the day, lead to the realisation that this concepts fails as well.

First, we need to clarify, which one of these raised capacities is/are necessary and which is/are sufficient. Is it sufficient to be reasonable or does a human being also need to be autonomous at the same time? Or is there something like a 'basic cognitive capacity' (e.g. self-consciousness) that is sufficient for attributing human dignity, as it is the condition for any other kind of capabilities? Or do we rather have to assume a 'minimal set' of capacities and capabilities that is composed of several different human traits?

Moreover, talking about specific capacities and traits, it is unavoidable to undertake a certain selection. There are so many potential 'candidates' of specifically human capacities and capabilities that it is impossible to do justice to all of them. Such a selection, however, would be hard to make as the raised 'candidates' cover a broad range of what is called human. In this context we also need to ask who might be the authority to make such decisions. To give such powers to individuals or groups can lead to terrible abuse and can have devastating consequences as recent history teaches us. Again, this concept would also contradict the principle of human dignity being anterior to the law.

Furthermore, the capacities and capabilities that are at disposal are ambivalent themselves. It is questionable whether all possible capacities and capabilities are positive ones at all. Many of them can be abused in order to harm people. Therefore, it would be a mistake to assume any of them as purely positive.

Even if we managed to find a solution for these problems, we then would need to decide whether a human being has to possess these capacities actually or only potentially. It is a very high requirement to actually possess a capacity for not every human being can meet this requirement constantly. Being asleep, in a coma or mentally disabled might bring me into a situation, where I am incapable of being self-conscious or reasonable, let alone autonomous. The notion of potentiality is able to relax these enormous requirements, because it only requires us to possess a certain capacities potentially, i.e., in another situation or under different conditions in the future. Having the potential for something hence is a much weaker requirement than having something.[19]

In addition, the argument of potentiality can also be constructed in retrospective. A person suffering from dementia or even a dead human being had been realising the capacities for self-consciousness or reason before she became ill or died.

However, the notion of potentiality is not absolutely without contradiction either. In the case of a conflict, the existing potentiality is less valuable than the existing actuality. Thus, we cannot draw the conclusion that given the different evaluation of both states, we accept them to lead to the exact same moral status.[20]

Moreover, we have to acknowledge that many of these capacities are distributed unequally among human beings. Most of them do not have an 'either/or character,' but rather are confusing on the individual level. Finding a boundary that determines the realm in which such capacities are considered to constitute human dignity is necessarily subjective and highly arbitrary.[21] Also, such a boundary would be of little help to distinguish the specific human dignity from a dignity of all other living creatures.[22]

Despite the differences, all these human capacities that are supposed to justify human dignity have one thing in common: They all require being alive. Only living people and, in fact, not even all of them, are capable of being self-conscious, reasonable, free willing or moral agents. We often share the assumption that with a person's death, not only her life comes to an end, but, accompanied by it, all her mental and physical capabilities vanish as well. After death no one is able to be reasonable, self-conscious, free willing or a moral agent anymore. However, if everything that constitutes human dignity in human beings is lost with death, then a dead human being cannot hold human dignity.

Acknowledging all these arguments, we have to admit that the only way to assume a specific human capacity of capability as the reason for human dignity, is a much more general one. We could say that a certain capacity of capability is typically human and, therefore, justifies human dignity. This is the only way to assure that all human beings are included in the concept of human dignity. Otherwise, all those, who are either so severely mentally disabled that they will never be able to possess any of the crucial capacities, or those who have never realised them during their life time would be excluded of the concept of human dignity. This consequence, however, would be highly counter-intuitive and little helpful for our problem. Besides, it would clearly contradict the principle of human dignity being anterior to the law yet again.

So, obviously, we are running into a dilemma. On the one hand, we share the intuition that dead human bodies are not at the mere disposal of others and deserve a treatment that respects their human dignity. On the other hand, we assume human dignity to be linked to certain human capacities that dead humans are definitely lacking.

One possible answer to this problem is to say that dead human bodies indeed do not have full-fledged human dignity, but instead a weaker form of dignity called residual or contingent dignity, which protects them from the mere disposal by others and guarantees them some *post mortem* rights[23] - to respect a last will or not to do anything to the corpse the person did not give her agreement to before she died. Nevertheless, this is not the 'full' human dignity.

However, this answer is misleading. The idea of a residual dignity is not reconcilable with the core notion that human dignity does not know any gradation. Moreover, these granted *post mortem* rights based on a residual dignity do not satisfy our intuition about the proper handling that dead human bodies actually deserve. Rules, derived from a residual dignity seem arbitrary and lack a sound justification. Why, for example, are US citizens allowed to keep the ashes of their loved ones at home, whereas in Germany ashes have to be buried in the cemetery?

So, we still hold two contradicting intuitions: we seem to simultaneously deny and recognise the human dignity of dead human bodies. How can this be correct? Does not one of these assumptions necessarily have to be wrong? Either our intuitive language of human dignity in connection with the handling of dead human bodies is wrong and misleading, or the limitation of human dignity to only living human beings is wrong.

In the following, I would like to suggest a way out of this dilemma. I claim that we only run into this dilemma because we subscribe to a misleading description of human dignity. Let me show you why our common idea of human dignity is deceptive, and what a better concept of human dignity can look like.

The fact that most conceptions of human dignity limit the scope of potential bearers of human dignity merely to living people is due to the ways they try to justify human dignity in general. These conceptions identify some human characteristics as crucial for the assigned special status of human beings. They do so in order to give convincing reasons for why human beings have dignity and, therefore, deserve certain rights and treatments.

All these proposals have their shortcomings, but what they all have in common is that they focus on something characteristic within the individual human being - i.e., something that characterises a human individual as being worth having the highest normative standard called human dignity. But this focus is off target. The commonly shared problem of all these concepts is that they always and necessarily exclude certain groups of people. Relating the attribution of human dignity to certain cognitive capacities means to ignore all the people who are temporarily or permanently lacking these capacities.[24] A comatose patient, a severely brain damaged, a profoundly mentally disabled person or even a healthy unborn or newborn infant is lacking most or all of these capacities. To account for human dignity by referring to one or a set of these qualities must fail because it requites too much. It is extremely misleading to ground the highest normative standard among human beings on supposed characteristics that a lot of people do not even share. The capacity for reason, self-consciousness, morality or free will might be typical for human beings. But the mere identification of a capacity as typical for most human beings is not a sound and plausible reason to make it crucial and essential for the constitution of a status that should be granted to every human being regardless of their natural capabilities.

Beyond that, these concepts are mistaken on another level: they only focus on the human individual. All concepts aim to justify human dignity from within every single human individual. They look at human beings as isolated existences, but overlook that this is a merely theoretical and unrealistic perspective. Human beings never exist isolated from other human beings, but rather in communities of various sizes and manifold structures. Even if it were possible for a single human individual to survive in total isolation, the idea of human dignity would and could not make any sense to her. Human dignity is an inherently relational idea that unfolds its importance only within the various relations and interactions among people. Human dignity, therefore, can only be constituted in a community of human beings, were all merge in certain relationships and engage in interactions with each other.

Concepts that make allowance for this criterion can be subsumed under the term of inheritance.

3.4   Concepts of Inheritance

An alternative concept of inheritance that avoids this mistake is founded on the fundamentals of the Christian ethics.[25] It considers all human beings to be God's children. Regardless what qualities they have they are all created in God's image[26] and it was God himself who gave them their human dignity.[27] However, secular concepts that try to rely on this argumentation are confronted with the lack of a theological authority like God, as an approach like this can only be convincing for those who believe in God. It is not the individual human being herself who is justifying her human dignity, but rather his or her relation to God. Accordingly, this concept does not need to be limited to the living human beings. Created by God and called back to Him after death, the dead can be considered equal bearers of human dignity as any other of God's children, as their relation to God does not end with their death but continues beyond.

However, this approach is problematic as not everybody believes in a God, let alone a Christian God. If a person's concept of the world is lacking the crucial theological authority, she will be unable to accept, religious arguments for humanity's special status and rights. A commonly acceptable and shareable concept of human dignity, however, has to take into account religious plurality and is, therefore, challenged to provide a justification comprehensible for everyone. Only a purely secular concept of human dignity will be accepted internationally, transculturally and transreligiously.

Unlike the religious approach, the preamble to the Charter of the United Nations[28] describes a modern and secular concept, in which the equality of all human beings is agreed on, regardless of their ethnicity, social status, nationality or religion. Everyone is born free in rights and dignity. Being human is the only condition one has to fulfil to have human dignity. This formulation is, above all, understandable as a strong refusal to all anti-semitic, racist and fascist ideologies, but remains problematic nonetheless, as it lacks a sound justification. Even though the attempt to enunciate human dignity's inherent aspects of universality, equality and un-graduality, is invaluable, the concept of inheritance fails to give a convincing justification beyond the divine authority or certain sets of mental capacities. The underlying concept of all people being born free and equal in rights and dignity might be a matter of course to people within the western world. But it could also be understood as a way of western cultural imperialism. We just do not know whether it is correct or not. Moreover, despite the fact that species membership is the only capacity all living and dead beings have, merely being a member of a particular biological species can hardly count for the justification of a moral status.[29] Philosophers like Peter Singer[30] point out that attributing rights and a special moral status to human beings merely on the groundwork of their 'membership' in the species, is a 'biological discrimination.'[31] The line between different biological species is drawn arbitrarily and lost to any good moral argument.

In addition, it is argued that this justification is a 'naturalistic fallacy.' To conclude an *Ought* out of a mere *Being* is an invalid conclusion. It is as invalid as concluding a certain status or rights from having a certain sex, being a member of a certain ethnic group or nationality. The belonging to a biological species is in fact irrelevant as it does not give any evidence about the needs, interests or (actual or potential) capacities of the human being. So, taking this argument of speciesism seriously, we have to give a sound reason why the belonging to the human species should be the reason for human dignity. As long as we cannot do that, this concept is inacceptable.

Although this concept does not provide a final solution, I would like to acknowledge that it is pointing in the right direction. Thus, it turns out that neither of these concepts can help us solve our problem. If we draw on certain mental capacities to justify human dignity we are doing so on good grounds, but we are unjustifiably excluding some groups of living people as well as human corpses. However, if we resort to the fact of being human as essential for human dignity, we do include all kinds of living and dead human beings, but we are failing to give good reasons for it. So, we are faced with a Hobson's choice. Either we accept a narrow concept or one that is lacking a sound justification.

What could be a way out? Although it is unsatisfying in total, what the genuinely Christian approach correctly emphasises is the relational moment of human dignity. According to this concept, human dignity is not only founded in any individual human being, but it is in fact constituted in his or her relation to God. I think this relational element of human dignity is the key to a satisfying concept of human dignity.

In order to develop a convincing concept of human dignity, we need to replace the idea of a divine authority with one that has the power to grant value.[32] This authority is the social interaction among human beings. It is, in fact, the social interaction all human being always naturally engage in that makes human dignity possible.

4.   An Interactional Concept of Human Dignity

Every time, two or more people interact with each other, they create a realm in which dignity arises. As social interaction is something all beings are bound to, it represents one cornerstone of human togetherness. It is exactly the fact that and the way how we interact with other people that constitutes human dignity.

It was Avishai Margalit who, in his work, *A Decent Society*,[33] developed this idea of a social concept of human dignity. He proceeds *ex negativo* by defining a violation of human dignity.

4.1   Humiliations

Essentially, violations are acts of humiliation. Humiliations are 'of any sort of behaviour or conditions that constitutes a sound reason for a person to consider his or her self-respect injured.'[34] Self-respect is the diametric opposite of a humiliation. It is a human being's dignity that is violated when she is humiliated. Yet, not every kind of humiliation is automatically a violation of human dignity.[35] A humiliation does not disregard a person's bodily and/or material integrity, but rather her claim of not being humiliated. So, to attribute human dignity to somebody means to respect his moral claim not to be humiliated.[36] The moral claim of treating other human beings in a certain manner is exactly constituted in the reciprocal interaction among people.

Hence, in order to violate a dead human body's dignity, it is necessary to humiliate her. This requirement seems to be off target, at first. A certain treatment or action can only be experienced as humiliating, if one is able to experience anything in general. The dead, however, do not possess the cognitive or emotional preconditions, so it seems easy to ignore this question.

Without questioning that the dead are lacking any capacity to experience the feeling of being humiliated, this answer falls short. According to Margalit, a humiliation is real, independently of someone experiencing the feeling of being humiliated. Put differently, a person need not to *feel* humiliated, in order to *be* humiliated. So the moral claim not to be humiliated is only satisfied by the abandonment of a humiliation.

But what about self-respect? Is it possible to hurt a dead one's self-respect?

4.2   Self-Respect

Unlike the self-esteem, which can be established from the mere outside environment, self-respect is an attitude that 'persons have to the fact of their being human.'[37] Self-respect *shows* in our behaviour, our thinking, feeling and believing, without *being* it. It is this self-respect that is violated, when a person is humiliated. Thus, a humiliation is more than just the violation of certain rights. It is the violation of self-respect that categorically questions the personhood, i.e., the 'Dasein' of someone as such. Again, it is not clear why this should apply to dead human beings as well. Why should they possess something like self-respect, if they are lacking all necessary capacities for it? They have no awareness of themselves neither of others, no self-reflexion and no emotional states. How can they be able to constitute and hold up something like self-respect? How can they respect themselves? As for the dead, there is no self anymore. In my opinion, the answer is hidden in the idea of 'Dasein.' A violation of self-respect questions a human being's 'Dasein.' 'Dasein' understood as 'being there' goes beyond the mere biological being there. It owns a continuity which goes beyond the biological death. The dead are still 'there.' They are present. By being present in the world, they define the ending points of human interaction, which opens up the realm in which human dignity is constituted.

The concept of 'Dasein' is strongly connected to the notion of presence. 'Dasein' includes being present. A dead human being can be present in two different ways - materially and immaterially - which I will explore more in detail later. At this point, I would like to stretch the idea that it is due to her presence that a dead human being can mark the one cornerstone of human interaction. When a violation of self-respect questions a human being's 'Dasein' and 'Dasein' is strongly connected to presence, a present human being - dead or alive - cannot be deprived of her self-respect. As we will see later on, presence of the dead is something that cannot be constituted by the present subject alone, but necessarily requires human interaction.

But what is the relation between self-respect and human dignity?

4.3   Respect and Human Dignity

So far, I was exploring the notion of self-respect and its importance for the concept of humiliation. But for the moral description of self-respect, it is essential to add the concept of human dignity. An act is a violation of human dignity, if it ignores the above stated standards which are independent of the individual experience. An act can be humiliating and disrespectful, even though the person concerned does not feel that way, as she is caring a wrong concept of self-respect.[38] And that is also the case with dead human bodies, when they do not have any concept of self-respect on their own anymore. The relation between respect and human dignity can thus be seen from two perspectives: those, whose claim not to be humiliated is done justice to, are respected. And those, who are respected, have dignity. To humiliate another human being hence means to violate her human dignity; to respect her, means to respect her human dignity. In addition, it is not crucial whether the human being concerned experience this humiliation or respect. The focus rather is on the human being who acts, i.e., who respects someone or humiliates someone and the relation that she constitutes with the other one.

Here, Margalit points out that the concepts of human dignity and respect always rely on human interaction. It is the way human beings treat and interact with each other that constitutes the realm in which the idea of human dignity makes sense.

As Axel Honneth puts it, self-respect is not constituted on certain achievements, but only on the awareness of the belonging to a human community.[39] While this formulation clearly requires the awareness and, therefore, the being alive of a human being, Margalit's approach can also be applied to the interaction with the dead, as he focuses on the perspective of the agent. The awareness of being a member of a human community has to be provided by the acting participant, by the one who respects or humiliates, not by the one who is the target of those actions. So, in the interaction with dead human beings, it is me, the living one, who has to have an awareness of their membership in the human community, not the dead. So, in order to treat the dead appropriately, I must be aware of my own and their belonging to the human community.

4.4   Human-Blindness and Exclusion from the Human Community

According to Margalit, the strongest way to humiliate a person is in fact, to exclude her from the community of human beings. This exclusion happens when people are treated as if they were not human beings. So when someone is humiliated, she/he treated as an object and not as a subject. But even worse than being treated as an object is to be treat *as if* one was an object. To treat people as objects shows that one is convinced not to interact with a human being at all. But recognising someone as a human being and yet treating her *as if* she were not human is humiliating. It means to be aware of the other's humanity and yet ignoring it.[40] To treat human beings as if they were not human means to 'be blind to the human aspect of persons.'[41]

This is exactly what happens when we feel a discomfort when confronted with a certain treatment of the dead. When dead human beings are instrumentalised for other people's ends, e.g. by plastinating and publicly exhibiting them, or by using them as crash test dummies, they are treated *as if* they were objects, although all people involved know and are aware of their being human. It means to recognise someone's humanity and ignore it.

This experience is the discrepancy that we feel when we veer between the idea that dead human beings are dead and somehow not existing anymore and the concrete experience of seeing their humanity. That is, when many people feel a diffuse intuition that dead human beings are not at the mere disposal of others, but rather deserve a treatment with dignity and respect. The intuition is diffuse because of the felt discrepancy. But we can say that in fact, it is based on a false assumption. We only experience it, when we treat dead human beings *as if* they were objects, instead of respecting it. We just cannot treat them as objects, as we still perceive their humanity. Not to see a human face in a dead human body just means to ignore his humanity.

But, according to Margalit, naturally, all human beings are capable of recognising other beings as human. To see people as not being human and requires an active effort: namely ignoring their humanity. Such a perception of human beings as if they were not human beings must be created actively and intentionally. So, if we actively try to see other human beings as if they were not human, we make ourselves guilty of what Margalit calls 'human-blindness.'[42] Acting human-blind does not mean one does not recognise the humanity in another person. It rather means to make an active effort to ignore another person's humanity. For Margalit, human-blindness is a pathological deficiency of social competence. There is no natural way of being unable to recognise others as human. In fact, it is a self chosen blindness. In most cases where people ignore the humanity of others, it requires an active effort to overlook another person's humanity. It requires to make oneself blind to the humanity of the other one. Margalit's crucial point is hence not that we have to respect and treat people as people, but stronger, that we, as human beings, are innately incapable to act differently.

This active and intentional exclusion from the human community is what happens, when we feel uncomfortable with a certain handling of dead human bodies. The discomfort we feel, when a dead human body is used as a crash test dummy or when it is carelessly disposed in a trash can, is due to the fact that what we see the corpse as a human being. Therefore, such a handling of corpses is ignoring their humanity; it is human-blind. In situations with dead human bodies, where we feel the diffuse discomfort that we try to name by saying: 'This is violating or disrespecting the dead person's dignity' we acknowledge that someone is recognising the corpse as human, but is treating him as if she were not a human being and hence is making herself guilty of being human-blind. By treating dead human bodies incorrectly, namely as non-human, we erroneously and unjustifiably exclude them from the community of human beings. And being excluded from the human community is humiliating and therefore violates one's human dignity.

4.5   Presence of the Dead

But in order to be excluded from the community of human beings, it is necessary to be a member in the first place. Thus, we must ask whether dead human bodies are still human beings. From the legal perspective (at least in Germany), they are entities between a 'person' and an 'object,' which leads to the odd formulation of 'personal objects.' Even some philosophers prefer the idea that dead human bodies, although they have certain rights, actually are objects.[43]

However, I think this is wrong. Philosophically, there are reasons to assume that dead human bodies are still human beings. Although, as stated at the beginning, a lot that we care about comes to an end when we die, it is not true for everything. Instead of limiting the membership in the human community to the living ones I want to argue for an overcoming of the boundary between life and death. This border might be incisive and morally relevant in several regards, but it is not when it comes to a proper handling of human bodies. Being alive or dead is not the crucial criterion for the treatment. Relevant is, in fact, that the realm of human dignity is not marked by the biological dimension between life and death, but rather by the social dimension between people. This social dimension is crucially determined by the notion of presence.

A dead human being is present on two levels. In most cases, when a person dies, there is a corpse, which represents her material presence. Moreover, the dead human being is present to his friends and families in an immaterial way. They remember their beloved one and recall her looks, way of speaking and thinking, actions and shared experiences. They keep photographs, letters, videotapes and other media that give prove of the former living existence of the now diseased.

The material presence, manifested in the human corpse, still represents the former functional unity of the human being.[44] However, this presence is necessarily transient. The natural process of degeneration and autolysis implicates severe physical changes, which, in the end, lead to the complete disappearance of the corpse.[45] The immaterial presence, however, is different. It is independent of any physical embodiment and thus can exit over a much longer period of time. It is not subject to external factors of change, but rather in the powers of the living people. It is in the powers of family and friends to keep the memory alive, and hence to keep the departed one present.

These thoughts show how the notion of presence is a much stronger criterion for the interaction among dead and living people than the biological border between life and death. So, there is no good reason to assume a significant and morally relevant difference between the claims for respect in interactions among living people, or between living and dead people. This becomes obvious when we look at the proper treatment of comatose or brain dead patients. In these situations we become aware that the mere fact of being alive is not as pivotal for the evaluation of a treatment as we might think. Like with a comatose patient, we might not be able to hurt a dead human body physically or psychologically, but we can harm him/her by ignoring his/her presence and by neglecting the status that he/she deserves as a member of the human community - dead or alive.

What is much more important for the question of human dignity in this case is the existence, the mere being there, the presence of the dead human being. As stated above, usually, when a person dies, there is a corpse. This corpse, although subjected to severe physical changes, is still recognisable as human. By this, she does not only provide the above mentioned notion presence, but does something more. By being there he/she calls for action. In the presence of a dead human body we cannot omit acting. No matter what we do, crucial is that we have to do something. We cannot do nothing. The material presence of the dead body requires our action. For Margalit, we are, towards human beings, always and necessarily acting beings.

This incapability of omitting acting in the presence of a human corpse, also continues when the material presence is over and only the immaterial presence remains. Then, it is in the powers of family and friends, to remember the departed one, to talk to and about him, to keep his life and stories 'alive,' to pass them on to the offspring and other people. No matter what family and friends decide to do, whether they want to keep the memory alive or prefer to forget the person, whether they look at photographs every day or prefer to burn them, they act. And yet again, the dead human being requires our action and constitutes a realm for interaction. For once more, it is this realm in which human dignity arises. By this postulation of human beings as necessarily acting beings, interaction among humans inevitably has to happen and, therefore, the possibility of the constitution of a realm of human dignity is given.

Where does this conception lead us to? Does it mean there is no difference between the interactions among living people or between living and dead people? As interpersonal interaction is closely related to the physical presence of its participants, we have to acknowledge that in cases of dead human bodies it is limited. As mentioned above, the human corpse is gradually disintegrating, which limits interaction. Imprisonment, torture or other ways of physical harm that we consider to be violations of human dignity are irrelevant.

However, dead human bodies are still potential victims of human dignity violations. The fact that dead human bodies are immune to some of the most common violations of human dignity does not mean that they are immune to *all* possible violations.[46] In fact, they belong to a group of people, like comatose patients, severely brain damaged or mentally disabled persons or unborn and newborn infants, who are limited in their interpersonal, interaction and thus extremely vulnerable, when it comes to the most fundamental violation of human dignity, i.e., the exclusion from the human community! Exactly because they cannot defend and protect themselves, others have to be particularly careful with them.

So, a proper handling of dead human bodies does not mean to treat a dead human body in the same way we would treat a living person. It means to recognise and treat her as human and thereby respect her human dignity. By ignoring her humanity, we automatically exclude her from the human community. And such exclusion would necessarily be intentional and human-blind, as it ignores the potential of identification that dead human bodies have for living people. By means of their presence, corpses enable people to recognise themselves in them. The realm in which human interaction takes place creates the basic requirement for the constitution of human dignity. When this realm that comes to existence naturally and directly between all human beings who interact with each other is neglected, it is our feeling of discomfort and the intuition that indicates that this is not the way to treat dead human bodies, because it is disrespecting their human dignity.

But even when the physical presence of a dead human being is not given anymore, interaction is still possible. No matter what family and friends do with the immaterial presence of a departed person, they always do something. Remembering as well as forgetting is an action.[47]

Thus, one can say, that as long as someone is keeping the memory of a departed one 'alive,' as long as there is any sort of interaction, the realm of human dignity arises and the criterion of human dignity and humiliation can be applied to judge a certain way of treatment as appropriate or not. Only when the former material and immaterial presence does not play any role for anyone anymore, this person cannot be violated in his or her claim of human dignity anymore.

Therefore, we are justified to use human dignity as the valid criterion for evaluating the treatment of dead human bodies. Our intuition is not doomed to be a naïve illusion, but is shown to be correct, as it is possible to formulate a concept of human dignity that reconciles itself to. And we see that the notion of presence of the dead plays a decisive role to justify this concept, as the presence of the dead is what functions as a fundamental groundwork for the constitution of the realm where human dignity arises.

Notes

[1] T. Hofstätter, 'Crashtests mit Leichen. Skandal rund um die Crash Test Dummies', *Via Medici Online*, April 2005, viewed on 10th August 2009, <http://www.thieme.de/viamedici/studienort_graz/aktuelles/crashtest.html>; Veröffentlichungen des Instituts für Deutsches, Europäisches und Internationales Medizinrecht, Gesundheitsrecht und Bioethik der Universitäten Heidelberg und Mannheim (eds), *Kommerzialisierung des Menschlichen Körpers. Leichen-Schau und Menschenwürde. Von Körperwelten, Kuriositätenkabinetten und Crash-Test-Dummies*, Springer Verlag, Berlin, 2007.

[2] A. Esser, 'Respekt vor dem Toten Körper', *Deutsche Zeitschrift für Philosophie*, Vol. 56, No. 1, 2008, pp. 119-134.

[3] This anthropocentric concept of the world is highly criticised. Many environmental ethicists and animal rights-activists deny that the species of human beings deserve a special moral status. Within the synergetic cooperation of living creatures, it is highly deficient to assume a dichotomy of human beings and 'the others,' which, above all has been established by Immanuel Kant, when he emphasised the capacity of reason as the crucial criterion of human dignity, and which exposes all other living creatures to the arbitrary powers of the human being. Their status is only established from their relation to the human species. They do not own any value on their own. Yet, for a contemporary and valid concept of human dignity, we do not have to accept this perspective. In fact, what we today call 'dignity of the creature' or 'animal dignity' expresses the very idea of not only human beings having dignity and, therefore, have certain rights and deserve a certain treatment. Cf. P. Singer, *In Defense of Animals: The Second Wave*, Blackwell, Malden, 2006; P. Balzer et al., *Menschenwürde vs. Würde der Kreatur*, Alber, Freiburg, 1999.

[4] This assumption leads to the so-called 'paradox of humiliation.' On the one hand, human dignity is characterised that one cannot lose or forfeit, on the other side, a violation of human dignity is clearly defined as an act that violates another human being's dignity; an act that impairs or even destroys it. Cf. R. Stoecker, 'Menschenwürde und das Paradox der Entwürdigung', in *Menschenwürde. Annäherung an einen Begriff*, R. Stoecker (ed), öbv&hpt, Wien, 2003, pp. 133-151.

[5] Cf. N. Hoerster, *Ethik des Embryonenschutzes*, Reclam, Stuttgart, 2002, pp. 21ff; D. Birnbacher, 'Menschenwürde - Abwägbar oder Unabwägbar?', in *Biomedizin und Menschenwürde*, M. Kettner (ed), Suhrkamp, Frankfurt am

Main, 2004, p. 249; F-J. Wetz, *Die Würde des Menschen ist Antastbar: Eine Provokation*, Klett-Cotta, Stuttgart, 1998, pp. 94ff; A. Schopenhauer, *Die Welt als Wille und Vorstellung*, Brockhaus, Wiesbaden, 1972, p. 726.

[6] This is for example the case with the debate on euthanasia, in which, in the name of human dignity, proponents and opponents equally argue in favour of a dignified dying.

[7] Cicero, *De Republica*, Reclam, Stuttgart, 2001; Cicero, *De Officiis*, Reclam, Stuttgart, 1986.

[8] V. Pöschl, *Der Begriff der Würde im Antiken Rom und Später*, Carl Winter, Heidelberg, 1989.

[9] Augustinus, *De Libero Arbitrio*, in *Werke*, Vol. 9, Schöningh, Paderborn, 2006.

[10] I. Kant, *Groundwork of the Metaphysics of Morals*, Cambridge University Press, Cambridge, 1998.

[11] G. W. F. Hegel, *Phenomenology of Spirit*, Clarendon Press, Oxford, 1977.

[12] United Nations, *Charter of the United Nations and Statute of the International Court of Justice*, United Nations, Department of Public Information, 1985.

[13] Cf. C. Menke and A. Pollmann, *Philosophie der Menschenrechte zur Einführung*, Junius, Hamburg, 2007, pp. 129-166; S. Gosepath, 'Zur Begründung Sozialer Menschenrechte', in *Philosophie der Menschenrechte*, S. Gosepath and G. Lohmann (eds), Suhrkamp, Frankfurt am Main, 1998, pp. 146-187.

[14] J. Maritain, *The Rights of Man and Natural Law*, Scribner, New York, 1949.

[15] Cf. R. Herzog, 'Die Menschenwürde als Maßstab der Rechtsphilosophie', in *Technologischer Fortschritt und Menschliches Leben*, H. Seesing (ed), Schweitzer, Frankfurt am Main, 1988; K. Stern, 'Menschwürde als Wurzel der Menschen- und Grundrechte', in *Recht und Staat im Sozialen Wandel - Festschrift für Ulrich Scupin*, N. Achterbach et al. (eds), Berlin, 1983; M. Stepanians, 'Gleiche Würde, Gleiche Rechte', in *Menschenwürde. Annäherung an einen Begriff*, R. Stoecker (ed), öbv&hpt, Wien, 2003, pp. 81-101; C. Menke, 'Von der Würde des Menschen zur Menschenwürde', *WestEnd*, Vol. 2, 2006, pp. 1-23.

[16] Cf. I. Kant, *Groundworks of the Metaphysics of Morals*, op. cit.

[17] Kant, op. cit.

[18] Augustinus, op. cit.; G. Pico della Mirandola, *On the Dignity of Man (De Hominis Dignitate)*, Bobbs-Merrill, Indianapolis, 1965.

[19] This argument is mostly brought up in the debate on the moral status of unborn human life. Cf. G. Damschen and D. Schönecker, *Der Moralische Status von Embryonen*, De Gruyter, Berlin, 2003, pp. 149-277.

[20] Cf. A. Leist, 'Menschenwürde als Ausdruck', *DZPhil*, Vol. 53, No. 4, 2005, p. 601.

[21] D. Jaber, *Über den Mehrfachen Sinn von Menschenwürdgarantien: Mit Besonderer Berücksichtigung von Art. 1, Abs. 1, Grundgesetz*, Ontos Verlag, Frankfurt am Main, 2001, pp. 86-87.

[22] Jaber, op. cit., p. 86.

[23] D. Sperling, *Posthumous Interests. Legal and Ethical Perspectives*, Cambridge University Press, Cambridge, 2008.

[24] Balzer et al., op. cit.; Boston University (ed), 'Symposium on the Identity and Dignity of Man 1969', in *Ethical Issues in Biology and Medicine*, Schenkman Pub. Co., Cambridge, 1973.

[25] R. Duffy and A. Gambatese (eds), *Made in God's Image. The Catholic Vision of Human Dignity*, Paulist Press, New York, 1999.

[26] The essential passages in the Bible are: Genesis 1, 26; 1, 27; 5, 1; Colossians 1, 15; Corinthians 44; Philippians 2, 6.

[27] Bible, Genesis, I, 26-27.

[28] United Nations, op. cit..

[29] P. Singer, *Practical Ethics*, Cambridge University Press, Cambridge, 1993.

[30] Singer, op. cit.

[31] Cf. Jaber, op. cit., pp. 887-888.

[32] Jaber, op. cit., p. 90.

[33] A. Margalit, *The Decent Society*, Cambridge University Press, Cambridge, 1996.

[34] Margalit, op. cit., p. 9. For Margalit, also conditions can be humiliating, but only in certain cases: 'Conditions are humiliating, however, only if they are the result of actions or omissions by human beings. Conditions ascribed to nature cannot be considered humiliating on my view.' Margalit, op. cit., p. 9.

[35] It is possible to think off situations, in which people are humiliated, but his/her human dignity is 'untouched' and only a contingent dignity is violated. Imagine talent-free candidates for casting shows, who are not afraid to present themselves in front of a harsh jury and a million people audience. Very often, they get disrespectful and humiliating responses and feed backs to their performances. Yet, it would be exaggerated to speak of violations of human dignity. It is rather their dignity as an artist that gets violated in such situations, but not their dignity as a human being as such.

[36] Balzer, op. cit., pp. 28-31.

[37] Margalit, op. cit., p. 51.

[38] Cf. The example of the submissive wife in T. Hill, *Autonomy and Self-Respect*, Cambridge University Press, New York, 1991, pp. 4-19.

[39] A. Honneth, *Die Zerrissene Welt des Sozialen*, Suhrkamp, Frankfurt am Main, 1999, p. 258.

[40] Margalit, op. cit., p. 115
[41] Margalit, op. cit., p. 96.
[42] Margalit, op. cit., pp. 96-101.
[43] S. Schenk, *Die Totensorge - Ein Persönlichkeitsrecht. Zivilrechtliche Untersuchung der Verfügungsbefugnis am menschlichen Körper*, Verlag Dr. Kovač, Hamburg, 2007; M. Weck, *Vom Mensch zur Sache? Der Schutz des Lebens an Seinen Grenzen*, Shaker Verlag, Aachen, 2003.
[44] Esser, op. cit., p. 130.
[45] Cf. M. Roach, *Stiff. The Curious Life of Human Cadavers*, Norton W. W. and Company, New York, 2004.
[46] The laws of many countries take this into account. German law, for example, guarantees personal rights after death; cf. Weck, op. cit.
[47] Again, German law takes this into account: There was the so called 'Mephisto case,' where the Federal Court of Justice in Germany bared a publishing house to distribute Klaus Mann's novel, *Mephisto - Roman einer Karriere*, as it, in the opinion of the Federal Court Schenk, portrayed the departed actor, Gustaf Gründgens, as a characterless symbol of the national-socialist regime. Even though the Federal Constitutional Court had negated the continuation of personal rights after death, as the bearer of such rights can only be a living person (according to the German Basic Constitutional Law, Art. 2 I), it acknowledges the human dignity which cannot be lost with death and which has to be protected by the state (German Basic Constitutional Law, Art. 1). Moreover, it is considered a criminal act to denigrate a person's memory (§ 189, StGB), Schenk, op. cit., pp. 72-73.

Bibliography

Augustinus, *De Libero Arbitrio*, in *Werke*. Vol. 9, Augustinus, Schöningh, Paderborn, 2006.

Balzer, P., Rippe, K. P., Schaber, P., *Menschenwürde vs. Würde der Kreatur. Begriffsbestimmung, Gentechnik, Ethikkommissionen*. Alber Freiburg, 1999.

Birnbacher, D., 'Menschenwürde - Abwägbar oder Unabwägbar?', in *Biomedizin und Menschenwürde*. M. Kettner (ed), Suhrkamp, Frankfurt am Main, 2004.

Boston University (ed), 'Symposium on the Identity and Dignity of Man 1969', in *Ethical Issues in Biology and Medicine*. Schenkman Pub. Co., Cambridge, 1973.

Cicero, *De Officiis*. Reclam, Stuttgart, 1976.

——, *De Republica*. Reclam, Stuttgart, 1956.

Damschen, G., and Schönecker D. (eds), *Der Moralische Status von Embryonen*. De Gruyter, Berlin, 2003.

Duffy, R. and Gambatese, A. (eds), *Made in God's Image. The Catholic Vision of Human Dignity*. Paulist Press, New York, 1999.

Esser, A., 'Respekt vor dem Toten Körper'. *DZPhil*, Vol. 56, No. 1, 2008, pp. 119-134.

Gosepath, S. and Lohmann, G. (eds), *Philosophie der Menschenrechte*. Suhrkamp, Frankfurt am Main, 1998.

Hegel, G. W. F., *Phenomenology of Spirit*. Clarendon Press, Oxford, 1977.

Herzog, R., 'Die Menschenwürde als Maßstab der Rechtspolitik', in *Technologischer Fortschritt und Menschliches Leben: Die Menschenwürde als Maßstab der Rechtspolitik*. H. Seesing (ed), Schweitzer, Frankfurt am Main, 1988.

Hill, T. (ed), *Autonomy and Self-Respect*. Cambridge University Press, New York, 1991.

Hoerster, N., *Ethik des Embryonenschutzes*. Reclam, Stuttgart, 2002.

Hofstätter, T., 'Crashtests mit Leichen. Skandal rund um die Crash Test Dummies'. *Via Medici Online*, April 2005, viewed on 10th August 2009, <http://www.thieme.de/viamedici/studienort_graz/aktuelles/crashtest.html>.

Honneth, A., *Die Zerrissene Welt des Sozialen. Sozialphilosophische Aufsätze*. Suhrkamp, Frankfurt am Main, 1992.

Jaber, D., *Über den Mehrfachen Sinn von Menschenwürdegarantien: Mit Besonderer Berücksichtigung von Art.1 Abs. 1 Grundgesetz*. Ontos Verlag, Frankfurt am Main, 2001.

Kant, I., *Groundworks of the Metaphysics of Morals*. Wilder Publications, Radford, 2008.

Leist, A., 'Menschenwürde als Ausdruck'. *DZPhil*, Vol. 53, No. 4, 2005, pp. 597-610.

Margalit, A., *The Decent Society*. Cambridge University Press, Cambridge, 1996.

Maritain, J., *The Rights of Man and Natural Law*. Scribner, New York, 1949.

Menke, C., 'Von der Würde des Menschen zur Menschenwürde: Das Subjekt der Menschenrechte'. *WestEnd*, Vol. 2, 2006, pp. 1-23.

Menke, C. and Pollmann, A., *Philosophie der Menschenrechte zur Einführung*. Junius, Hamburg, 2007.

Pico della Mirandola, G., *On the Dignity of Man (De Hominis Dignitate)*. Bobbs-Merrill, Indianapolis, 1965.

Pöschl, V., *Der Begriff der Würde im Antiken Rom und Später*. Carl Winter, Heidelberg, 1989.

Roach, M., *Stiff. The Curious Life of Human Cadavers*. Norton W. W. and Company, New York, 2004.

Schenk, S., *Die Totensorge - Ein Persönlichkeitsrecht. Zivilrechtliche Untersuchung der Verfügungsbefugnis am Menschlichen Körper*. Verlag Dr. Kovač, Hamburg, 2007.

Schopenhauer, A., *Die Welt als Wille und Vorstellung*. Brockhaus, Wiesbaden, 1972.

Singer, P., *In Defense of Animals: The Second Wave*. Blackwell, Malden, 2006.

——, *Practical Ethics*. Cambridge University Press, Cambridge, 1993.

Sperling, D., *Posthumous Interests. Legal and Ethical Perspectives*. Cambridge University Press, Cambridge, 2008.

Stepanians, M., 'Gleiche Würde, Gleiche Rechte', in *Menschenwürde. Annäherung an einen Begriff*. R. Stoecker (ed), öbv&hpt, Wien, 2003, pp. 81-101.

Stern, K., 'Menschenwürde als Wurzel der Menschen- und Grundrechte', in *Recht und Staat im sozialen Wandel - Festschrift für Hans Ulrich Scupin*. N. Achterberg, W. Krawietz, D. Wyduckel (eds), Duncker und Humblot, Berlin, 1983.

Stoecker R., 'Menschenwürde und das Paradox der Entwürdigung', in *Menschenwürde. Annäherung an einen Begriff.* R. Stoecker (ed), öbv&hpt, Wien, 2003, pp. 133-151.

United Nations, *Charter of the United Nations and Statue of the International Court of Justice*. United Nations, Department of Public Information, 1978.

Veröffentlichungen des Instituts für Deutsches, Europäisches und Internationales Medizinrecht, Gesundheitsrecht und Bioethik der Universitäten Heidelberg und Mannheim (eds), *Kommerzialisierung des menschlichen Körpers. Leichen-Schau und Menschenwürde. Von Körperwelten, Kuriositätenkabinetten und Crash-Test-Dummies*. Springer Verlag, Berlin, 2007.

Weck, M., *Vom Mensch zur Sache? Der Schutz des Lebens an Seinen Grenzen*. Shaker Verlag, Aachen, 2003.

Wetz, F. J., *Die Würde des Menschen ist Antastbar: Eine Provokation*. Klett-Cotta, Stuttgart, 1998.

Julia Apollonia Glahn is, after graduating in Philosophy in 2008, a research fellow at the Institute of History, Theory and Ethics of Medicine at the RWTH Aachen, Germany, where she is mainly working in philosophical thanatology. Currently her research and writing are devoted to various problems with death, dying and the dead. Moreover, she is interested in moral theory, ethics and applied ethics.

The Deathless Self: Death and Immortality in the Discourse of Vedanta

Dhruv RajNagar

Abstract
Death is the inevitable culmination of a life. It waits patiently as we go about our business in careless or deliberate forgetfulness. But the fact that one day we will cease to be looms over our entire waking life However, the Upanishads, ancient Indian philosophical texts, present to us a vision, according to which, the self, being of the nature of existence-consciousness, *sat-cit,* is immortal and does not perish at the time of death. In fact, our belief in the reality of death, according to the Upanishads, is *avicara-siddham,* that is, a belief formed without careful deliberation or reflection on the matter. Here, the teaching of Vedanta, which is the philosophy present in the Upanishads, will be unfolded in order to analyse our current understanding of death and, if possible, arrive at a more authentic conception of it, one that may also guide us towards a more authentic way to live. This is mediated through a juxtaposition of two ancient streams of thought - Vedanta and Buddhism (themselves representative of more general philosophical positions about the nature and reality of the self). In the process, we arrive at something that is capable of fundamentally altering our understanding of ourselves and of death. By unfolding a single vision behind the apparently opposed viewpoints, the analysis seeks to change our current relationship with death, asking it to come to our very doorstep, our present, instead of fearing it and relegating it to the future. This, it is argued, is only possible when one learns to die to oneself and becomes aware of the presence of death in the midst of life and activity.

Key Words: Consciousness, death, dying, identification, immortality, self, time.

*****

1. Introduction

The Katha Upanishad narrates an encounter between Naciketas, a young Brahmin boy and Yama, the Lord of Death. Naciketas questions Yama: 'There is this doubt about a man who is dead. "He exists," say some, others, "He exists not." I want to know this, so please teach me. This is the third of my wishes.'[1]

By a strange turn of events, Naciketas, who is condemned to death, is granted three wishes by Yama. His third and final wish pertains to the mystery of death and he pleads to Yama to explain to him the truth of the matter. Yama is hesitant and offers the young boy every gift worthy of mortal desire from wealth and beautiful maidens to prominence and longevity, but declines to expatiate upon the issue of death itself, which, according to him, is hard to understand and confounds the gods themselves. Such hesitance reflects Yama's discomfort with revealing the greatest of all secrets to a young boy. At the same time, the various lures act as a way of testing Naciketas's resolve to be content with nothing less than the ultimate truth itself. Naciketas is steadfast:

> What mortal man with insight, Who has met those who do not die or grow old, Himself growing old in this wretched and lowly place, Looking at its beauties, its pleasures and joys, Would delight in a long life? The point on which they have great doubts- What happens at that great transit - Tell me that, O Death! This is my wish, probing the mystery deep, Naciketas wishes for nothing other than that.[2]

The conversation sets the stage for a prolonged analysis of the phenomena of death and the answer given by Yama, which reveals to Naciketas the insights of the Upanishads into the phenomena of death. Death is a central motif of the Upanishads, whose purpose is to lead an individual towards self-knowledge. Their treatment of the question of death, like their treatment of all other questions, is intimately connected with the question of the self, on which hangs the fate of all other pursuits and enquiries, and the answer to which will simultaneously solve man's problems at all levels- intellectual, moral and existential. Once the question, 'Who am I?' has been answered, there is nothing more to ask, nothing more to be done. It is at once the answer to philosophical scepticism and existential disquiet. For Vedanta, therefore, it is the first as well as the last question. And its solution will instantly lay to rest all other doubts- logical, epistemological or metaphysical. Knowledge of the truth, of reality, *tattva-jñana*, is a direct consequence of self-knowledge, *atma-jñana*. The questions, 'Who am I?' and 'What is?' point to the same truth, one that can also lead us towards a more meaningful and coherent conception of death and dying.

The statement of the Upanishads regarding the matter of life and death is definite and singular - it is unreal. You can never really die because you are immortal by nature. It may appear that at the time of death we cease to be, but at most, death only signifies the cessation of my current relationship with the world, my sense of being surrounded with what is familiar. But how is this possible? After all, is not death a fact of experience, if only a second-hand one? In the *Tractatus,* Wittgenstein observes that death is not an event in life.[3] I do not experience my own death - because in order to experience death (or to experience anything at all) I must be alive at the first place. But I do observe the death of others. And death seems to be universally present in nature. Let us see what is precisely meant by such a claim.

2.   The Immortal Self
A.   Self and the Other

According to Vedanta, my sense of self, my personal identity, plays a crucial role in determining my relation with death. What precisely does Vedanta have to say about the self? This must be first clarified. According to Vedanta, the self is of the nature of consciousness. It is not even that 'being conscious' is a characteristic of the self. Rather, the self is consciousness itself. Moreover, this consciousness is alone what is. It alone has being. And the being of this consciousness is nothing else but my own being. If this is so, then how is it that in everyday life I perceive myself to be otherwise - a psycho-physical organism in continuous causal interaction with its surroundings? My ordinary experience does not reveal my existence as pure consciousness. Vedanta explains this through the process of identification. Let us understand what is meant by this.

At a very fundamental level we know ourselves to be somewhat different from the world we find ourselves in. My sense of self separates me from this world. I know myself to be a part of the physical universe and yet, somehow, I consider myself free from its causal inexorability and materiality. Each of us possesses a sense of self-identity, which sharply differentiates us from our surroundings. This sense of self that determines what is intimate to us and what is not. It is natural for the self to identify itself with all kinds of things that may be, at first, foreign to it, thereby reducing the non-self to itself. And just as the self identifies itself with something, it also, by a like act, alienates itself from something else. In this way the self constantly creates the other and negotiates with it, sometimes appropriating something from its domain and sometimes relegating something back to it. However, in this constant negotiation with the other, the lines never blur. The domain the self has appropriated for itself is special, intimate to itself. It is the 'I.' The other is always distant. However, though the borders between the self and the non-self are clearly etched, the passage from one to the other is fairly fluid. I can choose to identify myself with any object, person, or ideal. And at any moment I can choose to dissociate myself from them.

Moreover, whatever I identify myself with begins to exert control over me. My destiny now coincides with the destiny of the thing, person or idea I have identified with. To take an everyday example, the death of my neighbour's cat will not cause me half as much sorrow as the death of my own cat. In fact it may bring me no sorrow at all. The latter causes me grief because it is 'my' cat and for no other reason. In the same way the fate of any idea or ideal I have identified with is also my own fate. Its failure is often equivalent to my failure. It is for the same reason that when something causes me immense pain I may be compelled to completely detach myself from it, relegating it to the other. Once it has become the other, I am free from it.

Such an account of self-identity goes beyond thinking merely in terms of one's body. In fact, physicality has nothing to do with it. Rather, the self is seen as constantly outreaching itself to accommodate anything that may be physically separate from it. The cat, for instance, is an altogether different living entity. However, when it is my own pet cat there is a certain affinity which only points to an identification between myself and the cat. And this identification only means that somehow I have made the cat a part of my larger self, which is why it causes *me* pain when something painful occurs to the cat. Physically I may be an autonomous, independent entity that is localised in space. But the self is not merely corporal. And self-identity ought to be explicable in terms of the entire space that the self creates around itself that goes beyond mere physical space to also include psychological or noumenal space.

So far the analysis confirms to our common-sensical notions about ourselves. However, Vedanta takes the further leap by declaring that such a process of identification is at work not only with respect to things, people and ideas, but also my own body, mind and the ego. I identify myself with my body in just the same way as I identify myself with something else. Therefore, the status of my own body is no different from that of any other physical object. If I may so choose, I can dissociate my sense of self from my body, just as I can detach myself from any other object. The same is true for everything else constituting an organism. Vedanta accepts the psycho-physiology of Yoga according to which, apart from the body, *sarira*, a human being possesses a mind, *manas*, intelligence, *buddhi*, memory, *citta* and ego, *ahankara*.[4] All these together with the sense-organs and the body interpenetrate to create a thinking, acting, willing individual. The process of identification is at work at each one of these levels, the self identifying itself with all of them in the course of its daily existence.

If this is so then what is the real nature of the self, when it is not identified with anything at all? Who really am I? According to Vedanta, I am pure consciousness, self-existent and self-evident. The reasoning by which Vedanta arrives at this fact is referred to as *drg-drsya-viveka*,[5] that is, discrimination between the seer and the seen. It points out, in successive stages, certain self-evident facts about the self that finally lead to the seeing or understanding of the nature of the self. The logic is as follows. It is evident to us that we must be different from what we perceive. The fact that I perceive something implies that the thing is something separate from me. Perception, in some way or the other, presupposes distance or duality. Now even my own body and thoughts are something I perceive. Therefore, it follows that they must be something other than me, something apart from me.

After all, is not my own body also an experience of mine? The corporality and extension of the body are a part of the overall experience that I have so long as I am conscious of having a body. It may be true that my own body has a special status with respect to me as compared to other bodies or objects. I can 'feel' my own body in a manner that I cannot 'feel' other objects. I share a special intimacy with it. However, the point is that even this 'feel' or sense of intimacy are also experiences that I undergo. Being experiences, they must be themselves different from the experiencer. Moreover, my sentiency may only extend so far as the limits of my body (in particular, my sense of touch) allow it to, but the fact of sentiency itself is not enough to establish that the limits of the body are the limits of the self. The same logic can be applied to the mind. I can perceive my thoughts as they arise in the mind and I also perceive their disappearance. All this only implies that, as their seer, I am something separate from them.

B.   Self as Pure Consciousness

What does this discriminatory analysis between the perceiver and the perceived reveal about the nature of the self? If I experience my own thoughts, my body and all the numerous sensual perceptions, then who is this 'I' that is the subject of all these experiences? Who is this subject that is conscious of everything and yet itself is not something one can be conscious of? Certainly, it can only be consciousness. For, anything else can only form an object of consciousness, something which presents itself to consciousness. But the latter, accompanying every state and experience, is the eternal subject in which the entire world including my own body, mind and ego present themselves.

Moreover, even if I strip away all my identifications one by one, including that of my own mind and body, I still do not cease to be conscious. This conscious being that abides, irrespective of the presence and absence of any identification, is a pointer to what I really am. I can never doubt the fact that I am conscious. It may be argued that the fact, 'I am conscious,' does not itself lead to the further conclusion, 'I am consciousness.' But who is this 'I' who is conscious? Any answer we may give will only appeal to the domain of the perceived, the objectifiable in order to ascribe an owner to consciousness, which now becomes an attribute, a function of the one who possesses it. But whatever or whoever I take to be the owner or substratum of this consciousness is itself perceived in consciousness, in which and owing to which I am aware of it at the first place. The existence of anything, of any object that exists and for which we have a name, is known and recognized in consciousness. My own existence as a thinking, willing agent possessing a body is something I am conscious *of*, something I perceive in consciousness. Therefore, to assume the latter as an attribute that belongs to or arises from the former is to commit an error. Rather, the capacity to objectify that with which we mistakenly identify ourselves and the self-evidence of our own conscious being point to the one truth that my being can only be the being of consciousness.

In terms more familiar to Western thought, we may say that the logic of Vedanta relies on evidence of a phenomenological nature.[6] In this process certain facts may reveal themselves directly to the conscious subject. Such an approach was also characteristic of certain Continental thinkers of the last century, though they differ considerably in their approach as well as motives. In the context of Vedanta, however, it is illumining to consider a passage from Husserl's *Idea of Phenomenology* regarding what he calls the 'problem of transcendence':

> In all of its manifestations, knowledge is a mental experience: knowledge belongs to a knowing subject. The known objects stand over against it. How, then, can knowledge be sure of its agreement with the known objects? How can knowledge go beyond itself and reach its objects reliably? What appears to natural thinking as the matter-of-fact givenness of known objects within knowledge becomes a riddle. In perception, the perceived object is supposed to be immediately given. There stands the thing before my perceiving eyes. I see it; I grasp it. But the perception is nothing more than an experience that belongs to me, the perceiving subject ... How do I, the knowing subject, know - and how can I know for sure - that not only my experiences, these acts of knowing, exist, but also what they know exists? Indeed, how do I know that there is anything at all that can be set over against knowledge as an object?[7]

The problem is genuine. Though not the first, Husserl is here casting doubt on the very possibility of knowledge. Positing real existence of objects, of the world is questionable insofar as what is immediately given to me at any moment is always only my own experience. How can we talk of an agreement between thought or knowledge and reality if we always only have access to the former, never to the latter? It is this 'natural attitude' with respect to the world that Husserl is questioning. This is precisely what many philosophical traditions of the East and West, and Vedanta itself is driving at. But the similarity ends here. For where Husserl takes this as a challenge to be overcome, and prepares to redeem the objectivity of the world, Vedanta turns to consciousness itself as the only reality, the sole ground beneath the changing scenes of the world. Running right through the entire discourse of the Vedanta is this premise of consciousness as unnegatably present in all particular states and experiences, as well as in their absence. In fact, consciousness is that presence in which everything else presents itself or withdraws away.

A phenomenological analysis of experience, therefore, establishes the pervading presence of consciousness underneath and through all our particular experiences, thoughts and feelings. Vedanta carries this analysis into the states of dream and deep sleep to conclude that the continuity of consciousness is not broken even when one leaves the waking experiences behind. In sleep, the waking world may have withdrawn from consciousness but the latter does not cease to be. Moreover, the experience of dreams establishes something further. A dream is, so to say, sustained by the dreamer and its contents have no objective existence outside of us. And, moreover, it collapses as soon as I awake.[8] By analogy, Vedanta points out that the world present to us in the waking condition collapses when we enter into a dream or, for that matter, into deep sleep. In deep sleep, however, there is a complete absence of any objects or content of consciousness. Consciousness alone is - in itself and by itself.

The upshot of all this is that consciousness alone be taken be real, everything else - even one's own body, mind and everything else one considers as constitutive of oneself - being a mere appearance in consciousness. From this perspective, Vedanta leads us towards an understanding in which everything that seems to have an independent, objective existence is seen as existing in one's own consciousness. At any given moment, consciousness is one with whatever is arising. The trichotomy of the perceiver, perceived and the act of perception, therefore, dissolves into one unified 'perceiving' that alone is. And this 'perceiving' or 'seeing" is the intrinsic characteristic of consciousness. That is, it is *anubhavarupam.* So everything arises and vanishes in consciousness, but consciousness itself never ceases to be.

This is what is meant when Vedanta asserts that the self is of the nature of consciousness. Consciousness is identified with one's true self. In our normal waking life we cling to certain experiences mistaking them for our true self and thereby ascribing to these experiences an objective reality, an independent individualised existence. The seen is always mistaken for the seer. It is the seen that constantly arouses our curiosity and wonder. We study it, analyse it, and try to get into the very depths of it. The seer always escapes the scrutiny of the scalpel. Paradoxically, its existence stands unnoticed to itself. It remains oblivious to its own gaze. And the whole thrust of Vedanta is to direct the gaze of the seer back to itself, away from the seen. The self is this seer whose very nature is to be aware. In this seeing, moreover, the self sustains what is seen so that the object, the world have no independent existence outside one's consciousness. And our understanding of ourselves as psychophysical beings is only a consequence of the self as the seer identifying itself with certain experiences. Gaudapada, the author of the *Mandukya Karika*, sums it up as follows:

> All the Jivas (individuals) are, by their very nature, free
> from senility and death. They think, as it were, that they are
> subject to these and thus by this very thought they appear to
> deviate from their very nature.[9]

In identifying with the mortal, therefore, they seem to assume the fate of the mortal, which is change and death. Sankara (Adi Sankaracarya), in his commentary to the above mentioned work, explains that 'the Jivas are subject to senility and death on account of their identification, through thinking, with senility and death.'[10] So long as the self has identified itself with the body, it will also naturally make its own all that which comes to and occurs to the body. Therefore, if the body becomes inanimate, it is also taken as the end of the life of the self. But despite its mistaken sense of identity, the self can never really renounce its true nature, its *svarupa*, though it may appear to. In spite of all our unique, individual identities, we never cease to be what we really are - self-existent, self-evident consciousness.

And, as seen before, consciousness cannot cease to be. It is absurd to even speak of its birth or death. Everything else, which is an object of consciousness, is liable to change and perishing, owing to its being an object of consciousness. The very possibility of change belongs to the domain of what can be objectified. Consciousness, as we have seen, cannot be objectified because it is that in which any objectification takes place. All change, birth and death are phenomena perceived in consciousness. Thus consciousness itself, not being subject to what it perceives and what forms its object, is free from the fate of the perceived, that is, from birth and death.

The foregoing analysis has shed some light on the nature of the self unfolded by Vedanta. This served the purpose of leading us towards the understanding of death present in the Upanishads. Therefore, in as brief space as possible, the reasons behind the assertion of the impossibility of death have been explored. If I am not the body, then I am not subject to the fate of the body. Consciousness cannot die, just like it is never born. Therefore, if the self is indeed of the nature of consciousness then it must be immortal. Death only implies, at most, the cessation of certain kinds of experiences - those which we associate with the waking life.

3.   The Illusion of the Self

Death may be approached from another perspective. Wittgenstein's remark that death is not another event in life, not another experience because it implies the end of all possible experience is true only so long as one considers death an event external to life, as something that comes at the very end of it. However, death has also been viewed, not simply as something that brings an end to one's life, but as a constant concomitant to it. Such a view is typical of the Buddhist understanding of life. In fact, in Buddhism impermanence, *anityam*, is seen as the very essence of existence. Birth and death are not events that take place simply at the beginning and the end of one's life, but pervade the very fabric of existence.[11] We may highlight certain events in our life as beginnings and ends but in truth, reality is ever in a state of flux, ever being renewed. And renewal implies death.

A.   The Art of Dying

Ordinarily we live with the belief that one day we will cease to be. Obviously, the belief implies that I regard death as something that will happen to me in the distant future. Do I not in this process mentally separate life from death, creating an unbridgeable gap between the two? Moreover, is not living with such a belief living in continual fear? And continuously attempting to perpetuate our own existence as a consequence of that fear? Jiddu Krishnamurti, an Indian thinker of the last century, offers, in his conversations, a painstaking analysis of death and this human fear of death. Observing the trend of an ordinary life, he comments:

> When you look at all this - the beliefs, the comforts, the desire for comfort, knowing that there is an ending, the hope that next life you will continue, and the whole intellectual rationalisation of death - you see that you have separated dying from living ... everyday living with all its conflicts, the miseries, the attachments, the despairs, the anxieties, the violence, the suffering, the tears and the laughter. Why has the mind separated life from dying? The life that we lead, the everyday life, the shoddiness of it, the bitterness of it, the emptiness of it, the travail, the routine, the office year in and year out ... all that we call living. The strife, the struggle, the ambition, the corruption, the fleeting affections and joys and pleasures: that is what we call living. And we say death mustn't enter into that field because that is all we know, and death we do not know; therefore keep it away. So we cling to the known- please watch it in yourself- to the known, to the remembrance of things past, to memories, to experiences, which are all known and therefore the past. We cling to the past and that is what we call the known. And the unknown is death. So there is a wide gulf between the known and the unknown ... .[12]

To understand death, therefore, one must first understand life. And what does one discover when one contemplates over one's own everyday existence? Our life consists of a never-ending series of hopes, desires, efforts, beliefs, projects and experiences. And in their continuation is our own perpetuation. Death is understood as the end, the culmination of all such hopes, projects and experiences. For, I cannot imagine myself in their absence. I identify myself with them. I am them. The passage of my life consists of a continuous accumulation of experience. And my understanding of myself is born through such experience. Such knowledge of the self, of the 'I,' 'me' and 'mine' is perpetuated through one's life as one gathers more and more experiences. Therefore, experience is constantly strengthening the self. As Krishnamurti points out, 'consciousness as the "me" is the centre of recognition, and recognition is merely the process of the accumulation of experience.'[13] Recognition, therefore, as Krishnamurti observes, is the very basis of experience. This is an all-important point. He explains it thus:

> According to my memories, I react to whatever I see, to whatever I feel. In this process of reacting to what I see, what I feel, what I know, what I believe, experience is taking place, is it not? Reaction, response to something seen, is experience. When I see you, I react; the naming of that reaction is experience. If I do not name that reaction it is not an experience. Watch your own responses and what is taking place about you. There is no experience unless there is a naming process going on at the same time. If I do not recognize you, how can I have the experience of meeting you? It sounds simple and right. Is it not a fact? That is if I do not react according to my memories, according to my conditioning, my prejudices, how can I know that I have had an experience?[14]

Therefore, recognition, response and reaction comprise experience. As explained, it is impossible to have an experience without recognition playing a crucial part in the process. Recognition, moreover, is rooted in memory. It is possible due to the latter. It is impossible to have an experience, therefore, without the functioning of memory is some form or the other. This implies, moreover, that my understanding of myself is mediated through memory, because my self-identity also arises within experience. In fact, it may not be too much to say that the identity of individual existence is maintained through it. Thought too is a product of memory. Now if my conception of myself is rooted in memory, then my conception of my own end, that is, my death must also be understood in its context. Therefore, death, being the end of all experience, implies the end of memory, the end of the mind and the end of all identification.

If this is so then is it possible to end experience right now? If death implies the end of memory and accumulation of experience, then is it not possible to die at this very moment and thereby invite death at our doorstep? Can we cease thinking of death as an event in the distant future and 'begin to die' right here and right now? Is not the division of life as the known and death as the unknown an artificial one? Death, as we have come to see, is the end of the 'I.' Is it not possible to bring an end to this 'I' while still living?

According to Krishnamurti, not only is this possible, but to learn to die is the only true way to live. Dying, understood in this manner, means dying to one's identifications, one's experiences and one's thoughts and beliefs by letting go of them all. It means dying to oneself every moment. If I am able to end all my attachments here and now, then I have brought death into the very moment of living.[15] In doing so, I am also spontaneously free of any fear associated with death. To end all one's attachments means simply to end one's identifications with ideals, with beliefs, objects, habits and with one's own self-image. And this is what is meant by saying that one must die to the known, for all of the former is rooted in the past, in memory and, therefore, belongs to the field of the known.

But how is this possible? How can one die to oneself while one is still alive? To begin with, one does not really have to do anything because dying is already built into the very fabric of life. One merely has to recognise the truth of that fact. Moreover, if one made an effort to die, one would perpetuate the very thing one wants to end, which is experience. For, to take any ourse of action, to follow a plan, means to act on the basis of memory, recognition and accumulation. It means to strengthen the very 'I' that we want to end. Instead, the only possibility that offers itself is what Krishnamurti refers to as 'seeing oneself from moment to moment in the mirror of relationship.'[16] This 'seeing' could occur in one's relationships with anything - objects, people, ideas and feelings. The crucial thing is that one must follow every thought, feeling and action as it occurs without trying to either alter it or hang on to it:

> To understand that process, there must be the intention to know "what is", to follow every experience; and to understand "what is" is extremely difficult, because "what is" is never still, never static, it is always in movement. The "what is" is what you are, not what you would like to be; it is not the ideal, because the ideal is fictitious, but it is actually what you are doing, thinking and feeling from moment to moment.[17]

In this passive alertness and watchfulness to every thought and experience, I neither condemn anything nor identify myself with it. I simply watch myself from moment to moment without the process of accumulation. Therefore, in continually dying to all accumulation and identification, I pre-empt the birth of the process that strengthens the 'I,' a process which is rooted in memory. Dying, therefore, becomes a continuous activity embedded into the very fabric of living. It becomes a way of being.

4.   Seeing the Seer
A.   The Problematic

We have considered two apparently opposed notions of death - one that considers the self immortal and the other stating the very opposite - the continuous dying of the self. In fact, according to the latter, not only is death possible, but something of us is dying every moment. And to live is to recognise death as the very essence of life. The two notions are representative of the two age-old philosophical, religious and spiritual traditions of India - Vedanta and Buddhism. In fact, the question of the eternality or impermanence of the self has been the perennial point of contention between the two. At the same time, such views are not restricted to these two schools alone but are representative of larger philosophical positions about the nature of the self. In the history of thought, there has always existed one side that asserts the existence of an eternal, deathless substance and another that denies reality to any kind of permanence or constancy. But our consideration of the problem has made one thing clear - that the two are not as opposed as they have been made out to be and may indeed be reconcilable. And that it may be possible to break free from the dialectical constrains of thought to arrive at a genuine resolution - an answer that is not merely an overt synthesis of opposing positions but the truth of them both, revealing their inherent oneness and unity of vision.

To set up the opposition explicitly, according to Vedanta, the self is eternal. In fact, it is the sole reality, nothing else having an independent existence of its own. For, the being of everything is reducible to the being of consciousness. I am what is. According to Buddhism, not only is the self not eternal, but it has no intrinsic reality of its own, being merely a construction of the mind. We may have a sense of self but it is misleading. In reality there is no such thing. Now a resolution of this conflict is possible if it is discovered that the word 'self' has been understood differently by the two parties. Thus, in possessing different denotations, it may not even be referring to the same entity, thereby pre-empting any potential conflict. We may be, then, just quarreling over a word. Let us see if this is actually the case.

B.   Death and the Timeless

To kill the self, as Krishnamurti points out, is to kill all identification. It is to end the process of continuous accumulation through experience, which strengthens the 'I' or the ego. This 'I' is nothing but one's identification with one's experiences, holding on to that identification and perpetuating it. At this point it might be worthwhile to consider David Hume's famous denial of the self, not very different from the Buddhist's own argument against it:

> There are some philosophers who imagine we are every moment intimately conscious of what we call our self; that we feel its existence and its continuance in existence … . For my part, when I enter most intimately into what I call myself I always stumble on some particular perception or other, of heat or cold, light or shade, love or hatred, pain or pleasure. I never can catch myself at any time without a perception and never can observe anything but the perception.[18]

Krishnamurti's call for a continuous 'dying to the self' means precisely the recognition of this fact - that there is no abiding self. When one actually begins to study oneself moment to moment in the mirror of relationship, one transcends the process of the creation and perpetuation of the ego, which is nothing but the centre of accumulation of experience. One realises that the self is only a creation of memory and one's identification with the experiences rooted in that memory. And that the creation of self-identity is an artificial process of the mind.

However, the very denial of a self belies the truth of the opposite thesis, that is, its unnegatable existence. And it hints at the discovery of that other denotation of the word 'self,' which is spoken of by Vedanta. How is this possible? Hume's fundamental error lay in his attempt to search for the self in the domain of his perceptions, his experiences. However, if the self is the very subject of experience, then it is absurd to look for it in the domain of the objects, or that which can be objectified. Hume's criticism of the philosopher who claimed that he was conscious of a self is justified because there really is no such thing. But this is only so because it is impossible to be 'conscious of' a self, since the self is the very subject of consciousness. Even Buddhist criticisms of the existence of an abiding self center around the failure of finding an abiding substance in any rigorous self-examination or enquiry. The assumption, in both cases, lies in taking the subject, *visayi,* for a possible object, *visaya*, of consciousness. The culminating words of the dialogue between Yajnavalkya and Maitreyi in the Brhadaranyaka Upanishad drive the point home. Yajnavalkya, the great sage of this Upanishad, tells her:

'By what means can one perceive him by means of whom one perceives this whole world? Look - by what means can one perceive the perceiver?'[19]

So how is it possible to be 'conscious of' that by which one is conscious of everything? How can it ever be known? Sankara, in his commentary on the above verse, explains:

> ... when one sees something, through what instrument should know That owing to which all this is known? For that instrument of knowledge itself falls under the category of objects. The knower may desire to know, not about itself, but about objects. As fire does not burn itself, so the self does not know itself, and the knower can have no knowledge of a thing that is not its object. Therefore through what instrument should one know the knower owing to which this universe is known?[20]

The problem always lies in assuming that the self is some kind of entity, against which we are continually warned by Vedanta. And since it is not an entity, it is never available for observation or perception. The tendency to think of the self as an entity, in fact, to think of everything in terms of that, may have deeper roots in the substance metaphysics so intrinsic to our habitual modes of thinking, according to which the reality of anything is a function of its 'thing-ness.' If something *is* then it is *out there*. After all, we only know the existence of anything through our sense-organs and the latter can only reveal a world that is tangible, physical, perceptible, available to the touch. And, therefore, our understanding of what is real, in fact, of the word 'real' itself, proceeds from this evidence of the senses.

This belief that the existence of anything can only be a substantive existence is universally present in our thinking irrespective of what the object of enquiry is. By this account, therefore, the self too ought to be a kind of substance - perhaps not physical but a subtle, noumenal sort of substance nevertheless. It seems that it cannot be any other way because what we perceive is what guides us to make sense of words such as 'real' or 'existing.' And naturally, what we perceive, we call 'real' or 'existent.' Though here the element of circularity is easily seen. But more pertinently, the question arises, what is the metaphysical status, the 'reality' of the self who is the perceiver, the one to whom the whole world (including our own bodies) presents itself and asserts, 'I am here!?' Is this self existent or non-existent? Certainly no sensory evidence can be adduced for it. It cannot be perceived for it is the very perceiver. And for the same reason cannot possess any of the attributes by which we pronounce an object in the world real. If one goes looking for the self in the domain of the objects (of the senses or of the mind), one is never going to find it. That is why Yajnavalkya says in the Brhadaranyaka Upanishad: 'Not this, not this!'[21]

Therefore, it is apparent that when Vedanta speaks of the immortality of the self, it is referring to that subject which must be presupposed in all experience. The presence of change and impermanence can only be known on the assumption of something that abides through them. How else is awareness of change even possible? Therefore, the Upanishads are pointing to the very condition of possibility of any experience whatsoever. And not some abiding substance that lasts for eternity! The eternal nature of the self only points to the fact that since all possible change is perceived by the self, the latter itself must be free from change, and, therefor, from time. The seeming difference, therefore, between the skeptics and the saviours of the self vanishes when the notions of eternity and immortality are understood in the context of timelessness.

And here the difference in the possible denotations of the word 'self' becomes apparent. The self, spoken of by Vedanta, does not refer to the identity of individual existence, to the 'I,' the ego, which, as we have seen, is supervenient upon mind and memory. Rather, it attempts to lead the individual away from such identifications that constitute our ordinary sense of identity towards realising the self as pure consciousness alone, as that which is the very ground, the condition of possibility of any identification or experience. At any instant of my life, I cannot doubt the fact that I am. The question is only whether I am what I take myself to be in the course of my daily existence. And, regarding this point, Vedanta and Buddhism unanimously question the reality of the everyday self, which according to them, is derivative and does not have an intrinsic reality of its own. Therefore, both also attempt to remove erroneous notions and prescribe ways by which the truth of it may be seen and appreciated. One way or the other, one must learn to die to this derivative self. In the words of Krishnamurti:

> Immortality is not the continuation of the "me". The "me" and the "mine" are of time, the result of action towards an end. So there is no relationship between the 'me' and the "mine" and that which is immortal, timeless. We would like to think there is a relationship, but this is an illusion. That which is immortal cannot be encased in that which is mortal. That which is immeasurable cannot be caught in the net of time.[22]

When one sees the truth of this one not only ends the apparent conflict between death and immortality, but recognises that the immortality of the self can only be realised when one has mastered the art of dying. Wittgenstein may be right after all when he remarked that we never live to experience death. And to master the art of dying is not to have another experience, but to end all experience while still living. In the very same remark Wittgenstein continues: 'If we take eternity to mean not infinite temporal duration but timelessness, then eternal life belongs to those who live in the present.'[23]

Notes

[1] Katha Upanishad, *The Early Upanishads*, P. Olivelle (trans), Oxford University Press, New York, 1998, p. 379.

[2] Ibid., p. 381.

[3] L. Wittgenstein, *Tractatus Logico Philosophicus*, D. F. Pears and B. F. Mcuinness (trans), Routledge, London, 2004, p. 87.

[4] The English translations of these Sanskrit words slightly differ in meaning. At best they may act as a guide to the original words. In fact, in case of the word 'sarira,' Yoga speaks of each individual possessing, not one body, but various bodily sheaths, each encased in the other and differing in level of subtlety.

[5] B. Tirtha, *Drg-Drsya-Viveka*, S. Nikhilananda (trans), Advaita Ashrama, Kolkata, 2006.

[6] The question of precisely how phenomenology ought to be understood in the context of Vedanta, as distinct from its understanding in Continental thought, is a question outside the scope of our current enquiry. For now it will suffice to say that the Upanishads put a premium on first-person experiences as they present themselves to consciousness without taking the nature or reality of anything for granted, and following the evidence of the facts so revealed.

[7] E. Husserl, *The Idea of Phenomenology*, Kluwer Academic Publishers, Dordrecht, 1999, p. 17.

[8] Gaudapada, *Mandukya Upanishad & Karika*, S. Nikhilananda (trans), Advaita Ashrama, Kolkata, 2000.

[9] Ibid., p. 222.

[10] Adi Sankaracharya, Ibid.

[11] T. R. V. Murti, *The Central Conception of Buddhism*, Munshiram Manoharlal, New Delhi, 2006.

[12] J. Krishnamurti, *On Living & Dying*, KFI, Chennai, 2004, p. 56.

[13] J. Krishnamurti, *The First & Last Freedom*, KFI, Chennai, 2001, p. 36.

[14] Ibid., pp. 62-63.

[15] Krishnamurti, *On Living and Dying*, p. 12.

[16] Krishnamurti, *The First & Last Freedom*, p. 36.

[17] Ibid., p. 33.

[18] D. Hume, *Treatise of Human Nature*, Oxford University Press, New York, 2000, p. 162.
[19] Brhadaranyaka Upanishad, *The Early Upanishads*, P. Olivelle (trans),. Oxford University Press, New York, 1998, p. 71.
[20] Adi Sankaracarya, Brhadaranyaka Upanishad with Bhashyam, S. Madhavananda (trans), Advaita Ashrama, Kolkata, 2004, p. 259.
[21] Brhadaranyaka Upanishad, *The Early Upanishads*, p. 67.
[22] Krishnamurti, *On Living & Dying*, p. 12.
[23] Wittgenstein, op cit., p. 87.

Bibliography

Brhadaranyaka Upanishad, *The Early Upanishads*. P. Olivelle (trans), Oxford University Press, New York, 1998.

Gaudapada, *Mandukya Upanishad & Karika*. S. Nikhilananda (trans), Advaita Ashrama, Kolkata, 2000.

Hume, D., *Treatise of Human Nature*. Oxford University Press, New York, 2000.

Husserl, E., *The Idea of Phenomenology*. Kluwer Academic Publishers, Dordrecht, 1999.

Katha Upanishad, *The Early Upanishads*. P. Olivelle (trans), Oxford University Press, New York, 1998.

Krishnamurti, J., *On Living & Dying*. KFI, Chennai, 2004.

——, *The First & Last Freedom*. KFI, Chennai, 2001.

Murti, T. R. V., *The Central Conception of Buddhism*. Munshiram Manoharlal, New Delhi, 2006.

Sankaracarya, Adi, *Mandukya Upanishad & Karika*. S. Nikhilananda (trans), Advaita Ashrama, Kolkata, 2000.

——, *Brhadaranyaka Upanishad with Bhashyam*. S. Madhavananda (trans), Advaita Ashrama, Kolkata, 2004.

Tirtha, B., *Drg-Drsya-Viveka*. S. Nikhilananda (trans), Advaita Ashrama, Kolkata, 2006.

Wittgenstein, L., *Tractatus Logico Philosophicus*. D. F. Pears and B. F. Mcuinness (trans), Routledge, London, 2004.

Dhruv Raj Nagar is currently studying Vedanta and Paninian Grammar at the *Arsha Vijñana Gurukulam* , Vedapuri, India. Prior to this, he completed his M.Phil. in Philosophy in 2009 from the University of Delhi, after having graduated in Mathematics in 2005 from the same.

Sites that Cope, Cure and Commemorate:
Weblogs of Terminally Ill

Marga Altena and Nothando Ngwenya

Abstract
This text investigates weblogs of terminally ill created by patients to express emotions about dying and death, as well as to reflect about their life and how they want to be remembered. The authors analysed weblogs of terminally ill employed as research instruments in English hospices as well as weblogs created by individual patients in private settings in the Netherlands. Altena and Ngwenya find that weblogs provide an innovative means of funerary expression. They argue that weblogs are important mediators to help patients and their bereaved to cope with their illness, imminent death and mourning. Furthermore, the patients' comprehension and acceptance of their situation through the use of weblogs could possibly help in the prediction of their mental and physical health improvement.

Key Words: Bereaved, death, dying, health care instruments, hospice, LIWC, patients' agency, terminally ill, weblogs.

*****

1.   **Introduction**
        In the dealings with death and dying in Western Europe today, the Internet has become an important means of expression and communication. In the last twenty years, new reports and rituals have emerged on the internet that both reflected and affected people's daily lives, including funerary culture. People have been using the Internet to acquire information about illnesses, treatments and medicine, as well as about the performance of funerals. Patients, their family and friends employ websites to connect to like-minded people in order to share their feelings and thoughts. In digital diaries, weblogs, terminally ill patients record the way they cope with being ill and their impending death.[1] As care takers in institutions become aware of the beneficial effect of these weblogs, they encourage patients to keep weblogs. Next to this, weblogs of terminally ill are used by professionals in hospices as research instruments to acquire insight in the patients' daily lives and needs.
        This chapter investigates weblogs used by terminally ill people in England and in the Netherlands that came about by instigation of hospices and that were created by private initiative. Being researchers who investigate weblogs as a therapeutic intervention (Ngwenya) and weblogs as a new means of funerary ritual (Altena), we are interested in the ways people handle

death and grief and how they give shape to the events and emotions they have
to endure. By what texts and images do patients express themselves about
death and mourning; how do these weblogs relate to their non-digital lives;
do weblogs of terminally ill initiated by institutions differ from those that
were created individually; how are the dead present in people's weblogs; and
does this change in time?

Working in different fields of disciplines - psychology and visual
culture - we felt challenged to explore weblogs of terminally ill by
implementing methods that are quantitative and qualitative. On the one hand,
we studied the frequency of specific emotionally-laden concepts and the
importance these have for the author. On the other hand, we analysed the
weblog authors' contributions by looking at their choice of topics, words and
images, how these are appreciated and how weblogs function in people's
lives.

Weblogs draw on existing traditions, whether these are social or
cultural conventions. The success of a weblog depends strongly on its ability
to communicate and to connect to the larger traditions of mortuary
expression. Because of this, weblogs need to be studied in the context of the
author's everyday life. In studying the use of weblogs initiated by both
institutions and individuals we are especially interested in the way weblogs
are employed to help people cope with their disease; how these contribute to
an improved health; and how they help dying people and their bereaved to
find comfort.

In our effort to answer these questions we were inspired by several
authors and methods. With respect to weblogs as a coping instrument the four
concepts of Glaser and Strauss were useful, indicating the degrees of
awareness of approaching death among medical staff, patients and their
family: 'closed awareness,' 'suspected awareness,' 'mutual pretence' and
'open awareness,' later expanded by Taylor's notion of 'conditional
awareness.'[2] The quantitative analysis in the first case study employed the
tool of LIWC (Linguistic Inquiry and Word Count) which assesses the
frequency of emotionally-laden concepts in weblogs text.

As to the qualitative method of the second research case respecting
the innovation of people's expression about death and grief and the meanings
attributed to weblogs, the work of Brian de Vries and Judy Rutherford was
helpful.[3] De Vries and Rutherford stated that media such as films, television
shows and the Internet represent new opportunities for post death ritual.[4]
Although it seems obvious that this is the case with the new medium of
weblogs, an interesting question is in what ways weblogs by terminally ill
draw from existing traditions in funerary culture. As to how the weblogs
relate to the patients' real lives, the analysis was inspired by Tony Walter
who analysed the collective construction of a durable biography of the
deceased as a means to mourn and to incorporate the memory of the dead in

the lives of the bereaved.[5] As both the biographical and the social element are prominent in weblogs of terminally ill it will be interesting to explore how these contribute to this process of memory building, before death occurs.

Having introduced the weblogs that are the focus and the methods of analysis, the following part of this chapter presents two case studies coming from the authors' different fields of research. Each of these case studies will be analysed according to the questions presented above, highlighting their faculties to cope, cure and commemorate. We will conclude with an evaluation of our findings and of the concepts of analysis we applied

2. The First Case: Weblogs of Terminally Ill People in English Hospices

In Western Europe, the awareness and communication about dying and death has changed over time. In the eighteenth century, death was experienced as public and a subject that was openly discussed.[6] This all changed in the following century when death became invisible and very much a private affair. In the twentieth century, death became bureaucratised when all funeral rituals were taken from the home and passed onto funeral parlours. Society encouraged people to place their faith in technology and science and, as a result, grew used to deny death.[7] In daily practice and in medicine, isolation of dying patients was believed to help the transition into death.

The nineteenth and twentieth century have been typified as a period in which humans have either tried to defer or to deny death.[8] Death arouses many conflicting emotions in humans including sorrow, anger, helplessness and, most of all, fear. Hinton declared that the fear of dying and death has been a main force in the emerging medicalisation of death and the prolongation of life. The understanding of death as a taboo in the past two centuries has led to death being approached with an attitude that can be defined as a 'closed awareness' where medical staff and relatives kept patients ignorant of their impending death.[9] The twenty-first century has seen a slight change in the conceptualisation of dying and death as can be perceived from the different debate forums, conferences and considerable amount of literature that encourage open communication.

Glaser and Strauss divided people's awareness of dying into four sections: 'closed awareness,' experienced in the nineteenth and twentieth century, when death was not openly discussed and medical professionals kept patients ignorant of their upcoming death; 'suspected awareness,' where patients suspected their imminent death but were not informed; 'mutual pretence,' where the medical staff, relatives and the patient pretended that they did not know of the patient's imminent death; and 'open awareness,' where medical practitioners and the patient openly discuss the patient's imminent death.[10] Taylor added a fifth category, that of 'conditional awareness,' where medical practitioners employ moderating strategies when discussing a dying patient's prognoses.[11] Although the way people talk about death and dying has become more open, Ngwenya suggests that the current climate is experiencing what is known as Taylor's 'conditional awareness.' In this chapter, analysis shows that weblogs can contribute to the essential 'open awareness' for both the patients and relatives in the removal of uncertainties and fear and in helping them to deal with death.

Next to changes in people's conception of death, the changing epidemiology has brought about a decline in mortality in Western Europe.[12] In the nineteenth century, people died from infectious diseases because of unhealthy living conditions and the absence of professional treatment. Today, death occurs due to chronic illnesses affecting mostly elderly people. The dramatic change in both the sociology and epidemiology calls for an adaptation of the social norms and conceptualisations of the terms concerning death.

For people to accept death as part of nature and to deal with dying in a dignified manner, they need to understand the phenomenon. Zimmerman reported how a death denying society can complicate open communication and produce obstacles in discussions at the time of death.[13] A death denying society can also hinder choices for alternative options, like choosing the place of death or deciding to stop futile treatments. So far, the twenty-first century has seen a slight change of attitude concerning dying and death within society.

Death is becoming perceptible once more with a move towards 'open awareness' of death. The movement towards openness at the time of death has changed societal attitudes and improved communications and understandings of dying. In this process, new media like television and the internet play a prominent role. Deconstructing the expressions and experiences of terminally ill patients on weblogs may contribute to a better understanding of dealings with the dying process today.

Since Dame Cicely Saunders founded the first hospice in England in 1967, hospices have been promoting palliative care at the end of life. English hospices have grown considerably offering specialised care to terminally ill patients and their families. This care has tried to follow the needs of patients in different ways such as in-patient, out-patient, day-care, and home-care services. Although, hospices go a long way to meet the patients' needs, literature suggests that clinicians are still hesitant to create an 'open awareness' of death.

Weblogs supply open communication for terminally ill patients, being a platform where they can express themselves, where they can find information and where they can report their plans about terminal care. In weblogs, like in non-digital life, talking about dying and death to terminally ill patients helps them make meaning of their death as well as to inform the bereaved about the dying process which can assist in caring for dying patients.[14]

Terminally ill patients considered talking about dying and death very helpful as it encouraged them to explore the personal meaning of their death and to plan for terminal care. The taboo nature of death and dying may lead to misunderstanding within palliative care whereby a patient who talks about wanting to die may be mistaken as a request for assistive dying, whereas they may simply require palliative rather than restorative treatment.[15] Open discussion of their death has reassured patients and dispelled some fears and reservations they had about dying.[16] Cancer patients have reported increased support and enhanced quality of life through using the internet as a support mechanism.[17]

In recent years, there has been an increasing interest in the use of the Internet to remember the dead. Traditionally, public memorials were created at cemeteries in the form of tombstones and other stone memorials, with messages about as well as directed to dead loved ones.[18] Family fragmentation or geographical and time limitations, in case of visits to physical memorials, made people look for alternative media to establish memorials. Today, the Internet is embraced as a new medium of mourning giving individuals the opportunity to create permanent memorials and the ability to share memories with friends and family anywhere in the world.

The past decade has seen a rapid development of memorial websites both from personal and collective, commercial users, such as www.memoriallink.com, www.christianmemorials.com, and www.lightacandle.co.uk. These websites supply services varying from online biographical memorials, to dedicated Christian websites and other sites offering individuals to light a virtual candle in memory of their dead. Some of the sites are public; whilst others have the option of being private.

These websites are proof of people's need to continue bonds with their dead loved ones online. Aitkin has noticed that the language used when writing these blogs are words addressed to the dead as if they can read them.[19] Weblogs may be comforting to the bereaved as they feel that they are still in touch or somehow connected to the deceased. The continuation of relationships with the deceased in conventional media has been well-documented in literature and is now also present in weblogs and web memorials.

Although the 'presence' of the dead person in the life of the living is perceived as an important part of dealing with death and part of the process of grieving, this continued relationship has been suppressed, in the recent past.[20] As the Internet has grown into an important and central part of people's everyday lives and the way they communicate, it was to be expected that it also became a place to grieve.[21] The Internet seems to fill the void between the living and the dead in a way that helps the living to reach out to the dead. The usage of weblogs continues the bond between the dead and the living, a finding that not only encourages the debate on dying and death but that also has the potential to facilitate a death accepting society rather than a death denying society.

In the twentieth century dominant advice to the bereaved was to mourn and to get over it.[22] Today, the prevalence and increasing presence of weblogs of terminally ill and web memorials undeniably defy this advice. In weblogs individual patients as well as their bereaved choose to deal with death *their* way. This way, weblogs of terminally ill provide a medium that acknowledges - individually and collectively, publicly and privately - the presence of the death and mourning in society.

Despite the lack of 'open awareness,' terminally ill patients have found ways of openly talking about dying and death, whilst expressing themselves in a therapeutic way by means of weblogs. Research has shown that many palliative care users are employing the Internet for support and communication. Many terminally ill patients reported that they have found most information about their illness and how to cope with it on the Internet. The effectiveness of Internet-based interventions in hospices with an increase in virtual hospices and tele-hospices was also affirmed by research. These are interventions that rather enhance than replace traditional care, a circumstance that has contributed to their popularity.

Patients have accounted that keeping a weblog promotes catharsis, a statement that is confirmed by research and literature on therapeutic writing. Literature confirms that writing about a stressful or traumatic experience can result in physical and psychological health improvements. Pennebaker conducted several studies on therapeutic writing with participants reporting significant health benefits including reduced visits to the doctor, better lung and liver function as well as improved immune system functioning.[23]

Next to the patients, care takers in hospices employed weblogs to identify the reported improvements in health and to explore the emotional, cognitive and structural components of experiences of terminally ill people, focusing on the patients' language. Medical practitioners chose weblogs as a source of research as they are unobtrusive tools which can be used in a real life environment. It was a major advantage that participants could continue with their everyday lives rather than having the inconvenience of being monitored in a laboratory environment, whilst at the same time taking part in the research through their weblogs. The weblogs provided rich data as they give natural language samples. The participants were unaware of the variables under investigation, thus strengthening the external validity of the research.

Within the field of thanatology, so far there has been little discussion about the experiences and the actual expressions of the individuals who blog. Most of the studies remained limited to descriptions of web technology. Only very few have involved bloggers as co-researchers through in-depth interviews to explore their motivations and purposes for using this tool. Here, the analysis of the first case study consists of a linguistic inquiry to explore the expressions these individuals use through their language.

Research has shown that the use of words can expose important characteristics of people's social and psychological worlds serving as markers of personality, emotional state, health and cognitive styles.[24] The words that individuals use to express themselves can be diagnostic of their mental and physical health. Language can also be used to determine people's health, as well as to improve it by identifying individuals with specific needs and developing the most appropriate interventions for them. Examples would be the high percentage use of first person singular words that indicate depressed and suicidal individuals. The analysis of this case study is more interested in the words people use rather than the content of what they say.

The analysis of this case study employed the tool of LIWC (Linguistic Inquiry and Word Count) which is unobtrusive and allows for a reliable and quick analysis of the weblogs text. The quantitative analysis method conducted through the use of LIWC can assist in developing inferences about contextual- and text-based variables. The research source (weblogs) of the case study, and the analysis tool of the LIWC, were intended to avoid any inconvenience to the research participants and to limit any disruption to their lives during their illness and bereavement.

The LIWC method consists of more than seventy linguistic or psychologically relevant categories within its dictionaries and it is able to analyse any text-based sample. The text sample is defined by the percentage of words contained in it from all the different categories. The output of the LIWC program also holds descriptive information such as the total number of words in the text sample, mean number of words per sentence, and number of words longer than six letters. These are all part of the language composition category including the pronouns, articles and prepositions. Next to that, the LIWC method also captures the *emotional, cognitive, sensory,* and *social processes* under the psychological processes categories. Positive *emotion* words include optimistic words and positive feeling words, whereas negative emotion words include any words associated with negative feelings such as anxiety, fear, and anger. *Cognitive* processes include words that tap active thinking. Self reflection words such as 'realise' and 'know' suggest an understanding; whereas causal words, such as 'because', 'effect,' 'hence' make an attempt at explaining a cause. *Social processes* include references to others and *sensory* processes include references to any of the five senses, like hear, feel and see. *Relativity* is another category within the LIWC and refers to time, space and motion. The last category is *current concerns* which identify themes present in an individual's text sample.

The LIWC processes text files by analysing each file sequentially. LIWC searches the dictionary file for each word within the text and for each word that is found, the category to which that word belongs is incremented. LIWC 2007 has approximately 80 output variables including 22 standard linguistic features, 3 paralinguistic dimensions, 32 psychological dimensions, 12 punctuation categories, and 4 general descriptors.

The analysis of the naturally-occurring text in a patient's weblog identified linguistic markers of the author's emotional state. In this case study, one patient's blog was analysed to show the method of analysis and to reveal how blog analysis can be utilised to enhance hospice care. The use of a weblog as an unobtrusive research tool enabled a trend analysis across a length of time, an analysis which would have been quite difficult and inconvenient to perform in a psychological laboratory. As this was a family blog, only the posts from the last two years entered by the patient were used in this analysis. In order to process these blog posts with LIWC, each post was converted to a word file. There were 5 post entries taken, beginning from February 2008 and ending in June 2009. No observed regular frequency was observed in which the patient posted entries in their weblog.

The primary focus of this analysis was the emotional words used. Research has reported that people who use a higher rate of negative emotion words and less positive emotion words are more likely to suffer from depression.[25] The use of emotion words can also inform us of how an individual is experiencing a particular situation as emotional response is always prevalent in people's reaction to an event or the way they cope with a trauma.[26]

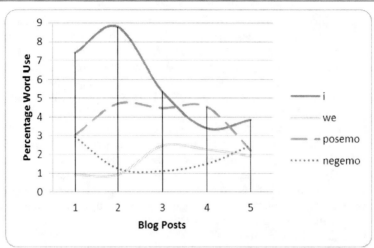

Figure 1: Trend analysis of emotion words, of first person singular and plural pronouns.

Figure 1 indicates that the patient initially has a high use of first person singular pronouns at 7.41% which slowly decreases to 3.86%. It is a decrease that is clearly illustrated by the trend analysis. There is also an increase in the use of first person plural pronouns as shown in the figure above from 0.93% to 1.93%. There is very low use of negative emotion words with the highest use being a percentage of 2.91%. During the blogging process, negative emotion word use decreases in blog posts 2 and 3 and increases again in blog posts 4 and 5. Positive emotion word use decreases from 3.04% in blog post 1 to 2.2% in blog post 5.

These results show that at the start of the blogging process, the patient had a more personal approach to their illness and was exploring personal thoughts and feelings of their experience. This is shown by the high word use of first personal singular pronouns. Within blog posts 1 and 2 which show an increased use of first person singular pronouns, the patient recalls their diagnosis and the feelings associated with this stressful time and the treatment they would have to undergo. These two posts were characterised by a continued use of negative emotion words as shown in Figure 1. It is a finding that has important implications indicating a possibly depressing time for the patient. This follows past research which states that high use of first personal singular pronouns is associated with depression or negative affective states.[27]

With time, the patient's use of first person plural pronouns elevated. A possible explanation for this could be an indication of social integration as the patient shared their experience with the social world online and formed online relationships. Figure 1 depicts the patient's use of this pronoun and shows the simultaneous decrease in the use of first person singular pronoun. This finding supports previous research which shows a drop in first personal singular pronouns and an increase in first person plural pronouns in online chat rooms following a traumatic experience.[28] An implication of these results is the possibility of predicting health improvement for patients as well as their emotional state.

The negative and positive emotion words used by the patient correlate with the events described in the blog posts. Blog post 5 is characterised by negative emotion words as the patient describes feelings about not being able to get a particular drug that is considered vital. The description of this event also shows a decrease in positive emotion words. The patient also describes an increasingly physical pain while getting sicker, more tired, and seemingly more immersed in the traumatic situation which is described as 'going downhill.'

These findings show how weblogs and LIWC can be used to indicate patients' psychological states and health changes. By identifying a possible depressive time for a patient, clinicians can respond to this by contacting the patient and sending relief or other suitable interventions. The findings suggest that text analysis of weblogs can be useful to enhance palliative outreach services, by indicating the patient's emotional state and by identifying the need for social support. Further work in this area could include the physiological outcomes to support and measure the accuracy of the text analysis on health predictions.

3.   The Second Case: Weblogs of Terminally Ill in Dutch Private Settings

In the last two decades in the Netherlands, the public attention for funerary culture has grown. In this country, as a result of the increasing secularisation, people have shown a growing interest in more personalised and creative funerary ceremonies.[29] In this process, internet weblogs have been discovered as an innovative medium that provides a great freedom of expression and the possibility to reach a large public.

As research of the Internet and its impact on social life is still young, so is the study of funerary expressions on the Internet.[30] Here, like in the work of De Vries and Rutherford, Altena argues that the Internet represents a powerful means of funerary innovation. The choice of weblogs as research objects is motivated by their particular relevance to how dying and bereaved create and appreciate digital diaries and memorials.

This case study focuses on a selection of ten Dutch weblogs about people suffering from cancer, created by the patients themselves, by their loved ones and by their bereaved. Because of their continuous high ranking in Google search results these weblogs could be recognised as ten of the most frequently visited weblogs about dying and deceased people diagnosed with cancer. The weblogs were visited in 2008 and 2009. The weblogs usually consisted of several chapters being: the introduction of the protagonist, the diagnosis and prognosis; a diary, the most prominent feature; a postal box for visitors comments and messages; a description of the funeral; and an overview of memorial activities. Often, the diary contributions were combined with inspiring quotes, photographs or films. The weblogs covered various periods of time, varying from a few years to more than a decade. The research method included a qualitative approach consisting of a close reading of the weblogs and the evaluation of their shape and content and attributed meaning and the way the weblogs were used in people's lives.[31] For reasons of privacy, illustrations were omitted as well as the names of the weblogs and their authors.

In the Netherlands, an unknown number of people suffering from a terminal disease as well as bereaved express themselves through virtual diaries, or weblogs. These weblogs contain life stories reporting on the experience of coping with a deadly illness, the prospect of having to die soon, and how the dying wants to be remembered. Bereaved people keep digital records about how they deal with the loss of a loved one, a child, a spouse, or a friend.

Next to a means of expression, weblogs provide people with an instrument of contact. Patients, who often have very little time or energy available to visit, or communicate with their family and friends in 'real life,' find an opportunity to do so online.[32] In one of the investigated weblogs, a father and mother report about the diagnosis of leukemia for their three months old baby daughter (Website J.d.K.). They inform family and friends about the treatment and share their anxieties, hopes and disappointments. The sometimes daily reports made by sick people consist of images - drawings or photos - that document radiation therapy, hair loss, and the new wig (Website M.). Authors take a confrontational approach in showing detailed images of operation scars; the deceased on a bier; the house clearing after the funeral; and a home memorial (Website C.l.P.; Website L.V.).

Weblogs allow patients to connect with fellow sufferers to exchange information and to reflect on being terminally ill. Next to the acquisition of information, the website offer relief to patients, spouses, parents and friends in relating their complaints and reflections to fellow-sufferers. Sometimes, these contain vexations caused by the inefficiency of hospital professionals: 'I wonder if I ever get to see a doctor' (Website C.l.P.). At another time, people share common emotions. A woman is able to laugh about her wig and realises that she can only share her feeling with her weblog community: 'This is only acceptable from fellow-patients' (Website M.).

In particular, parents of young deceased children find in weblogs a possibility to make themselves heard, sometimes only after many years of silence. In a weblog a parent states: 'After six weeks, society expects you to stop mourning' (Website F.d.R.). Another parent addresses the dead child in complaining: 'Nobody seems to want to know, how you live on in our hearts' (Website N.v.d.H.). Many of these parents feel a continuing need for public recognition of their dead children, a need in which individual expression and the desire to communicate are prominent. For these people, weblogs are an almost perfect solution.

Although a fairly modern medium, weblogs build on existing traditions. People have always needed images to remember dead loved ones. Portraits and objects of the dead not only helped people left behind to keep their memories alive, but they also re-defined the relations of the deceased and bereaved. Images and things reflected and constructed lost and new identities, and were tangible proofs of the ties between the living and dead loved ones. In the Netherlands at the turn of twentieth and twenty-first century, new funerary rituals emerged that made prominent use of popular media like television and the Internet. In this country, in 2008, television and the Internet have become broadly accepted means of communications about dying and death.

Like any new medium, weblogs build on recent funeral and mourning traditions in 'real life,' both socially and culturally. Obviously, weblogs draw on conventional handwritten diaries, extending its function by addressing a critical reading internet audience that comments and reflects on the entries. Despite the extra effort the construction of digital diaries requires, the chance to gain public access and feed-back make it worthwhile for the authors. Even stronger, the access to a public platform and the chance of mutual exchange are key concepts in the function of these weblogs.

Also, the creativity weblogs offer to terminally ill people is an important incentive. When funerary professionals in the Netherlands issued websites that imitated individual websites about death and mourning, the public hardly showed any interest. Obviously, the possibility to create a highly personalised site, containing the most individual records and expressions of the weblog author shaped into a specific format, is a decisive reason to create a weblog.

The weblogs' possibility to receive and discuss comments represents a major attraction. The guest book connected to the weblog collects messages from friends and family, next to those of anonymous visitors among whom are fellow patients and bereaved. The informed advices and words of consolation by unprejudiced people represent a priceless contact point for patients. Unlike family and friends who sometimes act overly worried, like-minded strangers provide practice based recognition and advice. Weblog comments constitute a social and emotional recognition people respond to with gratitude, they feel comforted and supported: 'It is fantastic... . Knowing that there are so many people who read my weblog ... supports me a lot' (Website M.). Another patient writes to weblog visitors: 'Without you, it would have been so much more difficult' (Website C.l.P.).

A striking characteristic of weblogs is the strong agency displayed by the protagonists. The weblog authors define the range of the topics and what can be shared with the audience. Their reflections are central in a way that is pretty much unique for the sound bite driven media culture of today. By employing the internet and because of the authors' creative input, weblogs provide patients with an agency to contact and help others, a possibility they enjoy. As one patient put it: 'It feels good to be able to help others' (Website R.S.).

Weblogs help to organise the authors' personal life as well as to construct their own public digital community. The weblog represents for parents and fellow mourners a much appreciated platform where they release feelings of sorrow, anger, and despair. A woman expresses her anxiety about her breast amputation: 'It is not going to be pretty' (Website M.). Another woman exclaims her frustration about the nerve breaking process of her child's therapy: 'Excuse me for complaining. I am so pissed' (Website J.d.K.). As in a traditional diary, people report that they experience their writing about their daily lives as an opportunity to organise their feelings. A woman declares: 'The more you talk about it, the better you are able to deal with it' (Website J.H.). The act of keeping a diary works as a strategy to attribute meaning to their experiences. It is an act of comfort, much to the surprise of some authors: 'Strangely enough, from the weblog I draw a lot of strength' (Website J.d.K.).

By taking control of the shape and content of their weblogs, authors experience that they can direct their 'real life,' too. Parents of dead children use websites as instruments to instruct people in their immediate sphere. In the case of the death of a young child, leaving little moments of remembrance, parents tend to create these afterwards. Next to texts, photos document the events in the life of the deceased child. Once put on the website, each photo proves to be an object the parents take pride in. They invite visitors to confirm that their child was beautiful and brave. A parent describes the photo of her deceased daughter: 'These are beautiful pictures of my beautiful sleeping girl' (Website A.). While looking at the pictures, the weblog visitor is addressed as if he or she was a visitor at a real life visit where parents expect that their guest provides the recognition the child deserves.

Parents and other bereaved state that the memory of their loved ones by means of a website meets an urgent need. After a civil servant refused to register the birth of a dead child, the injured father created a website dedicated to the same child (Website J.d.K.). Other parents explain that the website is supposed to confirm the dead child's existence. In the Netherlands, like in England, medical practitioners encourage bereaved parents to keep a log to support their mourning process (Website F.d.R.).

Bereaved parents explain the website as an ongoing confirmation that the dead person did exist. Weblog visitors are welcomed and told what the attention means to the weblog authors. The guests' comments, their numbers, and the various times of the day or night on which sites are visited, are all felt as proofs of acknowledgement (Webpage M.). The duration of the weblog is counted with a calendar counting days, hours, minutes and seconds, mirroring the time that is given to the patient since the diagnosis (Website M.). To the authors, the digital visibility of the deceased person, despite their experience with rejection in real life, is a source of consolation and inspiration. Because of this, websites function as a therapeutic instrument that contributes to the identity construction of both child and parents.

Weblogs on dying and death function on different levels: as a means of communication between the dying protagonist and his/her family and friends; between the bereaved; and in some cases even between the bereaved and the deceased through space and time. The awareness that the weblog represents the dead person's last thoughts and actions makes the site into a révered memorial, a sacred place. So, bereaved leave messages in the weblog's guest book, addressing the deceased as an intermediate between the living and the dead. One parent imagines her dead daughter to be her little guardian angel whom she asks to provide her and her husband with a new baby brother and sister (Website S.v.E.). Here, weblog messages are digital versions of conventional prayers and requests.

The perceived independence of the Internet from place and time, its possibility for people to communicate with whom, when and wherever they want to, has made the medium particularly attractive for memorial purposes. People bear witness of their memories of deceased loved ones and friends: 'We will never forget our fellow patients who did not make it' (Website J.d.K.).

The fact that it are mainly women who construct weblogs on death and mourning, affects the choice of topics as well as the way these have taken shape. Whereas men are usually acting as website providers leaving its content to women, three out of the ten weblogs analysed were written by men. When writing about dying and death, men find different topics describing physical processes, therapies, techniques and medications, instead of focusing on emotions and relations the way women authors do. One male author provided his weblog with links to Wikipedia, photos of scanning machines and information about medical health care insurance.

Women discover weblogs as instruments to design care givers' directories, instructing what family members or friends can come to visit, wash, cook or clean at a set day of the week: 'When you are going to visit him, please try to do some chores. At the moment, these are just too much for him' (Website C.l.P.).

Sick or mourning people make use of websites to inform friends and family about events in their lives, in order to limit phone conversations or visitors. Calling for getting (well cards, drawings) prayers or the burning of candles to support the patient or deceased through the internet. Website J.d.K., Website S.v.E. Next to these, the patient applauds the courage and support of caring family and friends Website M.; Website C.l.P. Such a digital directory, connects people and communicates with them, taking care of the patient's health and privacy, facilitating 'real life' visits or preventing unnecessary disturbances of the sick.

Another difference among weblog users is that of how they prove to be aware of the global range of the medium. As people generally make use of the Internet in the privacy of their homes - comfortably seated behind one's computer and working on their own familiar weblog - some people have trouble understanding that they are connected to a worldwide community. The deceptive intimacy of websites and the inconceivability of a world wide range makes that people ignore it, or they take public exposure for granted.

Intimate experiences and emotions are shared with complete strangers. Although the boundaries people have are not always obvious, people make clear decisions about what to share with an anonymous audience. Sometimes, they act surprised when they find unexpected visitor comments. Some prevent these by screening their site by means of a login code. In most cases however, the digital contact between website authors with an anonymous mass audience is a conscious choice.

Because a weblog is constructed over a long period of time, from the first diagnosis to the memorial celebrations, the shape and function of the site evolve through time. Initiated originally as a point of reflection and contact, the addition of messages and advices by visitors, and sometimes after the death of the author, turn these sites into information points. It is a function that website authors sometimes are conscious of from the start, as is shown by links to hospitals or self help groups. Others become aware of this function after some time, and then present themselves as advisors while drawing from their own experience.

After years, the weblogs function as a daily point of reference has been replaced by one of a memorial. Additional chapters announce new phases in the lives of the bereaved, referring to the birth of a new baby, a new love or a new job. It also happens that contributors decide to simply stop contributing to the website: 'The need is diminishing' (Website L.V.) or 'Writing the weblog has become a ritual.' To some of the bereaved, the finishing of the weblog is felt as the end of the mourning period (Website S.v.E.). After expressing their gratitude to supporting visitors, they close the website and the period connected to it. This does not necessarily mean that the website is deleted. It proceeds to exist but - as a static, unchangeable entity - it evolves into a memorial monument.

4.   Conclusion

Weblogs of terminally ill people in English hospice settings - used by medical professionals, patients, family, friends and bereaved - prove to be helpful in many respects. For patients, family and friends, weblogs engender the removal of uncertainties and anxieties and help them to deal with disease, therapy and death. For hospice professionals, weblogs represent research instruments that are not obstructive, which have revealed the positive effects of weblog for the patients' mental and physical condition. For medical practitioners weblogs are also efficient indicators for treatment adaptation. Because of this, Ngwenya argues, weblogs of terminally ill contribute to the essential 'open awareness' as formulated by Glaser and Strauss. Although these are striking findings, further study will be necessary to explore how psychometric properties of word use can be employed to assist and enhance palliative care.

Weblogs of terminally ill used in Dutch private settings provide patients, family, friends and anonymous website visitors with a new instrument to deal with heartfelt emotions they cannot express elsewhere; a means of information about diseases or funeral ceremonies; as well as a memorial platform. The weblogs' ability to establish relations between the ill and weblog visitors, leading to friendships even, supports Walter's view of the importance of the collective in the construction of memorials.[33] However, what is fascinating in weblogs is that the creation of these biographies already takes place *before* death and that weblog memorials come about with the aid of people who do *not* belong to the intimate circle of the patient. It is an ironic paradox that a dying person's weblog biography is made through contributions of strangers who have never met the man or woman involved.

Both weblogs of terminally ill employed in an institutional setting and in a private setting enable patients to take more control about their lives. Furthermore, these weblogs give people facing death the opportunity to convey and interpret their own meaning of the phenomenon. Weblogs can be appreciated as a medium that brings these subjects to a public platform encouraging broad debate and an understanding on how disease and death affect different people in society.

Notes

[1] M. Peelen and M. Altena, 'Voor Altijd een Stralende Ster op het Web: Digitale Herinneringen aan Vroeg Gestorven Kinderen', in *Rituele Creativiteit: Actuele Veranderingen in de Uitvaart- en Rouwcultuur in*

Nederland, E. Venbrux, M. Heessels, S. Bolt (eds), Meinema, Zoetermeer, 2008, pp. 75-88.

[2] B. G. Glaser and A. L. Strauss, *Awareness of Dying*, Aldine, New York, 1965; K. M. Taylor, 'Telling Bad News: Physicians and the Disclosure of Undesirable Information', *Sociology of Health & Illness*, Vol. 10, 1988, pp. 109-133.

[3] B. De Vries and J. Rutherford, 'Memorializing Loved Ones on the World Wide Web', *Omega*, Vol. 49, 2004, pp. 5-26.

[4] Ibid., pp. 5-26.

[5] T. Walter, 'A New Model of Grief: Bereavement and Biography', *Mortality*, Vol. 1, 1996, pp. 7-25.

[6] P. Ariès, *The Hour of Our Death*, Oxford University Press, Oxford, 1991.

[7] R. Blauner, 'Death and Social Structure', *Psychiatry*, Vol. 29, 1966, pp. 378-394.

[8] J. Hinton, *Dying*, Penguin Books, London, 1991.

[9] Glaser and Strauss, op. cit.

[10] Ibid.

[11] Taylor, op. cit., pp. 109-133.

[12] J. W. Riley, 'Dying and the Meanings of Death: Sociological Inquiries', *Annual Review Sociology*, 1983, pp. 191-216.

[13] C. Zimmermann, 'Death Denial: Obstacles or Instrument for Palliative Care? An Analysis of Clinical Literature', *Sociology of Health & Illness*, Vol. 29, 2007, pp. 297-314.

[14] E. J. Emanuel, D. L. Fairclough, P. Wolfe, L. L. Emanuel, 'Talking with Terminally Ill Patients and Their Caregivers about Death, Dying and Bereavement', *Archives of Internal Medicine*, Vol. 164, 2004, pp. 1999-2004.

[15] T. E. Quill, 'Initiating End-of-Life Discussions with Seriously Ill Patients', *Journal of the American Medical Association*, Vol. 284, 2000, pp. 2505-2507.

[16] Ibid.

[17] G. W. Alpers, A. J. Winzelberg, C. Classen, H. Roberts, P. Dev, C. Koopman, C. Barr-Taylor, 'Evaluation of Computerized Text Analysis in an Internet Breast Cancer Support Group', *Computers in Human Behavior*, Vol. 21, 2005, pp. 361-376.

[18] K. Veale, 'Online Memorialisation: The Web As A Collective Memorial Landscape For Remembering The Dead', August 2008, <http://www.veale.com.au>.

[19] A. Aitken, 'Online Life after Death', *Bereavement Care*, Vol. 28, 2009, pp. 34-35.

[20] R. Goss and D. Klass, *Dead but not Lost: Grief Narratives in Religious Traditions*, AltaMira Press, Lanham, Maryland, 2005.

[21] Aitken, op. cit., pp. 34-35.

[22] Goss and Klass, op. cit.

[23] J. W. Pennebaker, 'Writing about Emotional Experiences as a Therapeutic Process', *Psychological Science*, Vol. 8, 1997, pp. 162-166; J. W. Pennebaker and C. K. Chung, 'Expressive Writing, Emotional Upheavals, and Health', in *Handbook of Health Psychology*, H. Friedman and R. Silver (eds), Oxford University Press, New York, 2007, pp. 263-284; K. A. Baikie and K. Wilhelm, 'Emotional and Physical Health Benefits of Expressive Talking', *Advances in Psychiatric Treatment*, Vol. 11, 2005, pp. 338-346.

[24] Pennebaker, op. cit.; J. W. Pennebaker, M. R. Mehl, K. G. Niederhoffer, 'Psychological Aspects of Natural Language Use: Our Words, Our Selves', *Annual Review of Psychology*, Vol. 54, 2003, pp. 547-577.

[25] S. S. Rude, R. Wenzlaff, B. Gibbs, J. Vane, T. Whitney, 'Negative Interpretive Biases Predict Subsequent Depression Symptoms', *Cognition and Emotion*, Vol. 16, 2002, pp. 423-440.

[26] Y. R. Tausczik and J. W. Pennebaker, 'The Psychological Meaning of Words: LIWC and Computerized Text Analysis Methods', *Journal of Language and Social Psychology*, in press.

[27] C. K. Chung and J. W. Pennebaker, 'The Psychological Function of Function Words', in *Social Communication: Frontiers of Social Psychology*, K. Fiedler (ed), Psychology Press, New York, 2007, pp. 343-359.

[28] J. W. Pennebaker, 'What Our Words can Say about Us: Toward a Broader Language Psychology', *Psychological Science Agenda*, Vol. 15, 2002, pp. 8-9.

[29] E. Venbrux, M. Heessels, S. Bolt, *Rituele Creativiteit: Actuele Veranderingen in de Uitvaart- en Rouwcultuur in Nederland*, Meinema, Zoetermeer, 2008, pp. 75-88.

[30] A. Herman and T. Swiss (eds), *The World Wide Web and Contemporary Cultural Theory*, Routledge, New York, 2000; J. Katz and R. Rice, *Social Consequences of Internet Use*, MIT Press, Cambridge, MA, 2002; De Vries and Rutherford, op. cit.

[31] M. Altena, 'Making Memories: Filmmakers, Agency and Identity in the Production of Funerary Films in the Netherlands', *Mortality*, Vol. 14, 2009, pp. 159-172; M. Altena, C. Notermans, W. Widlok, 'Tradition, Place and Community in Internet Rituals', in *Ritual, Media and Conflict*, Oxford University Press, Oxford, forthcoming Fall 2009.

[32] Peelen and Altena, op. cit.

[33] Walter, op. cit.

Bibliography

Aitken, A., 'Online Life after Death'. *Bereavement Care*, Vol. 28, 2009, pp. 34-35.

Alpers, G. W., Winzelberg, A. J., Classen, C., Roberts, H., Dev, P., Koopman, C., Barr-Taylor, C., 'Evaluation of Computerized Text Analysis in an Internet Breast Cancer Support Group'. *Computers in Human Behavior*, Vol. 21, 2005, pp. 361-376.

Altena, M., 'Making Memories: Filmmakers, Agency and Identity in the Production of Funerary Films in the Netherlands'. *Mortality*, Vol. 14, 2009, pp. 159-172.

Altena, M., Notermans, C., Widlok, W., 'Tradition, Place and Community in Internet Rituals', in *Ritual, Media and Conflict*. Oxford University Press, Oxford, forthcoming Fall, 2009.

Altena M. and Venbrux, E., 'Television Shows and Weblogs as New Death Rituals: Celebrating Life in the Dutch Production *Over My Dead Body*', in *Abstrakter Tod - Konkrete Leiche*. D. Groß, J. Glahn, B. Tag (eds), Campus Verlag, Frankfurt am Main, forthcoming Fall 2009.

Ariès, P., *The Hour of Our Death*. Oxford University Press, Oxford, 1991.

Baikie, K. A. and Wilhelm, K., 'Emotional and Physical Health Benefits of Expressive Talking'. *Advances in Psychiatric Treatment*, Vol. 11, 2005, pp. 338-346.

Blauner, R., 'Death and Social Structure'. *Psychiatry*, Vol. 29, 1966, pp. 378-394.

Bot, M., *Een Laatste Groet. Uitvaart- en Rouwrituelen in Multicultureel Nederland*. Marrie Bot, Rotterdam, 1998.

Chung, C. K. and Pennebaker, J. W., 'The Psychological Function of Function Words', in *Social Communication: Frontiers of Social Psychology*. K. Fiedler (ed), Psychology Press, New York, 2007, pp. 343-359.

Enklaar, J., *Onder de Groene Zoden. De Persoonlijke Uitvaart. Nieuwe Rituelen in Rouwen, Begraven en Cremeren*. Alpha, Zutphen, 1995.

Emanuel, E. J., Fairclough, D. L., Wolfe, P., Emanuel, L. L., 'Talking with Terminally Ill Patients and Their Caregivers about Death, Dying and Bereavement'. *Archives of Internal Medicine*, Vol. 164, 2004, pp. 1999-2004.

Faunce, W. A. and Fulton, R. L., 'The Sociology of Death: A Neglected Area in Sociological Research'. *Social Forces*, Vol. 36, 1958, pp. 205-209.

Glaser, B. G. and Strauss, A. L., *Awareness of Dying*. Aldine, New York, 1965.

Goss, R. and Klass, D., *Dead but not Lost: Grief Narratives in Religious Traditions*. AltaMira Press, Lanham, Maryland, 2005.

Herman, A. and Swiss, T. (eds), *The World Wide Web and Contemporary Cultural Theory*. Routledge, New York, 2000.

Hinton, J., *Dying*. Penguin Books, London, 1991.

Katz, J. and Rice, R., *Social Consequences of Internet Use*. MIT Press, Cambridge, MA, 2002.

Ngwenya, N., Mills, S., Kingston, P., 'Analysis of Terminally Ill Patients' Weblogs Using the Linguistic Inquiry and Word Count (LIWC) Program', in *Proceedings of the Sixth Annual Conference on Death and Dying*. N. Hinerman (ed), Inter-Disciplinary Press, Oxford, 2009.

——, 'Weblogs as Therapy and Memory Reservoirs', in *The Social Context of Death, Dying and Disposal*. 8th International Conference 12-15th September 2007, 'Mortality: Promoting the Interdisciplinary Study of Death and Dying', Vol. 12, Supplement 1, 2007.

Peelen, M and Altena, M., 'Voor Altijd een Stralende Ster op het Web: Digitale Herinneringen aan Vroeg Gestorven Kinderen', in *Rituele Creativiteit: Actuele Veranderingen in de Uitvaart- en Rouwcultuur in Nederland*. E. Venbrux, M. Heessels, S. Bolt (eds), Meinema, Zoetermeer, 2008, pp. 75-88.

Pennebaker, J. W., 'Writing about Emotional Experiences as a Therapeutic Process'. *Psychological Science*, Vol. 8, 1997, pp. 162-166.

——, 'What Our Words can Say about Us: Toward a Broader Language Psychology'. *Psychological Science Agenda*, Vol. 15, 2002, pp. 8-9.

Pennebaker, J. W. and Chung, C. K., 'Expressive Writing, Emotional Upheavals, and Health', in *Handbook of Health Psychology*. H. Friedman and R. Silver (eds), Oxford University Press, New York, 2007, pp. 263-284.

Pennebaker, J. W. and Graybeal, A., 'Patterns of Natural Language Use: Disclosure, Personality and Social Integration'. *Current Directions in Psychological Science*, Vol. 10, 2001, pp. 91-93.

Pennebaker, J, W. and King, L, A., 'Linguistic Styles: Language Use as an Individual Difference'. *Journal of Personality and Social Psychology*, Vol. 77, 1999, pp. 1296-1312.

Pennebaker, J. W., Mehl, M. R., Niederhoffer, K. G., 'Psychological Aspects of Natural Language Use: Our Words, Our Selves'. *Annual Review of Psychology*, Vol. 54, 2003, pp. 547-577.

Quill, T. E., 'Initiating End-of-Life Discussions with Seriously Ill Patients'. *Journal of the American Medical Association*, Vol. 284, 2000, pp. 2505-2507.

Riley, J. W., 'Dying and the Meanings of Death: Sociological Inquiries'. *Annual Review Sociology*, 1983, pp. 191-216.

Rude, S. S., Wenzlaff, R., Gibbs, B., Vane, J., Whitney, T., 'Negative Interpretive Biases Predict Subsequent Depression Symptoms'. *Cognition and Emotion*, Vol. 16, 2002, pp. 423-440.

Sliggers, B. (ed), *Naar het Lijk. Het Nederlandse Doodsportret 1500-Heden*, Walburg Pers, Zutphen, 1998.

Tausczik, Y. R. and Pennebaker, J. W., 'The Psychological Meaning of Words: LIWC and Computerized Text Analysis Methods'. *Journal of Language and Social Psychology*, in press.

Taylor, K. M., 'Telling Bad News: Physicians and the Disclosure of Undesirable Information'. *Sociology of Health & Illness*, Vol. 10, 1988, pp. 109-133.

Thorne, D., 'Adding Technology to Care - Is this Progress?'. *Progress in Palliative Care*, Vol. 7, 1999, pp. 53-54.

Van den Akker, P., *De Dode Nabij. Nieuwe Rituelen na Overlijden*. Dela, Tilburg, 2006.

Veale, K., 'Online Memorialisation: The Web As A Collective Memorial Landscape For Remembering The Dead'. August 2008, <http://www.veale.com.au>.

Venbrux, E., Heessels, M., Bolt, S., *Rituele Creativiteit: Actuele Veranderingen in de Uitvaart- en Rouwcultuur in Nederland*. Meinema, Zoetermeer, 2008, pp. 75-88.

Vries, De B. and Rutherford, J., 'Memorializing Loved Ones on the World Wide Web'. *Omega*, Vol. 49, 2004, pp. 5-26.

Walter, T., 'A New Model of Grief: Bereavement and Biography'. *Mortality*, Vol. 1, 1996, pp. 7-25.

Willis, L., Demiris, G., Parker-Oliver, D., 'Internet Use by Hospice Families and Providers: A Review'. *Journal of Medical Systems*, Vol. 31, 2007, pp. 97-101.

Zimmermann, C., 'Death Denial: Obstacles or Instrument for Palliative Care? An Analysis of Clinical Literature'. *Sociology of Health & Illness*, Vol. 29, 2007, pp. 297-314.

Marga Altena is a historian of visual culture affiliated to Radboud University, Nijmegen, The Netherlands. Participating in a research project about funerary innovation in the Netherlands, she investigates biographical accounts of dying and bereaved people in funerary films, television shows and the Internet.

Nothando Ngwenya Ph.D. (Staffordshire University, UK), is a Senior Research Associate at University Hospitals Birmingham, currently investigating the use of web based (weblogs) interventions in hospice and palliative care. Other research interests include ethnic minorities and their use of hospice care services, as well as sexual health in palliative care.

Survivor's Guilt in Caretakers of Cancer

Shulamith Kreitler, Frida Barak, Yasmin Alkalay, Nava Siegelman-Danieli

Abstract
The paper deals with survivor's guilt. The purpose was to describe the phenomenon and to study some of its correlates, functions and consequences in the context of the caretakers of cancer patients. The first part presents a brief review of what is known about survivor's guilt, focusing on its frequency, the circumstances in which it has been observed and explanations offered in the frameworks of the psychoanalytic, the social-evolutionary and existentialist approaches. The second part presents findings of an empirical study of survivor's guilt by the authors. The participants were 113 caretakers of cancer patients, to whom questionnaires were administered 2-3 weeks before the patient's death and 2-3 weeks following it. Interviews were conducted with 42 caretakers 6 months later. Survivor's guilt was reported by 65.4% of the caretakers. The major results were that survivor's guilt is distinct from the emotions of guilt and remorse, and that it is only moderately related to demographic, emotional, circumstantial and other variables characterising the relationship to the deceased. Interviews after 6 months showed that most of those with survivor's guilt were engaged in voluntary pro-social activities and showed evidence of enhanced 'contact' with the deceased whose presence was maintained in their life space.

Key Words: Cancer, caretakers, guilt, survivor's guilt.

*****

1. Review of the Literature about Survivor's Guilt
A. Guilt

Guilt is usually defined as an affective state that occurs when an individual believes that he or she has violated a moral standard either by having done something that one believes one should not have done, or conversely, by not having done something one believes one should have done, and that one is responsible for that violation.[1] Thus, the major necessary antecedents for guilt are the following three cognitions: the cognition that one has done or not done some behavior, the cognition that this entails violation of some moral standard, and the cognition that one is responsible. Guilt is closely related to shame from which it differs in crucial respects.[2]

Early theorists distinguished between guilt and shame by emphasising that shame is a reaction to public or external exposure of some disapproved act while guilt is a private internal event, limited to the relations between one's self and ones' conscience.[3] Later conceptualisations emphasised that both shame and guilt are negative evaluations of the self by the self, but while shame is a more global evaluation guilt refers to specific acts.[4] Further developments in theorising about shame and guilt were affected by ethological, social and evolutionary approaches, emphasising the dependence of guilt on the constructs of attachment and empathy.[5] Accordingly, guilt came to be seen as related to altruism and the tendency to feel empathy towards the suffering of the other[6] arising from the belief that one has hurt another.[7] This view assumes that guilt is rooted in the need to help or at least not to harm others, as part of the adaptive tendency of human beings to maintain their ties to those who are close to them - family members, friends, and other loved ones. More psychologically-oriented investigators emphasise that individuals suffering from guilt may in some cases have deliberately harmed or wished to harm another; but more often their feeling of guilt has to do with a fear of hurting others, not because they want to hurt them, but because they believe that by attempting to further their own interests, they may cause harm to others even without wanting or intending to do so.[8]

Weiss' conception serves to highlight another important distinction concerning guilt, based on the degree to which actual harm has been perpetrated. Thus, on the one hand, there may be so-called 'neurotic' guilt, that reflects the individual's assumption that he or she is responsible for some morally evil event, which actually may not be the case; and on the other hand, there is so-called real guilt experienced because of some harm, pain or inconvenience that the person has been involved in inflicting, directly or indirectly.

Neurotic guilt can be irrational, for example, because it refers to things about which the person has no control; or because it is displaced, i.e., transferred from the real source of the guilt to another less-threatening situation; or because it is disproportionate relative to the harm. It seems likely that the two kinds of guilt - neurotic and real - define a continuum that reflects differential degrees of irrationality and proneness to psychopathology.

However, the irrational components that may attach to guilt, do not change the basic conception shared by most investigators that guilt is a highly adaptive emotion, buttressed by affinity to moral standards, and serves to maintain attachments to others for the purpose of stabilising a comfortable social existence.[9] The conception of guilt as an interpersonal emotion, based on the individual's fear of harming others in the pursuit of his or her own goals, gave rise to a differentiation of several distinct though related categories of guilt: separation/disloyalty guilt, omnipotent responsibility guilt, and survivor guilt.

Separation guilt is characterised by feeling that one is harming one's parents or other loved ones by separating from them or by differing from them and thereby being disloyal. It is based on the belief that one's right to life depends on preserving one's similarity and intimate bonds to one's parents and other loved ones.[10] Omnipotent responsibility guilt is characterised by feeling anxiety and concern about real and particular acts concerning others that may have caused them wrong or discomfort in any way and for which reparation needs to be undertaken. It is based on the belief that one is responsible for the happiness and well-being of others, mainly one's loved ones. Finally, survivor guilt is characterised by the feeling that one has harmed others, especially loved ones, by the mere fact of having been spared some misfortune or even death that have befallen them.

All three kinds of guilt manifest their rootedness in the interpersonal context. Hence one component they share is concern for the others - maintaining the relation with them, their well-being and their physical survival. However, there seems to be another component they share, no less important than the mentioned one, and this is: preserving the presence of the other - by continuing to be a part of the other, by improving the other's well-being and by promoting the other's physical existence. This component has been less discerned than the first component of 'concern for others' and rarely mentioned in previous discussions of guilt. However, it seems to us to be of crucial psychological importance for the individual. Just as 'concern for others' reflects mainly altruism and fulfils an important social role for the community, 'preserving the presence of the other' reflects egotism and fulfils an important psychological role for the individual. The latter component is manifested most clearly in survivor's guilt, which forms the focus of the present chapter.

B.   What is Survivor's Guilt

Survivor's guilt or survivor's syndrome is generally defined as the mental condition resulting from the appraisal that a person is guilty by the mere fact of having survived a traumatic event whereas others did not. Freud referred to survivor guilt in the wake of his father's death, in a letter to Wilhelm Fliess, in which he noted '... that tendency toward self-reproach which death invariably leaves among the survivors ... .'[11] It was first diagnosed in the 1960s when several therapists identified a set of symptoms including survivor's guilt in holocaust survivors.[12] The traumatic events that may engender survivor's guilt usually refer to combat, natural disasters and significant job lay-offs, but includes also political concentration camps, automobile accidents, wartime bombing attacks, and deaths from disease.[13] The others in regard to whom survivor's guilt is felt may include family members, friends, colleagues but also unknown strangers. There has been some unclarity about the differential diagnosis between survivor's guilt and post-traumatic stress disorder, with the result that the latter but not the former was included in the DSM-IV.[14]

Nevertheless some unclarity seems to persist, because survivor's guilt is still sometimes listed as one of the symptoms of post-traumatic disorder and sometimes as a completely distinct category of trauma-related guilt. Yet, although both post-traumatic stress disorder and survivor's guilt develop following a trauma, they are very different phenomena. A basic distinction between them is that post traumatic stress disorder is a psychopathological phenomenon, whereas survivor's guilt appears to be an expression of a normal concern for other human beings singly and as a society.

Similarly, survivor's guilt differs from the guilt sometimes felt by rescuers who blame themselves for not having done enough to help others in emergencies or the guilt that therapists may feel for their patients' suffering. In both of the latter cases the guilt refers to not having done something for saving the others or alleviating their suffering whereas in survivor's guilt the guilt is based solely on the survival per se.

C.   In which Contexts or Circumstances Survivor's Guilt Arises?

Some investigators emphasise that survivor's guilt hits people who have not done anything wrong or have not done much of anything at all. In order to better characterise the phenomenon, it is necessary to focus on the original circumstances in which it occurs. As noted, survivor's guilt appears after a disaster or a trauma. The person who feels the guilt has not been hit or affected by the trauma but there was a fair probability that he or she could have been a victim. Further, survivor's guilt is more frequent in people who have suffered themselves in the circumstances in which the disaster occurred than in those who did not. Again, it is more frequent in people who have been somehow involved in the disaster than in those who observed it from a safe distance. The suffering of those who feel the survivor's guilt may have been serious, for example, it may have involved death risk, hunger, oppression, severe worries but in any case it was more moderate or at least ended better than in the case of the other victims, who may have died, or undergone imprisonment, torture or lay-off from work.

An interesting case of survivor's guilt is described in Kurt Vonnegut's novel, *Bluebird*. The protagonist Rabo Karabekian's father had survivor guilt from witnessing some parts of the Armenian genocide by hiding in a deserted village. In contrast, his wife who actually witnessed the killings and pretended to be dead while hiding under corpses, did not feel any survivor's guilt.

In regard to rescuers, the survivor's sense of guilt may be enhanced if the rescuer died while saving one's life. Another example of a similar effect would be when a soldier switches a patrol with a friend, and the friend dies during that particular patrol. The surviving friend thinks that it should have been him and is left with survivor's guilt. Further, survivor's guilt has been observed in situations that involve being put in a place where one was not able to revive or otherwise prevent the death of someone one may have loved, in short, situations where nothing can be done for the victim.

D.   What are the Symptoms and Manifestations of Survivor's Guilt?

The characteristic symptoms of survivor's guilt include primarily guilt and self-blame, as well as anxiety, depression, sleep disturbances, emotional liability, loss of drive, lower motivation and morale (e.g., increased absences from work if the trauma was lay-offs), and sometimes physical complaints. In general, survivor's guilt has been related to longer mourning period and complicated bereavement.

In the survivors of concentration camps of World War II, survivor's guilt was sometimes manifested in more subtle forms, for example, behaving as if they themselves were dead, inhibiting themselves from success or engaging in self-destructive acts in response to survivor's guilt in regard to a dead parent or sibling.[15]

E.   How Common is Survivor's Guilt?

Studies have detected survivor's guilt in a great variety of contexts. According to a literature review survivor's guilt occurs in: patients after a death takes place within a treatment setting for chronic illness;[16] people who keep their job when others are fired; homosexual men who have tested negative for the human immunodeficiency virus whereas their friends tested positive ('spared at random'); survivors of the Vietnam war; 'survivor-friends' (bereaved friends) who have experienced the death of a close friend;[17] individuals faced with the sudden death of a partner in an extramarital relationship (secret survivors);[18] after death in the family, more survivor's guilt in widows if the death was by suicide than by accident;[19] mothers of children who died of leukemia; psychotherapists working with the unique group of patients of holocaust survivors;[20] in a surviving twin, or siblings of a cancer patient child who died;[21] in survivors who suffer increased guilt due to not having completed certain courses of action prior to death of loved one and may blame themselves for failure to achieve an appropriate death for their loved one, or for not having perceived clues of impending death;[22] in survivors of beloved ones, more so when death has been sudden than if not.

F.   What are the Reasons for or Causes of Survivor's Guilt?

There are various theoretical approaches to survivor's guilt that will be briefly presented.

(a)   The Psychoanalytic Approach
         According to Freud,[23] guilt in general is the product of intra-psychic conflicts between the superego and the ego, and can be considered as a kind of weapon used by the superego to influence the ego's decisions in cases that involve prohibited or tabooed id impulses. Accordingly, survivor's guilt would be the result of repressed impulses that the survivor has had in regard to the deceased, such as aggressiveness, wishes of death or tabooed sexuality (e.g., incest).
         Rank,[24] another proponent of psychoanalysis, considered guilt as a function of the individuation process, originating in the infantile attachment to mother and in the fear and anxiety over breaking that attachment. Accordingly, guilt operates as a force that perpetuates that relationship. Survivor's guilt reflects the guilt over enhanced individuation resulting inevitably from the deceased death. Hence, the ubiquity of survivor's guilt. Actually, Rank equates survivor's guilt with separation guilt.
         A somewhat different perspective on survivor's guilt is presented by another group of psychotherapists who assume that individuals have 'an unconscious bookkeeping system' which considers the distribution of the available 'good' within a given family so that the current fate of all family members will determine how much 'good' one possesses. Thus, if fate has dealt harshly with other members of the family, the survivor may feel guilty because he or she have apparently obtained more than their share of the 'good.'[25] Similarly, survivor's guilt may be interpreted as due to the irrational belief people may have that the attainment of good things or the simple promotion of one's own interests is unfair or is at the expense of those who have not attained them and may in addition make others feel bad by comparison.[26]
         A most interesting claim has been raised by a group of dynamically-oriented investigators who assume that survivor's guilt originates in the survivor's identification with the victim, which according to the mimetic theory of trauma, is an attempt to understand psychologically the painfully incomprehensible.[27] The fantasy-based identification with the harmed one or the dead consists in incorporating the image of the victim in oneself. This has the further benefit of enabling the survivor to uphold the sense of immortality, which is integral to human existence. The dead are experienced unconsciously as if they were still living on in the survivor. However, on the conscious level the survivor knows that the victims are dead and that the proper order of things has been irreparably disrupted, which is the source of the guilt the survivor experiences.[28]

(b)   The Evolutionary-Social Approach
         According to evolutionary theorists the preservation of relationships is vital for survival and reproduction.[29] Hence, human guilt is assumed to

have emerged from natural selection because it prevented human beings from performing destructive actions that might damage their relationships with others. In view of the importance of maintaining the group, it is likely that guilt mostly reflects an offense against the group.[30]

Guilt is assumed to help maintain beneficial relations, such as reciprocal altruism in various ways.[31] For example, a person who feels guilty because he or she have harmed someone else or failed to reciprocate kindness, is less likely to get involved in conflicts with other group members, harm others or behave selfishly. In this way, that person reduces the chances of retaliation by other group members, and increases the chances of his own and the group's survival. Further, if a person who has harmed another feels guilty and demonstrates sorrow and regret, the harmed person or those close to him are likely to forgive.

The mentioned elements play a role also in survivor's guilt. In addition, survivor's guilt is considered as rooted in the empathy system which seems to depend to a large extent on mirror neurons that enable to feel the other's suffering as if it were our own.[32] Empathy may support the belief that we should do something to relieve or avoid the suffering of others. If we cannot help the other or fail in our efforts to help, we experience guilt which turns into survivor's guilt if the other is irreparably harmed. Thus, on the whole group functioning and cohesion benefit from having a large number of individuals who tend to feel guilt, and even more so survivor's guilt, which extends the beneficial impact of guilt beyond the life span of the harmed one.[33]

The social interpersonal approach considers guilt from the perspective of its role in communal relatedness, supported by its biological importance for survival and reflected in the affective responses of empathy, belongingness and attachment. Hence, guilt serves three broad functions for relationships. First, it motivates relationship-enhancing patterns of behaviour, by helping to enforce the communal norms prescribing mutual concern, respect, and positive treatment in the absence of self-interested return. Secondly, it may operate as an interpersonal influence technique that allows even a relatively powerless person to get his or her way. Thirdly, guilt helps to redistribute emotional distress within the dyad following a transgression. If the transgressor feels guilty his or her enjoyment is diminished, and the victim may feel better. Accordingly, survivor's guilt helps to restore emotional equity experienced by family members, friends, and co-workers in regard to significant others. In this way survivor's guilt contributes to promoting fair, equitable, and durable relationships.

(c)   The Existentialist Approach

The existentialist approach redresses the balance and returns guilt into the domain of the individual. The major emphasis of the existentialist approach is that guilt remains a personal emotional experience, beyond any other role it may have. The existentialist-oriented thinkers consider guilt as a normal part of life and of grieving. Guilt is the affective reaction of human beings to the existential predicament of the necessity to realise to the full the human potentiality of existence.[34] Human potentialities may be conceptualised in terms of three dimensions: the physical world of objects, defined by the struggle between survival and death; the social world of other people, defined by the contradictions between our need to belong and the possibility of our isolation; the personal dimension, defined by the tension between integrity and disintegration. The basic need of human beings is to find or construct meaning in regard to each of these existential dimensions.[35] Guilt is the feeling we tend to have when we fail to extract or construct meaning in each of these dimensions.[36] The struggle and need for meaning become particularly poignant when we face the 'tragic triad' of pain, guilt and death, which confront us with awareness of human suffering, of human fallibility and transitoriness of human life.[37]

It seems to us that survivor's guilt is involved most intimately in the tragic triad of existence. The death or misfortunes of one or more human beings makes us aware of the missed opportunities for life, and underscores the fact that as human beings we have not succeeded in preventing or diminishing the suffering, our own fallibility or the death of fellow human beings. Survivor's guilt is the manifestation of our awareness of our limitations as human beings physically, socially and personally.

Various additional circumstances may contribute to enhancing survivor's guilt. For example, survivor's guilt may reflect the decreased sense of vitality the grievers may feel because of their 'embracing' of death, for example, by their previous readiness to give up their own life for the deceased, their identification with the dead one or their decreased motivation for life now that the beloved deceased is no longer with them.

G.   What is there in Survivor's Guilt for the Surviving Individual?

In dealing with psychological issues it is often necessary to distinguish between explanations of antecedents and causes for the phenomenon and the functions of the phenomenon for the individual. The three approaches to explaining survivor's guilt differ in the answer they provide to the question about the role of survivor's guilt for the individual. According to the psychoanalytic approach the role would be to seek expiation or forgiveness for one's meditated, intended or carried out deeds that violated some real or fictional norm.

According to the evolutionary-social approach survivor's guilt serves to cement the cohesion of the group and thus indirectly contributes to the well-being of the individual. According to the view that guilt is a tool of social control, survivor's guilt should be manifested in submissive behaviour, expressions of regret and behaviours designed to placate the harmed one so as to elicit his or her forgiveness.

Notably, it has been argued that individuals with proneness to high levels of empathy-based guilt may be likely to suffer from anxiety and depression, but they are also more likely to cooperate with others and behave altruistically. This suggests that guilt-proneness may not always be beneficial for the individual, or within-group competition, but may be highly beneficial in between-group competition.[38]

According to the existential approach, survivor's guilt should benefit the survivor by enhancing his or her motivation to live, to realise one's potential for existence in the full sense of the term, and to use his or her survival for expanding and deepening the meaningfulness of one's life by changing himself for the better and by changing the world so that it becomes a better place for human beings.

The psychoanalytic and evolutionary-social approaches lead us to expect that the individual with survivor's guilt would show a tendency to be punished, or in the very least to confess to one's 'sin,' apologise and make some kind of reparation. Acts of this kind are assumed to alleviate the guilt. However, empirical studies have failed to demonstrate that survivor's guilt stimulates a wish for punishment.[39] If there is no evidence for regretting, confessing and craving for punishment on the part of the individual with survivor's guilt, there is no reason to expect that the individual would feel relieved and freed of the unpleasantness of the experienced guilt. No data is available about the enhancement of motivation for life elicited by survivor's guilt.

So what is there in survivor's guilt for the individuals - who seem to be on the losing side in both respects: they have been separated socially or physically from other people, mostly close to them, and they have been afflicted with survivor's guilt about which they seem to be able to do very little. One suggestion which may contribute to resolving the problem has been mentioned earlier: survivor's guilt seems to preserve for the individual the presence of the other who has been harmed. It occurs possibly by means of identification with the victim, which consists in incorporating the victim's image and personality into oneself in a psychological manner, and it is apparently maintained by means of the guilt itself. This function of preserving the presence of the victim is of special importance when the harm inflicted on the other is death or some other trauma that introduces distance in time or place between the harmed individual and the one afflicted with survivor's guilt. This aspect of survivor's guilt is among those handled in the study to be reported.

2.   The Study

This second part of the paper reports findings of a study of survivor guilt in the caretakers and family members of cancer patients.

A.   Purpose

The objectives were (a) to check the frequency of survivor's guilt in the family members and caretakers of cancer patients; (b) to identify demographic, circumstantial and psychological correlates of survivor's guilt; and (c) to explore the behavioural and experiential consequences of survivor's guilt.

B.   Method: Participants

The participants in the study were 195 family members of cancer patients who had been involved in taking care of the patients and had a continuous relationship with them.

The sample of caretakers was chosen for the following reasons: (a) the sample is potentially large and fairly homogenous in the circumstances of contact with the deceased; (b) the sample enables testing the participants prior to the death of the patient and following it, so as to determine the impact of the death itself on survivor's guilt and also to explore the immediate as well as long-term effects of survivor's guilt.

C.   Method: Procedure

A part of the participants (n=82) were studied only prior to the patient's death (2-3 weeks), and the rest (n=113) both prior and after the patient's death (2-3 weeks) and 42 of these also six months later. All participants were recruited in oncology wards in different hospitals and clinics in Israel.

D.   Method: Tools

The participants were administered two questionnaires: (a) the Profile of Mood States which assessed the participants' current levels of different emotions, such as depression and anxiety, to which guilt and remorse were added;[40] (b) a questionnaire that referred to the relationship of the participant with the patient and the nature and reasons for possible reactions of guilt and remorse, and reactions to it. This questionnaire was constructed on the basis of interviews with 20 pre-test participants, prior to the study itself, who were caretakers of cancer patients and were asked about possible reasons for guilt feelings following death of a close person. The following reasons that were referred to by at least 50% of the participants were incorporated into the questionnaire: (a) Things they have not done in regard to the treatment and relationship with the patient but should have done; (b) Things they have done in regard to the treatment and relationship with the patient but should not have done; (c) Feelings they had in regard to the patient or feelings they did not have; (d) Death wishes they have had in regard to the patient or feeling glad/relieved at patient's death; (d) Being/staying alive whereas patient is dying/dead.

E.   Results
The results showed that the major emotions reported by the participants prior to the patient's death were remorse, guilt, anger and confusion, and following the death the major emotions were remorse, guilt, fatigue and confusion. Hence, following the death, anger was replaced by fatigue.

Sixty two percent of the sample reported guilt above the medium level after the patient's death. The scores for guilt were significantly higher after the patients' death than before it.

Further, comparing the means of the emotional responses prior and after the patient's death shows that that there were declines in anger, anxiety and energy, and increases in depression, fatigue, confusion, guilt and remorse. Comparing the results in the first months after the death with those six months later showed that there were significant declines in depression, anger, confusion, anxiety and fatigue, and a slight increase in energy. Guilt persisted as a reported emotion, but its level was lower than before.

The major focus of the study was placed on three variables that seemed to us as closest to the theme of survivor's guilt. These were the feelings of guilt and remorse experienced before and after the death of the patient and the feeling of survivor's guilt, which was assessed only after the death of the patient. On a scale of 1-4, the means and standard deviations for guilt and remorse prior to the death of the patient and after it were 1.70 (.67), 1.66 (.66), 3.05 (.66), 2.92 (.65), respectively. After the death, 65.4% admitted they had survivor's guilt and the rest reported they had none. The justification for retaining for our further analyses all three variables - guilt, remorse and survivor's guilt, all assessed after the death of the patient - was the finding that they were not correlated significantly with each other, except for the significant relation between survivor's guilt and remorse ($t=2.494$, $p<.01$). There are two important conclusions based on these findings. The first is that guilt and remorse are two separate emotions; the second is that guilt as such and survivor's guilt are two separate emotions. Hence, a person may feel guilty after the death of someone but experience neither remorse nor survivor's guilt. Again, a person may experience survivor's guilt but not guilt following the death of others. However, the person who experiences survivor's guilt does tend to feel remorse concerning the other.

We explored the correlates of these three variables - guilt, remorse and survivor's guilt - in terms of the four following sets of variables: (a) Demographic variables: age and gender of the caretaker, being a close relative of the deceased, disease duration of the deceased, number of months the caretaker took care of the deceased, and the degree of treatment (how many hours per week); (b) Interpersonal contact characteristics and things or actions bothering the caretaker: things concerning the treatment of the deceased that the caretaker thinks he/she should not have done but did; things concerning the treatment of the deceased that the caretaker thinks he/she should have done but did not do; things concerning the relationship with the deceased that the caretaker thinks he/she should have done but did not do; things concerning the relationship with the deceased that the caretaker thinks he/she should have done but did not do; feelings and intentions that the caretaker has had concerning the treatment of the deceased; feelings and intentions that the caretaker has had concerning the overall relationship with the deceased; death wishes in regard to the deceased because of the suffering; (c) Feelings experienced by the caretaker prior to the death of the deceased: depression, vigour, confusion, tension, anger, fatigue, remorse and guilt; (d) Feelings experienced by the caretaker following the death of the deceased: depression, vigour, confusion, tension, anger, fatigue, remorse and guilt.

In the statistical analyses each of the four sets of correlates listed above was used as a set of independent variables, whereas remorse, guilt and survivor's guilt were used as dependent variables, each separately. In the case of guilt and remorse, we used regression analyses, and in the case of survivor's guilt we used logistic regression.

Results concerning guilt: overall results were significant only when the predictors were the set of feelings experienced after the death of the deceased ($F=3.25$, $df=9/92$, $p<01$). The variables with significant contributions were vigour ($t=2.25$, $p<05$), confusion ($t=2.27$, $p<.05$) and fatigue ($t=2.28$, $p<.05$). This indicates that caretakers who experienced guilt after the death of the deceased also experienced less vigour, more fatigue and more confusion. Hence, the feeling of guilt after the death of the patient may be considered as a natural part of the emotional state of the caretaker after the patient's demise. In addition there were several variables of other sets with significant contributions to predicting the emotion of guilt: the duration of the patient's disease ($t=2.16$, $p<.05$; the longer it lasted, the lower the guilt); things one has done in regard to the treatment ($t=1.89$, $p=.07$) and things one has done in regard to the relationship with the deceased (the fewer, the higher the guilt; $t=1.95$, $p=.05$); and the level of confusion prior to death (the lower, the higher the guilt; $t=2.01$, $p<.05$).

Results concerning remorse: overall results were significant only when the predictors were the set of interpersonal contact characteristics and things or actions bothering the caretaker ($F=2.42$, $df=9/92$, $p<01$). The variable with the significant contribution in this set was things that have been done in regard to the relationship (the fewer things, the higher the remorse; $t=3.51$, $p<.001$). In addition there were several variables of other sets with significant contributions to predicting the emotion of remorse: the feeling of vigour after the death of the deceased (t=1.94, p=.05) and the feeling of anger prior to the death (t=2.33, p<.05). These findings indicate that remorse had fewer correlates than guilt. It was related mainly to things done in regard to the relationship with the deceased. Further, the emotions to which it was related were energy-laden, in contrast to guilt that was related to emotions marked by confusion and fatigue.

Results concerning survivor's guilt: results in regard to each of the four sets of predictors were similar in the sense that all the variables in the set enabled a significant prediction of survivor's guilt: correct identification of the individuals with survivor's guilt by means of the demographic variables in 64.4%, Critical Ratio=2.102, p<05; by means of the interpersonal contact variables in 68.8%, Critical Ratio=2.707, p<.01; by means of the emotions after the death of the deceased in 67.3%, Critical Ratio=2.536, p<.01; by means of the emotions prior to the death of the deceased in 65.3%, Critical Ratio=2.201, p<.05). However, only in one case there was evidence for a significant contribution of any of the single variables in the set to the prediction. This was in the case of remorse felt after the death of the deceased (t=5.376, p<.05). These findings indicate that survivor's guilt is related but not closely to demographic, emotional and circumstantial characteristics of the caretaker and his or her relationship to the patient.

Further analyses showed that survivor's guilt is not related to having come from a holocaust family; the number of deaths in the family in the previous five years; the participant's marital status and number of children; and the participant's religiosity (or observance of religious habits/procedures).

As noted, 42 of the participants were available for interviewing also six months after the patient's death. The obtained information made it possible to explore the long-term effects of survivor's guilt. In the case of all 42 subjects, the level of mourning for the deceased was reported to have become low (1 or 2 on a scale of 4). Out of the 42, 34 participants still reported survivor's guilt (80.95%), whereas 8 did not. All those who reported survivor's guilt at this stage also reported it following the patient's death. A comparison of the subjects with and without survivor's guilt showed that 67.65% of the participants with survivor's guilt were engaged six months after the death in pro-social voluntary work, such as collecting food for the needy, helping victims of burglaries and robberies or taking care of hospitalised patients. Only two participants without survivor's guilt engaged in similar voluntary activities.

Another important finding yielded by the interviews six months after the death of the patient is that the majority of the participants with survivor's guilt reported they felt close to the deceased in various respects. The indices of closeness included the following: thinking about the deceased more than once every day, 'talking' in fantasy to the deceased at least once a week, talking about the deceased to others at least once in three days, having images of the deceased at least once a week, having insights about different things the deceased has said or done while alive and long before the disease. Reporting 5 or 4 of these indices can be considered as evidence for maintaining close contact with the deceased, while reporting 2 or 3 of these indices may be considered as evidence for medium contact, and reporting 0 or 1 as evidence for low degree of contact. These degrees of closeness were scored as 3, 2 and 1, respectively. Notably, the mean of closeness in the participants who reported survivor's guilt was 2.5 while in the group of those with no survivor's guilt it was 0.4. This indicates that one of the outcomes of survivor's guilt, which is possibly one of its functions too, is to help maintain the presence of the deceased in the inner life space of the survivor.

F.   Some Conclusions

The findings of the study are to be considered as preliminary. The results found so far show that survivor's guilt is prevalent among the caretakers of cancer patients. It is distinct from the experiences of guilt and of remorse. Further, the findings that survivor's guilt is unrelated to demographic, circumstantial and habitual common emotional responses, including gender, age, duration of treatment of the deceased, the relationship with the deceased, number of deaths in the family, marital status, number of children and religiosity, suggest that survivor's guilt is an affective response rooted in deeper layers of the personality. Most importantly, the observations about the correlates of survivor's guilt six months following the patient's death support the theses that survivor's guilt exerts a pro-social impact on the person's behaviour and that it helps maintain the presence of the deceased in the life space of the survivor. Both of these effects led the deceased a kind of metaphorical immortality, thus helping the survivor preserve his or her own sense of immortality and the sense of continued contact with the deceased. In these respects survivor's guilt contributes to overcoming death, at least on the psychological level. Notably, the results concerning the roots of survivor's guilt correspond partially to the theoretical accounts provided in the frameworks of all three above reviewed approaches: the psychoanalytic, the social-evolutionary and the existentialist.

The more general implication of these findings is that survivor's guilt should not be treated as a pathological phenomenon to be reduced, alleviated and mitigated at all costs. Rather it may be an intrinsically human response to the occurrence of death which leads to pro-social behaviours designed to strengthen the human bond as well as to fantasy acts designed to psychologically preserve the presence of the deceased, and thereby to transcend the existential plight of limited existence.

Notes

[1] B. R. Strickland, 'Guilt', *Encyclopedia of Psychology*, 2nd Edition, Gale Group, Farminton Hill, MI, 2001.

[2] J. P. Tangney, P. Wagner, R. Gramzow, 'Proneness to Shame, Proneness to Guilt, and Psychopathology', *Journal of Abnormal Psychology*, Vol. 10, 1992, pp. 469-478.

[3] D. P. Ausubel, 'Relationships between Shame and Guilt in the Socializing Process', *Psychological Review*, Vol. 62, 1955, pp. 378-390; R. Benedict, *The Chrysanthemum and the Sword: Patterns of Japanese Culture*, Houghton Mifflin, Boston, 1946.

[4] H. B. Lewis, *Shame and Guilt in Neurosis*, International Universities Press, Madison, CT, 1971; R. Janoff-Bulman, 'Characterological versus Behavioral Selfblame: Inquiries into Depression and Rape', *Journal of Personality and Social Psychology*, Vol. 17, 1979, pp. 1798-1809.

[5] M. Hoffman, 'Is Altruism a Part of Human Nature?', *Journal of Personality and Social Psychology*, Vol. 40, 1981, pp. 121-137; R. Plutchik, 'Evolutionary Basis of Empathy', in *Empathy and its Development*, N. Eisenberg and J. Strayer (eds) Cambridge University Press, Cambridge, 1987, pp. 38-46.

[6] Hoffman, pp. 47-80.

[7] M. Bush, 'The Role of Unconscious Guilt in Psychopathology and Psychotherapy', *Bulletin of the Meninger Clinic*, Vol. 53, 1989, pp. 97-107; M. Friedman, 'Towards a Reconceptualization of Guilt', *Psychoanalysis*, Vol. 21, 1985, pp. 501-547; H. Sampson, 'Pathogenic Beliefs and Unconscious Guilt in the Therapeutic Process: Clinical Observations and Research Evidence', *Bulletin # 6*, San Francisco, The Psychotherapy Research Group (The Mount Zion Psychotherapy Research Group), Department of Psychiatry, Mount Zion Hospital and Medical Center, 1983; J. Weiss, 'Notes on Unconscious Guilt, Pathogenic Beliefs, and the Treatment Process', *Bulletin # 6*, San Francisco, The Psychotherapy Research Group (The Mount Zion Psychotherapy Research Group), Department of Psychiatry, Mount Zion Hospital and Medical Center, 1983; J. Weiss, 'Unconscious Guilt', in *The Psychoanalytic Process: Theory, Clinical Observation, and Empirical Research*, J. Weiss and H. Sampson (eds), Guilford Press, New York, 1986, pp. 43-67; J. Weiss, *How Psychotherapy Works: Process and Technique*, Guilford Press, New York, 1993.

[8] Weiss, 'Notes on Unconscious Guilt', op. cit.; Weiss, *How Psychotherapy Works*, op. cit.

[9] L. E. O'Connor, J. W. Berry, J. Weiss, M. Bush, H. Sampson, 'Interpersonal Guilt: The Development of a New Measure', *Journal of Clinical Psychology*, Vol. 53, 1997, pp. 73-89.

[10] A. H. Modell, 'On Having the Right to a Life: An Aspect to the Superego's Development', *International Journal of Psycho-Analysis*, Vol. 46, 1965, pp. 323-331.

[11] S. Freud, 1896; cited from E. L. Freud (ed), *Letters of Sigmund Freud: Selected and Edited by Ernst L. Freud*, T. Stern and J. Stern (trans), Basic Books, Inc., New York, 1960, p. 111.

[12] W. G. Niederland, 'The Problem of the Survivor', *Journal of the Hillside Hospital*, Vol. 10, 1961, pp. 233-247.

[13] R. J. Lifton, *Death in Life*, Simon & Schuster, New York, 1967.

[14] Freud, op. cit., p. 111.

[15] A. H. Modell, 'The Origin of Certain Forms of Pre-Oedipal Guilt and the Implications for a Psychoanalytic Theory of Affects', *International Journal of Psychoanalysis*, Vol. 52, 1971, pp. 337-346; Lifton, *'Death in Life'*, op. cit.

[16] M. Vamos, 'Survivor Guilt and Chronic Illness', *Australian and New Zealand Journal of Psychiatry*, Vol. 31, No. 4, August, 1997, pp. 592-596.

[17] F. Sklar and S. F. Hartley, 'Close Friends as Survivors: Bereavement Patterns in a "Hidden" Population', *Omega: Journal of Death and Dying*, Vol. 21, No. 2, 1990, pp. 103-112.

[18] R. W. Weinbach, 'Sudden Death and Secret Survivors: Helping those Who Grieve Alone', *Social Work*, Vol. 34, No. 1, January, 1989, pp. 57-60.

[19] D. E. McNeil, C. Hatcher, R. Reubin, 'Family Survivors of Suicide and Accidental Death: Consequences for Widows', *Suicide and Life-Threatening Behavior*, Vol. 18, No. 2, 1988, pp. 137-148.

[20] Y. Danieli, 'Confronting the Unimaginable: Psychotherapists' Reactions to Victims of the Nazi Holocaust', in *Human Adaptation to Extreme Stress: From the Holocaust to Vietnam*, J. P. Wilson, Z. Harel, B. Kahana (eds), The Plenum Series on Stress and Coping, Plenum Press, New York, 1988, pp. 219-238.

[21] J. Woodward, 'The Bereaved Twin', *Acta Geneticae Medicae et Gemellologiae: Twin Research*, Vol. 37, No. 2, 1988, pp. 173-180.

[22] M. Porot, A. Couadau, M. Plenat, 'Le Syndrome de Culpabilité du Survivant/The Survivor's Guilt Syndrome', *Annales Médico-Psychologiques*, Vol. 143, No. 3, 1985, pp. 256-262.

[23] S. Freud, *New Introductory Lectures on Psycho-Analysis*, J. Strachey (trans), Norton, New York, 1964 [1933].

[24] O. Rank, *The Trauma of Birth*, Harcourt, Brace, New York, 1929.

[25] Modell, 'On Having the Right to a Life', pp. 323-340.

[26] Weiss, 'Unconscious Guilt', pp. 43-67.

[27] R. Leys, *Trauma: A Genealogy*, University of Chicago Press, Chicago, 2000.

[28] R. Leys, 'Image and Trauma', *Science in Context*, Vol. 19, 2006, pp. 137-149; R. J. Lifton, *The Broken Connection: On Death and the Continuity of Life*, Basic Books, New York, 1983.

[29] R. L. Trivers, *Social Evolution*, Benjamin-Cummings, Redwood City, CA, 1985.

[30] Ausubel, pp. 378-390.

[31] S. Pallanti and L. Quercioli, 'Shame and Psychopathology', *CNS Spectrum*, Vol. 5, 2000, pp. 28-43.

[32] G. Rizzolatti and L. Craighero, 'The Mirror-Neuron System', *Annual Review of Neuroscience*, Vol. 27, 2004, pp. 169-192.

[33] J. Tooby and L. Cosmides, 'The Evolutionary Psychology of Emotions and Their Relationship to Internal Regulation Variables', in *Handbook of Emotions*, 3rd Edition, M. Lewis, J. M. Haviland-Jones, L. Feldman Barrett (eds), Guilford, New York, pp. 114-137.

[34] M. Buber, 'Guilt and Guilt Feelings', *Psychiatry*, Vol. 20, 1957, pp. 114-129.

[35] V. E. Frankl, *The Unheard Cry for Meaning: Psychotherapy and Humanism*, Washington Square Press, New York, 1984.

[36] E. van Deurzen-Smith, *Everyday Mysteries: Existential Dimensions of Psychotherapy*, Routledge, London, 1997; M. Hersen, J. C. Thomas, D. L. Segal, *Comprehensive Handbook of Personality and Psychopathology*, Wiley, Chichester, UK, 2005.

[37] V. E. Frankl, *The Doctor and the Soul: From Psychotherapy to Logotherapy*, Vintage Books, New York, 1986.

[38] Tooby and Cosmides, pp. 114-137.

[39] M. Friedman, 'Toward a Reconceptualization of Guilt', *Contemporary Psychoanalysis*, Vol. 21, 1985, pp. 501-547; M. L. Hoffman, 'Development of Prosocial Motivation: Empathy and Guilt', in *The Development of Prosocial Behavior*, N. Eisenberg (ed), Academic Press, San Diego, CA, 1982, pp. 281-313; H. B. Lewis, *Shame and Guilt in Neurosis*, International Universities Press, Madison, CT, 1971; C. Zahn-Waxier and G. Kochanska, 'The Origins of Guilt', in *The Nebraska Symposium on Motivation 1988: Socioemotional Development*, R. A. Thompson (ed), Vol. 36, University of Nebraska Press, Lincoln, NE, 1990, pp. 182-258; R. F. Baumeister, A. M. Stillwell, T. F. Heatherton, 'Guilt: An Interpersonal Approach', *Psychological Bulletin*, 1994, Vol. 115, No. 2, pp. 243-267.

[40] D. M. McNair, M. Lorr, L. F. Droppleman, *Manual for the Profile of Moods States*, Educational and Industrial Testing Service, San Diego, CA, 1971.

Bibliography

Ausubel, D. P., 'Relationships between Shame and Guilt in the Socializing Process'. *Psychological Review*, Vol. 62, 1955, pp. 378-390.

Baumeister, R. F., Stillwell, A. M., Heatherton, T. F., 'Guilt: An Interpersonal Approach'. *Psychological Bulletin*, Vol. 115, No. 2, 1994, pp. 243-267.

Benedict, R., *The Chrysanthemum and the Sword: Patterns of Japanese Culture*. Houghton Mifflin, Boston, 1946.

Buber, M., 'Guilt and Guilt Feelings'. *Psychiatry*, Vol. 20, 1957, pp. 114-129.

Bush, M., 'The Role of Unconscious Guilt in Psychopathology and Psychotherapy'. *Bulletin of the Meninger Clinic*, Vol. 53, 1989, pp. 97-107.

Danieli, Y., 'Confronting the Unimaginable: Psychotherapists' Reactions to Victims of the Nazi Holocaust', in *Human Adaptation to Extreme Stress: From the Holocaust to Vietnam*. J. P. Wilson, Z. Harel, B. Kahana (eds), *The Plenum Series on Stress and Coping*, Plenum Press, New York, 1988, pp. 219-238.

Deurzen-Smith, van E., *Everyday Mysteries: Existential Dimensions of Psychotherapy*. Routledge, London, 1997.

Frankl, V. E., *The Unheard Cry for Meaning: Psychotherapy and Humanism*. Washington Square Press, New York, 1984.

——, *The Doctor and the Soul: From Psychotherapy to Logotherapy*. Vintage Books, New York, 1986.

Freud, E. L., *Letters of Sigmund Freud: Selected by Ernst Freud*. T. Stern and J. Stern (trans), New York Basic Books, New York, 1960 [1896].

——, *New Introductory Lectures on Psycho-Analysis*. J. Strachey (trans), Norton, New York, 1964 [1933].

Friedman, M., 'Toward a Reconceptualization of Guilt'. *Contemporary Psychoanalysis*, Vol. 21, 1985, pp. 501-547.

Hersen, M., Thomas, J. C., Segal, D. L., *Comprehensive Handbook of Personality and Psychopathology*. Wiley, Chichester, 2005.

Hoffman, M., 'Is Altruism a Part of Human Nature?'. *Journal of Personality and Social Psychology*, Vol. 40, 1981, pp. 121-137.

——, 'The Contribution of Empathy to Justice and Moral Judgment', in *Empathy and its Development*. N. Eisenberg and J. Strayer (eds), Cambridge University Press, Cambridge, 1987, pp. 47-80.

Hoffman, M. L., 'Development of Prosocial Motivation: Empathy and Guilt', in *The Development of Prosocial Behavior*. N. Eisenberg (ed), Academic Press, San Diego, CA, 1982, pp. 281-313.

Janoff-Bulman, R., 'Characterological versus Behavioral Selfblame: Inquiries into Depression and Rape'. *Journal of Personality and Social Psychology*, Vol. 17, 1979, pp. 1798-1809.

Lewis, H. B., *Shame and Guilt in Neurosis*. International Universities Press, Madison, CT, 1971.

Leys, R., *Trauma: A Genealogy*. University of Chicago Press, Chicago, 2000.

——, 'Image and Trauma'. *Science in Context*, Vol. 19, 2006, pp. 137-149.

Lifton, R. J., *Death in Life*. Simon & Schuster, New York, 1967.

——, *The Broken Connection: On Death and the Continuity of Life*. Basic Books, New York, 1983.

McNair, D. M., Lorr, M., Droppleman, L. F., *Manual for the Profile of Moods States*. Educational and Industrial Testing Service, San Diego, CA, 1971.

McNeil, D. E., Hatcher, C., Reubin, R., 'Family Survivors of Suicide and Accidental Death: Consequences for Widows'. *Suicide and Life-Threatening Behavior*, Vol. 18, No. 2, 1988, pp. 137-148.

Modell, A. H., 'On Having the Right to a Life: An Aspect to the Superego's Development'. *International Journal of Psycho-Analysis*, Vol. 46, 1965, pp. 323-331.

——, 'The Origin of Certain Forms of Pre-Oedipal Guilt and the Implications for a Psychoanalytic Theory of Affects'. *International Journal of Psychoanalysis*, Vol. 52, 1971, pp. 337-346.

Niederland, W. G., 'The Problem of the Survivor'. *Journal of the Hillside Hospital*, Vol. 10, 1961, pp. 233-247.

O'Connor, L. E., Berry, J. W., Weiss, J., Bush, M., Sampson, H., 'Interpersonal Guilt: The Development of a New Measure'. *Journal of Clinical Psychology*, Vol. 53, 1997, pp. 73-89.

Pallanti, S. and Quercioli, L., 'Shame and Psychopathology'. *CNS Spectrum*, Vol. 5, 2000, pp. 28-43.

Plutchik, R., 'Evolutionary Basis of Empathy', in *Empathy and its Development*. N. Eisenberg and J. Strayer (eds), Cambridge University Press, Cambridge, 1987, pp. 38-46.

Porot, M., Couadau, A., Plenat, M., 'Le Syndrome de Culpabilité du Survivant/The Survivor's Guilt Syndrome'. *Annales Médico-Psychologiques*, Vol. 143, No. 3, 1985, pp. 256-262.

Rank, O., *The Trauma of Birth*. Harcourt, Brace, New York, 1929.

Rizzolatti, G. and Craighero, L., 'The Mirror-Neuron System'. *Annual Review of Neuroscience*, Vol. 27, 2004, pp. 169-192.

Sampson, H., 'Pathogenic Beliefs and Unconscious Guilt in the Therapeutic Process: Clinical Observations and Research Evidence'. *Bulletin # 6*, San Francisco, The Psychotherapy Research Group (The Mount Zion Psychotherapy Research Group), Department of Psychiatry, Mount Zion Hospital and Medical Center, 1983.

Sklar, F. and Hartley, S. F., 'Close Friends as Survivors: Bereavement Patterns in a "Hidden" Population'. *Omega: Journal of Death and Dying*, Vol. 21, No. 2, 1990, pp. 103-112.

Strickland, B. R., 'Guilt', in *Encyclopedia of Psychology*. 2nd Edition, Gale Group, Farmington Hill, MI, 2001.

Tangney, J. P., Wagner, P., Gramzow, R., 'Proneness to Shame, Proneness to Guilt, and Psychopathology'. *Journal of Abnormal Psychology*, Vol. 10, 1992, pp. 469-478.

Tooby, J. and Cosmides, L., 'The Evolutionary Psychology of Emotions and Their Relationship to Internal Regulation Variables', in *Handbook of Emotions*, 3rd Edition, M. Lewis, J. M. Haviland-Jones, L. Feldman Barrett (eds), Guilford, New York, pp. 114-137.

Trivers, R. L., *Social Evolution*. Benjamin-Cummings, Redwood City, CA, 1985.

Vamos, M., 'Survivor Guilt and Chronic Illness'. *Australian and New Zealand Journal of Psychiatry*, Vol. 31, No. 4, 1997, pp. 592-596.

Weinbach, R. W., 'Sudden Death and Secret Survivors: Helping those Who Grieve Alone'. *Social Work*, Vol. 34, No. 1, 1989, pp. 57-60.

Weiss, J., 'Notes on Unconscious Guilt, Pathogenic Beliefs, and the Treatment Process'. *Bulletin # 6*, San Francisco, The Psychotherapy Research Group (The Mount Zion Psychotherapy Research Group), Department of Psychiatry, Mount Zion Hospital and Medical Center, 1983.

——, 'Unconscious Guilt', in *The Psychoanalytic Process: Theory, Clinical Observation, and Empirical Research*. J. Weiss and H. Sampson (eds), Guilford Press, New York, 1986, pp. 43-67.

——, *How Psychotherapy Works: Process and Technique*. Guilford Press, New York, 1993.

Woodward, J., 'The Bereaved Twin'. *Acta Geneticae Medicae et Gemellologiae: Twin Research*, Vol. 37, No. 2, 1988, pp. 173-180.

Zahn-Waxier, C. and Kochanska, G., 'The Origins of Guilt', in *The Nebraska Symposium on Motivation 1988: Socioemotional Development*, Vol. 36, R. A. Thompson (ed), University of Nebraska Press, Lincoln, NE, 1990, pp. 182-258.

Yasmin Alkalay, has a M.A. in Sociology and is the Head of Unit for Statistical Data Analysis, Social Sciences Faculty, Tel Aviv University. Her major interests are multivariate statistical models of data.

Frida Barak, MD, is the Director of Oncology, Barzilai Medical Center, in Ashkelon, Israel. Her fields of interest and research are: Epidemiologic, genetic and physiological characteristics of cancer patients

Shulamith Kreitler is a PhD., Professor of Psychology at Tel-Aviv University (Israel), Haifa University (Israel) and Freud University (Vienna) and Head of Psychooncology Research Center at Sheba Medical Center, Tel Hashomer (Israel). She has published over 200 scientific papers and 10 books. Her major research interests are psychooncology, creativity, and psychological impact on physical health.

Nava Siegelmann-Danieli, MD, is the Director of Oncology Service Line, at the Maccabi Health Services in Israel. Her major interests and research are: Medical, physiological, epidemiological, genetic and psychological factors decreasing the occurrence of oncological diseases and improving the state of health in oncology patients.

Part 2

Death, Presence, and Ritual

The Haunt/Demons and the Complex of Noon

Tolulope Onabolu

Abstract

Above the Gate of Intrepid is painted the inscription 'He who follows this path alone and without looking behind him, will be purified by Fire and Air; and if he strives to conquer the dread of Death he will emerge from the underworld, and will behold the Light once more, and will be worthy to be admitted into the company of wise men and men of valour.'[1]

This is the moment when the sun, at its zenith divides the day into equal parts, each governed by the opposing signs of rise and decline. This, then, is the moment when the forces of life and light yield to the powers of death and darkness. In ancient Greece, noon was in fact the *hour of transition* marking the boundary between the reign of the Uranian and of the infernal gods.[2]

To make a 'nonsensical' reading of dying, or of death, is problematic - for a subject which is taken so seriously - the tone set up in the call for papers implies such (discussions on euthanasia, abortion, suicide, homicide, genocide, infanticide, etc.) However, (as part of a creative practice) is not this 'nonsensical' reading precisely what is required for a theme which is caught up in the form of its description (making sense of) - precisely what is the sense (or nonsense) of dying and death? Between the sovereignty of initiation, sacrifice and the rites of passage, and the death of the soul implied in ennui (specifically psychasthenia and acedia with reference to Caillois),[3] this paper will attempt (by expanding on Lequeu's Gothic House, also known as 'The Haunt of Magicians,' and Caillois' 'The Noon Complex'[4]) to make sense of dying and death. As implied in The Haunt,[5] we will argue that the transformation in dying/death is indeed 'an awakening.'[6]

Key Words: Becoming(s), creative practice, death, desire, initiation, sympathetic magic, transformation, virtual.

*****

1. Preface

In this paper, I attempt a creative approach to death, within a Deleuzian thesis of becomings.[7] Thus, taking cue from Caillois, death becomes a threshold for virtual becomings: a transformation from a previous state of being, emerging from a state of boredom, drudgery, or delirium[8] and located within a propositional framework - in this case, a paradoxical, or affirmed and negated (fictive) architecture.

There are three seemingly unrelated issues in this paper: acedia or sinful sadness, legendary psychasthenia or the maligned perception of self, and finally, initiation. What these three have in common is death.

In acedia, there is a protracted death of the soul, born out of boredom; in legendary psychasthenia, there is a death of self - from a dissolution of perceived reality (the subject does not distinguish between itself and its environment); and in initiation, there is a death to a previous state of being and a subsequent transformation into 'something else.' In all three, 'something else,' something phantasmatical happens after death - this is what I have termed (borrowing from Tolstoy) an awakening. As such, the awakening is a transformation into something other than one's previous state of being or in another sense, a magical becoming.

Further, there are three unrelated authors: Lequeu, Caillois, and Tolstoy. These authors in various ways support a love of and a desiring into death; viewing death as a transformative process, which one must necessarily go through to achieve the transformative becomings argued in this paper. In Lequeu and Tolstoy, through a materialist mysticism, and in Caillois though delirium.

We will confront these awakenings and magical becomings through the transformative texts of these authors.

2.   Introduction

Initiating this magical reading into Dying and Death, I open from the third part of 'Memories of a Sorcerer' in Deleuze and Guattari's '1730: Becoming-intense, Becoming Animal, Becoming Imperceptible…':

> A man totters from one door to the next and disappears into thin air: "All I can tell you is that we are fluid, luminous beings made of fibres." All so-called initiatory journeys include these thresholds and doors where becoming itself becomes, and where one changes becoming depending on the "hour" of the world, the circles of hell, or the stages of a journey that set scales, forms, and cries in variation. From the howling of animals to the wailing of elements and particles.[9]

In presenting the three disparate concepts of death previously stated, will discuss some events between Volumes 1 and 2 of Tolstoy's *War and Peace*, demonic transformations in Caillois, and a site of one such transformation (The Haunt of Magicians) rendered by the 18th century architect, Jean-Jacques Lequeu.

A nonsensical reading of death is, therefore, a virtual sense of death, as opposed to any representation of death itself, which, I believe

,permanently eludes us, i.e. death knows us, but we cannot know death. Thus, in speaking about demons, we are actually speaking about phantoms of the undead: those awakened or transformed beings which elude representation.

Starting with Lequeu, we will explore the Haunt of Magicians, a formless form, where one goes through an initiatory process by dying (passing through the realm of the dead); then proceeding to Caillois to uncover the demonology of the hour of the dead, and the resulting excess leading to delirium and war; and finally concluding in a treatise on war (through Tolstoy), itself a confirmation of excess, springing from an entering or desiring into death.

What is argued in this paper is that the initiatory death in Lequeu is akin to the death in war, i.e. the initiate must go through The Haunt, to enter into a becoming, just as the warrior must go to war to enter into a dying (by entering into war, one is entering into dying). In both cases, the field of battle (death) is rife with its own excesses and inflections. Therefore, death is in itself not an instant, but a process leading to other transformations, or awakenings; or to use a Deleuzian term, death is the process of transformation where 'becoming' itself becomes. In this, The Haunt of Magicians becomes The Field of Battle and The Circle of Hell through the given Hour of The World.

The Haunt enters into a transformation of becoming war and becoming field of battle.

3.   **Lequeu**

Jean Jacques Lequeu was an 18th century French architect. In the foreword to Philippe Duboy's volume on him, Middleton draws to our attention in the opening lines the impact of a materialist mysticism in art (to a certain degree, and with reference to Bataille, a sort of artistic eroticism).[10] Central to Duboy's representation of Lequeu, is representation itself, and along with it the history of art, exemplified in the exclamation 'a blank page!' against the outlined statement 'Science of natural shading and wash for finished drawings' - on the first page, under 'A Certain Chinese Encyclopaedia,'[11] a statement made by Foucault in *The Order of Things*, on the classifications of Borges - itself an analysis of the history of representation.[12]

In the collection of works that constitute the volume by Duboy, we are presented with a somewhat enigmatic Lequeu - a sort of creative genius; whereas Lemagny in *Visionary Architects* has him down as a tormented mind - 'a motionless and disturbing universe.'[13] Again we are presented with the undeniable impact of representation. The words or gaze upon a thing, within which it is described, i.e. its signifier.

In my reading of Lequeu, (taking a cue from Duboy) I attempt a similar non-representational reading. Hence in 'The Haunt of Magicians,' which I will discuss below, I make no allusion to any representation of a building.

A.   'The Haunt of Magicians'[14]
        In 'The Haunt of Magicians', which is alluded to in both the abstract and title of this paper, Lemagny presents us with a somewhat sombre representation of the building. He states: 'From one of the grilled openings comes "moaning and weeping." We are unmistakably in the age of tales of terror.'[15] By contrast, in Duboy, we are presented with a frivolous/delirious Lequeu who wishes to impose a Masonic initiation on his public. What is clear from both Duboy and Lemagny is that 'The Haunt of Magicians,' or the 'Gothic House' as it is also known, is a temple of initiation, of which Death is a threshold that must be crossed.
        In describing this path of initiation, or confrontation with death by Lequeu, Lemagny, citing Metken, states:

> All the steps along his road to true knowledge appear again in Lequeu's picture, where they are accompanied by explicit legends. The aspirant's first trial is "Tartarus," a "fiery furnace" hung with instruments of hellish torture. From the centre of this grotto emerges a statue symbolic of fire. Farther on, "the forbidden River Cocytus ... [with] waterfall and pool" opens up. A statue symbolising water stands in its midst. Next, in the hollow pedestal of a colossal statue of wisdom, there is a mesh of wheels, pins, and pulleys. They command the opening to the sanctuary itself. Finally, within the sanctuary is the full cup of water of forgetfulness, "Mnemosyne's potion." Here in the "place where true wisdom is learned." It is "the sanctuary of the initiated, the content."[16]

B.   The Haunt/Demons
        We thus have three elemental constituents of the 'Gothic House': Tartarus, Cocytus, and Mnemosyne, all of which have Death at their core. We know from *The Theogony* of Hesiod that Tartarus, third after Chaos and Earth, and last before Eros, is both deity and abyss located in Hades (the mythological abode of the dead); also, that [it] 'is the unbounded first-existing "thing"' from which is born Light and Cosmos.[17]
        Again, from Greek Mythology, Cocytus is a river which flows in the domain of the dead, but represented as a lake (frozen by the flapping wings of Lucifer) in Dante's *Divine Comedy* as the ninth and lowest circle of hell, and home to traitors (the biblical Cain, Judas Iscariot, etc.).

Finally, Mnemosyne, mother of the nine Muses by Zeus, and the presider over one of the pools in Hades, of which initiates of Orphic poetry were encouraged to drink so as to enter into forgetfulness.

We can thus conclude that for Lequeu, The Haunt of Magicians was a place where one descended into the very depths of the underworld (Hades/ Hell), to come out renewed. Hence the inscription on the drawing:

> Above the Gate of Intrepid is painted the inscription… "He who follows this path alone and without looking behind him, will be purified by Fire and Air; and if he strives to conquer the dread of Death he will emerge from the underworld, and will behold the Light once more, and will be worthy to be admitted into the company of wise men and men of valour."[18]

Whether or not it is the protracted form of a Masonic initiation according to Duboy remains the subject of a different sort of speculation. We will now proceed to Caillois for the demonology of the hour of death, and the conditions and excesses of the said hour.

4. Caillois

In *A Caillois Reader*, Claudine Fink suggests, in the 'Introduction to The Noon Complex', that Caillois might have written the essay as a treatise on laziness, and of what I might add, boredom. Fink suggests that between *Les Démons de midi* (The Demons of Noon), and 'The Noon Complex,' Caillois addresses one of the questions central to the College of Sociology: of what has replaced the excess of the archaic festival?[19]

In *Man and the Sacred*, Caillois suggests that the period of excess, which was marked by festival, has come to be replaced by the vacation, that the escape from the drudgery of organised life which culminated in the orgiastic festival has been replaced by the ephemeral pleasure of the vacation. He asks: 'Is not the ephemeral pleasure of vacation one of those false senses of well-being that mask death throes from the dying?'[20]

In this we see a suggestion of the relationship between laziness, drudgery, boredom, and death (in the form of a prohibition, or denial of orgiastic excess). In fact, Caillois suggests that this state of existence was reserved exclusively for those under sovereign exception, i.e. sacred beings (the ideal being that they did nothing).

A. 'The Noon Complex'

Referencing Virgil's *Georgics*, Caillois states that Servius' assertion that the demons appeared mostly at noon provided sufficient grounds for his research into solar mythology.[21]

In a similar vein, I will present Caillois's essay as adequate for a demonology of noon, or what I have termed (borrowing from his 'Noon - Hour of Transition') 'The Hour of The World.'

Caillois' essay on the 'Noon Complex' is fascinating in terms of its revelation. We have the transitional phase of day into night occurring at noon, similarly the transformation from the reign of (heaven/the sky) Uranus, to the reign of (Hades) the Abyss, and through a form of sympathetic magic (where the soul is identified with the body's shadow), the re-emergence of the dead (those who cast no shadow). This is a fairly simple analogy, which when associated with Bataille ('Solar Anus'),[22] becomes fairly complicated. Thus, we will take it in its simple form, as the hour when the sun is at its zenith.

At its zenith, the intensity of the directly overhead sun brings with it certain physiological conditions that were related to these infernal beings (those who cast no shadow). Caillois states:

> The sun's burning heat is unforgiving at this time of day. Heat stroke, sun stroke, cerebral fever, and their attendant mental and physical ailments offered sufficient proof of demonic activity to persuade people that they existed.[23]

This strain of thought is followed by a discussion of the decline of the pre-eminence of noon through Christianity, and the invention of the chiming clock, but again undermined by the human condition of hopelessness experienced at noon. Caillois states:

> At noon, it would seem like life takes a pause, organic matter returns to an inorganic state, and everything blazes pointlessly and without ardour in a futile desire for luxury and display. Activity of any kind seems to involve unpleasant and risible agitation. All heartbeats come to a halt. The supreme triumph of all the positive forces dissolves into renunciation, their surging forth into slumber and their plenitude into resignation. The will to live withdraws somewhere unknown, as if absorbed by thirsty sands. This silent exaltation of every abdication, like a flood invincibly overwhelming all morality, swiftly drowns any uncertain inclination or remorse it might find.[24]

Caillois thus suggests that at this time, and with particularly association to medieval monks, there is a feeling of boredom, drudgery, and insuperable laziness - the acedic condition, overwhelmed by carnal desire.

Elsewhere, he suggests that the demon of noon would disguise itself as a nun, assault the monk during its siesta, and caress it like a prostitute. He states:

> The ailing monk comes to feel an overwhelming revulsion for his life, for his monastery and companions. He is overcome with insuperable laziness. Daily work disheartens and repels him; even reading fills him with disgust. He is weary and yet ravenously hungry, with a kind of morbid need to sleep as the sixth hour is drawing near - the fearful hour of noon. At that time, he keeps on watching the sun, judging that its decline towards the sun is too slow. ... Here then is acedia: ... . Acedia is a sense of apathy towards life, the dull anxiety of a frustrated heart, and an intellect confused by irrationality. ... And beneath it all we find the lure of sexuality: the acedic subject will like to visit a woman with no one to support her. Sometimes the sexual obsession is more explicit.[25]

Caillois concludes his essay by suggesting that if the tendency in nature is towards a state of delirium, and the irrationality of the monk is justified as a state of absolute becoming,[26] again suggesting that human excess manifests itself in this state of becoming.

We can conclude that the death being sought in Caillois is one brought about in the excess of the orgiastic event, (again, with reference to Bataille) in the ejaculatory eruption of blood, sweat, and semen.[27]

In Lequeu, we have located the place, and the demonic constitution of death, and in Caillois, the demonology of the hour of dying. With a certain empirical twist, we may suggest the event necessary for a transformative becoming (dying) - war; for as is in orgiastic event, in war we have all the eruptions of excess (blood, sweat, and semen).

B.   War: Legendary Psychasthenia, Boredom and Delirium

In 'Mimicry and Legendary Psychasthenia,' Caillois introduces a form of dematerialised space, what Lacan terms 'dark space,'[28] and Deleuze 'black holes.'[29] Dark space is any non-geometric definition of space: the space of music, of groping, of hallucination - a space where one feels oneself permeable to ones surroundings.

Within a similar framework, The Haunt of Magicians is a dark space, transformed into a field of battle by the very act of initiatory transformation that occurs within it. As such, the architecture of Lequeu becomes the dematerialised/deterritorialised architecture of the battle field. Further, the demons of The Gothic House become the asthenic conditions of the battlefield: boredom, fear, delirium, and the eruption of excess.

We know that the asthenic conditions of Caillois' insects (which he termed Legendary Psychasthenia), where the insect became indiscernible to its kind, was not as a form of protective or defensive camouflage, but an eruption of excess (as it no longer knows what to do with itself), culminating in cannibalism (the insects appeared as food to each other).[30]

5.   War and Peace

In my reference to war, I draw upon Volumes 1 and 2 of Tolstoy's *War and Peace.*

In Tolstoy's recollection of war, and in some other fictional works on war, the movie *Jarhead* and Sebastian Faulk's book, *Birdsong*, some of the most demonic manifestations are boredom and delirium, followed by excess: torture, looting, the use of women, etc. Tolstoy brings this to bear in many ways; from the inanity of aristocratic life to actual psychological turmoil in the field of battle. While it might appear outrageous to engage the acedic or asthenic condition with warfare, Tolstoy already provides us with the conditions: boredom, sexual tension and anxiety; from the teenage girls in the Rostov household to members of the infantry's preoccupation with climbing over a convent wall.

> …"No, but what I'd like" he added chewing a little pipe with his handsome, moist mouth, "is to climb in there." He pointed to the convent with its towers, visible on the hilltop. He smiled, his eyes narrowed and lit up "…At least to put a fright to those little nuns. There are some Italian ones, young ones they say…" "They must be bored, too' an officer, a bolder one said laughing."[31]

Elsewhere, we experience delirium in Rostov, while he is advancing with his regiment, he is finding difficulty keeping awake, and begins daydreaming, again an engagement with dark space - psychasthenia:

> "It must be snow - this spot; a spot - une tache," thought Rostov. "Tache or no tache… ."
> "Natasha, my sister, dark eyes. Na…tashka… (She'll be so surprised when I tell her how I saw the sovereign!) Natasha…take the…tashka…"
> A young, childish sleep was irresistibly coming over him.
> "…Yes, yes! Na-tashka…at-tack a… attack who? Hussars. Whose hussars? The hussar you saw ride down the boulevard, remember, just across from Guryev house… Old man Guryev. …"[32]

Further on, we experience the excesses of war, in the place of the bodies of the dead and wounded over the battle field, and a robbery. Denisov robs the infantry supplies transport, he is court-marshalled, but gets shot and ends up in hospital. In the hospital, again, more death, decay and disease; the description of the hospital wards is so invoking, that one almost experiences the stench and decay of the multitude of human bodies. Even more remarkable is the doctor's indifference to death.

In all, war which is also an engagement with death brings with it transformations of a sort not usually associated with it.

> One step beyond that line, reminiscent of the line separating the living from the dead, and it's the unknown, suffering, and death. And what is there? Who is there? There, beyond this field, and the tree, and the roof lit by the sun? No one knows, and you would like to know; and you're afraid to cross that line, and would like to cross it; and you know that sooner or later you would have to cross it and find out what is there on the other side of the line, as you will inevitably find out what is on the other side of death... .[33]

Is this any different from the Masonic initiation of Bezukhov that is folded into the story, especially in volume 2, where he is encouraged to embrace death, to love death ...? "'Whatever happens to you," he said, "you must courageously endure everything, if you are firmly resolved to enter into our brotherhood... .""[34]

Also, in the virtues of which he is supposed to uphold, the love of death (the seventh virtue) is tantamount to his redemption.

> "Seventh" said the rhetor, "try by frequent thoughts of death to bring yourself to the point where it no longer seems a fearsome enemy to you, but a friend...who delivers the soul grown weary in the labours of virtue in this calamitous life and leads it to the place of recompense and peace."[35]

Between books 1 and 2 of *War and Peace*, a number of deaths are recorded. Beginning with Count Bezukhov, the uncountable deaths and fields filled with masses of dead and wounded soldiers during the war with Napoleon's army, the blissful and somewhat heroic and puzzling death of Andrei Bolkonsky, the duel between Bezukhov and Dolokhov over the latter's intimacy with Bezukhov's wife, the death of Andrei's wife and the birth of their son at the moment of his return from the dead.

These deaths, or seeming deaths and their associated becomings/transformations constitute the war machine of Tolstoy.

The transformations in the characters, especially Andrei Bolkonsky, through his actual engagement and erstwhile purported heroic death in battle, and Pierre Bezukhov's transformation through Masonic initiation, also an engagement with death through a form of sympathetic magic a la Lequeu, become the dark space or 'night of senses' of death in this paper.

The principles of their engagement can be summarised in the three central principles of Bezukhov's initiation:

- Self-knowledge - for man can only know himself through comparison
- Perfection - for it is achieved through struggle
- The main virtue - The Love of Death

6.   Conclusion: Becoming-Myth/Desiring into Death

At the onset of this paper, we set out to confront the magical becomings (myths of dying) from a desiring into death. We can conclude as follows:

We have seen that death is in-itself a transformation into 'something else,' we have seen that whether in war, delirium or initiation, one is entering into death; as such, death is a sort of 'dark space' through which one must necessarily enter to re-emerge transformed in a demonic becoming.

In speaking about a desiring into death, we have been speaking about sorcery, or would-be sorcerers: Deleuze, Lequeu, Caillois, and Tolstoy, and their planes of composition: The Haunt of Magicians, The Circle of Hell, The Hour of the World, and The Field of Battle. We have argued that each (plan(e)) becomes the other through constant transformations or demonic awakenings centred on a desiring into death. And especially, that The Haunt of Magicians that we started with, in this empirical twist (becoming) enters into a becoming - Battle Field (the dark space of demons).

Finally, whether in Lequeu, Caillois or Tolstoy, we have been encouraged to embrace death (in a becoming-sorcerer/ becoming-demon): through initiation and strife in Lequeu and Tolstoy; and through orgiastic excess, boredom, and delirium in Caillois.

7.   Afterword: Death, Deleuze and Becomings
A.   Sovereign Exception, Destitution and The Sacred

Viewed from a certain perspective, the philosophy of Gilles Deleuze is a philosophy of death;[36] but what kind of death? In Deleuze, we have a death as liminal space, as threshold for transformations (or specifically, for becomings); however, absent from this thesis, or rather, contained within this thesis, is a negated form of ideological (divine) presence, or with reference to

Levinas, God. Following this, we encounter the paradox of the sacred removed from its ideological consistency. We can refer to this form of the sacred through an inversion of Agamben's *homo sacer*, 'it is the originary figure of life taken into the sovereign ban, *but excluding*[37] the memory of the originary exclusion through which the political dimension was first constituted.'[38] The political which Agamben describes is of an intermingling of the sacred and the profane within a religious framework. In this we may say that the becomings in Deleuze are banal transformations, incapable of a sovereign becomings/ concrete subjectivity (immortals). The exclusion of the divine in Deleuze's transcendentalism renders any subjective becoming impossible. In Deleuze, death is (any-death-whatsoever) a mystification of mere animal or machinic becoming.

In the above, the reference to immortals is from Alain Badiou's thesis on the Subject (contra any-becoming-whatsoever) and it is this death and the ensuing presence that is the interest of this essay. Hopefully, it should be clear at the end, that within The Haunt of Magicians, we have ghosts; not traces of the mortal dead, but of immortal becomings, which we lose through simulated events (psychasthenia, the mythology of noon and the battlefield). Thus the appearance of demons at noon and all the other such becomings (like the Cheshire Cat in *Alice*) can be equated with mere appearings (any-becomings-whatsoever), as they are not constituted within any transcendental divine, nor in the words of Badiou, are they constituted in fidelity to any event nor in excess of any situation.

Similarly, the notion of presence as contained in Heidegger will be extended in favour of the thesis of the immortal. For Heidegger, presence is of an already constituted *thing,* it is not an in-itself of an evental trace, it is static being, and even when he denies the objectness of *thing*, the *thing* remains object and presences as such because the transcendental dimension (dwelling) is simulated.[39]

Between Nietzsche and Badiou, the Immortal (concrete subject) is he[40] who resists death by affirmation and negation, i.e. he enters into death only to conquer it, in this, he becomes truly human and separates himself from a being-for-death, a mere animal which is incapable of an affirmation of life in the presence of death. Only the immortal can declare his sovereignty in the face of death.

> The mortals are human beings. They are called mortals because they can die. To die means to be capable of death as death. Only man dies. The animal perishes. It has death neither ahead of itself nor behind it. Death is the shrine of Nothing, that is, of that which in every respect is never something that merely exists, but which nevertheless presences, even as the mystery of Being itself. As the

shrine of Nothing, death harbours within itself the presencing of Being. As the shrine of Nothing, death is the shelter of Being. We now call mortals mortals - not because their earthly life comes to an end, but because they are capable of death as death. Mortals are who they are, as mortals present in the shelter of Being. They are the presencing relation to Being as Being.[41]

B.   Destitution and The Sacred

'To the extent that it is the subject of truth, a subject subtracts itself from every community and destroys every individuation.'[42]

The notion of presence pursued here is of The Haunt: The dwelling of the dead or the place of immortal becomings, of those who enter into death and dwell among the living, i.e. a declaration of entering into death of a living-being and the re-entering into living of this (dead) being. The examples pursued are of the initiate, the lovers and the warrior (those whom by this very declaration have entered into a state of exception). As a result of this exception, they are destitute, and must live away from community, or be killed without charge of homicide; they become in Agamben's words *Homo Sacer*.

The fate of the immortal is thus one of destitution. In this essay, what becomes destitute is architecture, as object, as thing. However, as we have established, only a subject is capable of immortality and destitution, therefore the deterritorialisation of The Haunt of Magicians (the place of initiation) to the nomadic/dispersed architecture of the battlefield through the mystification of noon, is the transformation/becomings of Deleuze. Deleuze's liminality (or death) is of a machinic or animal becoming.

Notes

[1] J-J. Lequeu in P. Duboy, *Lequeu: An Architectural Enigma*, Thames and Hudson, London, 1986, p. 72.

[2] R. Caillois, 'The Noon Complex', in *The Edge of Surrealism: A Caillois Reader*, C. Frank (ed), C. Frank and C. Naish (trans), Duke University Press, Durham and London, 2003, p. 125.

[3] R. Caillois. 'Mimicry and Legendary Psycasthenia', in *The Edge of Surrealism: A Caillois Reader*, C. Frank (ed), C. Frank and C. Naish (trans), Duke University Press, Durham and London, 2003.

[4] Caillois, 'The Noon Complex', op. cit.

[5] The Haunt is a shortened form for Lequeu's drawing 'The Haunt of Magicians' also known as 'The Gothic House' that I have adapted for this essay, viewed on 1st September 2009,

<http://visualiseur.bnf.fr/ark:/12148/btv1b7703097t>.

[6] See L. Tolstoy, *War and Peace*, Vintage, London, 2007.

[7] See G. Deleuze, *Logic of Sense*, Continuum, London, 2004; see also, G. Deleuze and C. Parnet, *Dialogues II*, Continuum, London and New York, 2006.

[8] See Caillois, 'Mimicry and Legendary Psycasthenia', op. cit.

[9] G. Deleuze and F. Guattari, *A Thousand Plateaus: Capitalism and Schizophrenia*, Continuum, London, 2004, p. 274.

[10] Middleton, foreword to *Lequeu: An Architectural Enigma*, op. cit.

[11] Duboy, op. cit.

[12] See M. Foucault, *The Order of Things: An Archaeology of the Human Sciences*, Routledge, London and New York, 2008, pp. xvi-xxvi.

[13] J-C. Lemagny, *Visionary Architects: Boullée, Ledoux, Lequeu*, Hennessy and Ingalls, Berkeley, CA, 2002.

[14] See Duboy, op. cit., '*Le Repaire des Magiciens*' ('The Haunt of Magicians'), p. 75, illustrations on p. 84, p. 215. See also: viewed on 1st September 2009, <http://visualiseur.bnf.fr/ark:/12148/btv1b7703097t>.

[15] Lemagny, op. cit., p. 187.

[16] Ibid.; G. Metken, 'Jean-Jacques Lequeu ou L'Architecture Rêvée', *Gazette des Beaux-Arts*, April, 1965, pp. 223-225.

[17] Hesiod, *The Theogony*, H. G. Evelyn-White (trans), viewed on 1st September 2009, <http://www.sacred-texts.com/cla/hesiod/theogony.htm>. See also, A. Pérez Gómez, *Built upon Love: Architectural Longing after Ethics and Aesthetics*, MIT Press, Massachusetts, 2008, pp. 32-33.

[18] Lequeu, op. cit.

[19] C. Fink, 'Introduction to The Noon Complex', in *The Edge of Surrealism: A Caillois Reader*, op. cit., pp. 124-125.

[20] Ibid.

[21] Caillois, 'The Noon Complex', op. cit., p. 125.

[22] G. Bataille, 'Solar Anus', in *Visions of Excess: Selected Writings*, 1927-1939, *Theory and History of Literature*, Vol. 14, University of Minnesota Press, Minneapolis, 2006, pp. 5-9.

[23] Caillois, 'The Noon Complex', op. cit., p. 126.

[24] Ibid., p. 127.

[25] Ibid., p. 128.

[26] Ibid., p. 129.

[27] See G. Bataille, '"Story of The Eye" by Lord Auch', J. Neugroschal (trans), Penguin Classics, London, 2001.

[28] J. Lacan, 'The Mirror Stage as Formative of the *I* Function as Revealed in Psychoanalytic Experience', in *Écrits*, B. Fink (trans), W. W. Norton and

Company, Inc., London and New York, 2006, pp. 75-81; Lacan, op. cit., pp. 93-100.

[29] See Deleuze and Parnet, *Dialogues II*, op. cit.

[30] Caillois, 'Mimicry and Legendary Psycasthenia', op. cit.

[31] Tolstoy, op. cit. p.138.

[32] Ibid., p. 266.

[33] Ibid., p. 143.

[34] Ibid., p. 355.

[35] Ibid., p. 357.

[36] A. Badiou, *Deleuze: The Clamour of Being. Theory out of Bounds*, Vol. 16, L. Burchill (trans), University of Minnesota Press, Minneapolis and London, 2000.

[37] Italics mine, the original text has it as 'and preserves', see G. Agamben 'Sacred Life', in *Homo Sacer: Sovereign Power and Bare Life*, D. Heller-Roazen (trans), Meridian, Crossing Aesthetics, Stanford University Press, California, 1998, p. 83.

[38] Ibid.

[39] M. Heidegger, 'The Thing', in *Poetry, Language, Thought*, Harper & Row Publishers Inc., New York, 1971, pp. 163-180; see also S. Žižek, 'Radical Intellectuals or, Why Heidegger Took the Right Step (Albeit in the Wrong Direction) in 1933', in *In Defence of Lost Causes*, Verso, London and New York, 2008, pp. 95-153; also A. Badiou, 'Outline of A Theory of Evil', in *Ethics: An Essay on the Understanding of Evil*, P. Hallward (trans), Verso, New York, 2002, p. 73.

[40] The masculine (he/his) is used here as a position, and bears no relation to sexualised being (man or woman), as either can fill this position.

[41] M. Heidegger, op. cit., pp. 178-179.

[42] A. Badiou, 'Democratic Materialism and Materialist Dialectic', in *Logic of Worlds: Being and Event II*, A. Toscano (trans), Continuum, London and New York 2009, p. 9.

Bibliography

Agamben, G., *Homo Sacer: Sovereign Power and Bare Life*. D. Heller-Roazen (trans), Meridian, Crossing Aesthetics, Stanford University Press, California, 1998.

Badiou, A., *Deleuze: The Clamour of Being. Theory out of Bounds*. Vol. 16, L. Burchill (trans), University of Minnesota Press, Minneapolis and London, 2000.

——, *Ethics: An Essay on the Understaning of Evil.* P. Hallward (trans), Verso, New York, 2002.

——, *Logic of Worlds: Being and Event II.* A. Toscano (trans), Continuum, London and New York, 2009.

Bataille, G., '"Story of The Eye" by Lord Auch'. J. Neugroschal (trans), Penguin Classics, London, 2001.

——, *Visions of Excess: Selected Writings, 1927-1939, Theory and History of Literature.* Vol. 14, University of Minnesota Press, Minneapolis, 2006.

Caillois, R., *The Edge of Surrealism: A Caillois Reader.* C. Frank (ed), C. Frank and C. Naish (trans), Duke University Press, Durham and London, 2003.

Deleuze, G., *Logic of Sense.* Continuum, London, 2004.

Deleuze, G. and Guattari, F., *A Thousand Plateaus: Capitalism and Scizophrenia.* Continuum, London, 2004.

Deleuze, G. and Parnet, C., *Dialogues II.* Continuum, London and New York 2006.

Duboy, P., *Lequeu: An Architectural Enigma.* Thames and Hudson, London, 1986.

Foucault, M., *The Order of Things: An Archaeology of the Human Sciences.* Routledge, London and New York, 2008.

Heidegger, M., *Poetry, Language, Thought.* A. Hofstadter (trans), Harper Perennial, New York, 2001.

Hesiod, *Theogony, Works and Days, Testimonia.* G. W. Most (trans), Loeb Classical Library, Harvard University Press, Cambridge, Massachusetts, London, 2006.

Lacan, J., *Écrits.* B. Fink (trans), W. W. Norton and Company, Inc., London and New York, 2006.

Lemagny, J.-C., *Visionary Architects: Boullée, Ledoux, Lequeu*. Hennessy and Ingalls, Berkeley, CA, 2002.

Levinas, E., *Outside The Subject*. Continuum, London and New York, 2008.

Pérez-Gómez, A., *Built upon Love: Architectural Longing after Ethics and Aesthetics*. MIT Press, Cambridge, MA, 2008.

Tolstoy, L., *War and Peace*. Vintage, New York, 2007.

Žižek, S., *In Defense of Lost Causes*. Verso, London and New York, 2008.

Tolulope Onabolu holds a PhD in Architecture (by Creative Practice) from Edinburgh College of Art. His research interests are in Architecture and Urbanism, Computation, Subjectivity and Sovereignty and the Posthuman. He is a tutor in Design and Contemporary Architectural Theory at the University of Edinburgh.

Planning a Funeral: The Encounter between Bereaved and Officiant

Glenys Caswell

Abstract
Although only a minority of the population attend a church on a regular basis, most Scottish funerals are conducted by a minister of religion. This means that there is potentially a lack of convergence between the beliefs of the individual who is conducting any given funeral and the bereaved relatives who are organising it. Many funeral ceremonies now make reference to the deceased in some way, and, as far as funeral planning is concerned, one result of this is that officiant and bereaved need to work together to decide what is going to be included in the service. The planning occurs during the course of an encounter between individuals who may have been strangers to each other before the death happened. This paper suggests that such an encounter can be a complex, multi-faceted occasion, and that Norbert Elias's game model is a useful tool with which to analyse the social event that is such an encounter. Using examples drawn from a study exploring Scottish funeral practices, the chapter identifies and describes six different games that may be involved in the funeral planning process and the effect each may have on the balance of power in the officiant/bereaved relationship.

Key Words: Bereaved, funeral officiant, funeral planning, Game Model, power balance.

*****

1. Introduction

Death in Scotland is usually followed by a funeral which consists of two separate parts: the disposal of the corpse and some form of ceremony to acknowledge the death. This chapter is concerned with the process by which the funeral ceremony is planned, and its purpose is to explore the relationship that comes into existence between the individual who will be conducting the funeral and the bereaved family. To this end Elias's theorisation of game models will be used to examine the different possible configurations that a meeting to plan a funeral can take, and data from research exploring Scottish funeral practices will be used as illustration.[1] The majority of cultures employ some form of funeral ritual when a member of the society dies, although the composition of the ritual depends upon the particular social setting, and the intentions which underpin it. The purposes of funeral ritual may be diffuse, and they may also be unacknowledged or unknown to those involved in any given funeral. The purpose of a funeral can be concerned with ensuring the welfare of the deceased in the afterlife, while simultaneously taking steps to safeguard the wellbeing of the bereaved and the wider social group. The first part of the chapter will, therefore, consider differing perspectives that may be taken with regard to funerals before moving on to introduce the Scottish funeral.

Since the Reformation in the sixteenth century Scotland has been an essentially Protestant country, and this continues to influence the form and content of funerals in the twenty-first century.[2] The paper will, therefore, provide some historical background to the Scottish funeral before introducing the research from which the data used are drawn. The chapter will then go on to discuss the different perspectives that individuals and groups in Scotland take with regard to the nature of death, and the difficulties that this can sometimes pose for the creation of an appropriate funeral. Perspectives on the funeral to be found in Scotland come from a wide spectrum that extends from the funeral as a service for the worship of God in which no mention should be made of the deceased, to the funeral as a celebration of the life of the deceased in which God should not be mentioned. The majority of funerals, however, fall somewhere between these two extremes.

Ministers, elders and priests from the varying religions, and non-religious funeral celebrants are usually clear about their belief systems. Bereaved individuals and families who are organising a funeral may also have firm beliefs, but sometimes they may hold vague or poorly formed ideas about religion and its place in their lives. A divergence in beliefs between minister or celebrant and the bereaved can make the planning of a funeral difficult, and Elias's game model will be introduced as a precursor to its use in the analysis of the interaction between funeral officiants and bereaved.[3] Six models of funeral planning games will be identified, namely the non-confrontational game; the rules of the game; the holders of expert knowledge game; the clarity of belief game; the choice of officiant game and the numbers game. After the models have been introduced one specific funeral planning encounter will be analysed to illustrate the complexity and socially situated nature of such encounters. First, however, the potential purposes of a funeral will be explored.

2.   Purpose of a Funeral

Although the form and content varies over time and place, human societies are alike in that deaths are marked by ritual practices embodied in a funeral ceremony, and there is:

> Perceived to be a need for a public celebration of the life
> that has been lived; for the decent disposal of human
> remains; generally speaking, for committing the dead
> person to a known or indeterminate future state; for giving

freedom to family and friends to express grief at their loss;
and for beginning the process of reintegrating the bereaved
into their community.[4]

The specific rituals enacted depend upon what death means within the belief systems held by those involved, and on whether the death is regarded predominantly as the loss of a unique individual or the loss of a member of a social group. In a setting where the loss of the deceased has created specific gaps in the social fabric which must be filled by another individual, the funeral ritual can offer the opportunity to begin the building of the new social structures so that the group can continue to function. Durkheim suggested that when a member of a group dies the living members come together in order to renew their 'collective sentiments.'[5] They do this through collective participation in formal mourning practices, and these are an expression not only of the grief felt by each individual, but mourning practices also represent the individuals' obligations to the society of which they are members. Such practices are concerned with the living and not with the fate or welfare of the soul or spirit of the deceased, but some ways of viewing funeral ritual relate to both the living and the dead.

The rites of passage described by Van Gennep may be applied to funerals. The rites of passage involve three separate stages, the first of which is separation when the individual is separated from his or her old status. The second phase is that of transition, which marks the time when the individual makes the move away from the previous status position towards the new one, and the final stage is that of incorporation which describes the process by which the individual is absorbed into the new status.[6] It may be argued that the funeral represents the transitional stage, during which the deceased make the move to the world of the dead and the bereaved begin their move back to the world of the living, but the funeral can also be described as the phase of incorporation when the deceased or the bereaved have been fully drawn into their new worlds. The rites of passage provide a useful way of viewing a process during which the individuals involved must move on to another status or role, but they take no view on what that new status involves for the dead. Religions, however, tend to have a clear perspective on both what death means for the deceased and what a funeral service should accomplish.

For adherents of religion, the funeral has the purpose of committing the deceased to the future, within the context of faith and integrity in the particular tradition,[7] and depending on the particular beliefs it may also involve rituals intended to ensure the welfare of the deceased in the afterlife.[8] In the Church of England, for example, purposes ascribed to funerals include commending the deceased to God, reminding mourners of their own mortality, and proclaiming faith in the existence of everlasting life.[9] Such a funeral would not include prayers for the deceased, but for a Roman Catholic praying for the dead is an important component of the ritual as it is considered that such prayers assist the dead on their progress through purgatory, a transitional phase through which most deceased must pass.[10] Traditional Japanese Buddhist funeral rituals were based around the belief that the souls of the newly dead continued in existence and could be dangerous to the living. The purposes of the rituals performed, therefore, included the breaking of the connection between the spirit and the dead body and assisting the deceased to achieve Buddhahood, and there were also rituals performed which were intended to smooth the transition of the deceased into their new status as an ancestral spirit which would guard the household.[11] Religions thus ascribe purposes to a funeral that come from the specific set of beliefs held about death and the afterlife, but even a religious funeral can have social or individual aims, which usually are centred upon the bereaved and other mourners.

Some commentators suggest that the purpose of a funeral is related solely to the needs of the living, because for the survivors to be able to return to their everyday lives, the dead must 'be given the opportunity to move securely to their destination,' whatever that destination may be.[12] Sometimes a funeral may be described in terms of allowing the mourners to grieve and make a public acknowledgement of their relationship with the deceased and in the process of doing this the mourners may be offered some measure of comfort.[13] Such a funeral may also, in a similar manner to that described by Durkheim, bring together a family that rarely meets and allow them to begin the process of filling the gap created by the death of a family member. The funeral does this by providing an occasion during which new family structures may be developed and existing ones affirmed.[14] Thus different purposes are ascribed to funerals, and the next section will introduce the Scottish funeral before going on to describe the purposes that research informants placed upon funerals.

3.   Scottish Funerals

As previously noted, since the sixteenth-century Scotland has been an essentially Protestant country, and this has influenced the kinds of funerals that take place in the country. The national church is the Church of Scotland, and it is one of a number of Presbyterian denominations in the country. Derived from Calvinist roots, which forbid praying for the dead and discourage ceremonial display, prior to the eighteenth century church ministers had no involvement with the burial of the dead, unless they attended funerals as mourners. From the eighteenth century onwards, however, ministers began to conduct funerals in the family home, although in some parts of the country it was not until the second half of the twentieth century that the minister began to accompany the coffin to the cemetery.[15] For Scottish Presbyterianism, the important factor was worship of God, not the deceased and his or her life and character. By the end of the twentieth century many changes had taken place, so that funerals in Scotland rarely took place in the family home, and women had become involved in funerals in a way unknown in the past.[16] Despite regional variations, there was a trend discernible towards focusing the funeral service on the life of the deceased.[17]

The data on which the remainder of the paper draws are from a qualitative sociological research project exploring Scottish funeral practices, the fieldwork for which was carried out in 2007. Interviews were conducted with 56 professionals working in the organisation and conduct of funerals, such as the ministers, priests and secular celebrants who conduct funerals, crematorium and cemetery staff and funeral directors. Ten interviews were also carried out with bereaved people who had arranged funerals, in a manner commensurate with the demands of ethical practice[18] and the potentially sensitive nature of the subject.[19] Fieldwork was carried out in three locations, in order to sample a range of practices, and these sites were Stornoway on the Isle of Lewis which is situated off the north-west coast of Scotland, Inverness in the Highlands and Edinburgh, Scotland's capital.

Today, Protestant ministers still lead the majority of funerals, even though by the middle of the twentieth century only 12 per cent of Scots attended church regularly on Sundays.[20] Ministers of the Church of Scotland have a duty under the Church's own laws to conduct funerals for anyone living within the boundaries of their geographical parishes, so that its ministers conduct more funerals than any other group, and it is not unusual for a parish funeral to be for people the minister has never met before.[21] It is also the case that the minister will possibly not know whether the deceased or the bereaved have a religious faith and what any such faith might consist of. However, the Church of Scotland is not the only provider of funerals. Different Protestant denominations and different religions, both Christian and non-Christian provide funerals for their adherents, and the Humanist Society of Scotland will conduct funerals with no religious references for atheists, and in 2007 the Humanist Society was responsible for four per cent of funerals in the country.[22] A typical Church of Scotland funeral includes prayers, readings, hymns, a tribute to the deceased, recorded music and a committal of the deceased. A secular humanist funeral typically includes poetry, readings, a tribute to the deceased, music and the committal of the deceased. As Garces-Foley found in the United States of America[23] the secular funeral takes a broadly similar shape to the religious funeral, as the practices of the dominant church have been absorbed into Scotland's wider social customs.

4.   The Purposes of Scottish Funerals

All professional informants were asked what they believed to be the purpose of a funeral, and most of them suggested a number of different aims and intentions they would have in mind when planning a funeral. For ministers of religion the prime purpose centred on their belief in God and the funeral as a service for the worship of God. In the smaller, strict Presbyterian denominations the purpose might extend to the provision of comfort to the bereaved, but this would be through 'putting things in the right perspective' and directing mourners' attention to God.[24] The focus of these funerals is firmly on God rather than the deceased, and comfort for the bereaved is to be found through this religious focus. For ministers of the Church of Scotland, while they acknowledge the importance of God in the funeral context, they were more likely than their conservative colleagues to speak also about honouring the deceased and giving thanks for his or her life, as well as providing an opportunity for family and friends to come together in mutual support.

Amongst religious informants, the most open responses to this question came from the chaplains who worked in either general hospitals or hospices for the terminally ill. They tended to speak of the funeral in terms of providing an opportunity for mourners to say goodbye to the deceased, for them to remember and reminisce about the life of the deceased, and for the bereaved to express the love they felt. For the chaplains their religious faith and their belief in God informed everything that they would say and do in the funeral context, but this would not necessarily be outwardly expressed. For secular humanists the purpose of the funeral is bound up with their atheist beliefs. They described the funeral as a way of paying tribute to the deceased, with the specific purpose of celebrating the life lost and of being of therapeutic value to the bereaved.

For those who conduct funerals their perspective on the meaning of death and the existence of an afterlife is clear and this has consequences for what they see as being the purpose of a funeral. The situation with regard to the views of the deceased and the bereaved, however, is fraught with complications and questions. When the bereaved family are members of a particular church the likelihood is that they will ask their minister to conduct the funeral. Often, however, the deceased was perhaps a church regular while the surviving relatives are not, or the deceased was an atheist while some of the bereaved are also atheists but some are not. The possible permutations of belief within a bereaved family are many, and this is particularly pertinent with regard to the planning of a funeral, since the beliefs of some or all of the family may be vague or unformed, making it potentially difficult for them to decide on an appropriate funeral context. The majority of bereaved families in Scotland employ the services of a funeral director, and he or she will often be the one who suggests the individual who will conduct the funeral in the absence of any prior allegiance on the part of the bereaved. Some funeral directors will contact the Humanist Society on behalf of non-believers, but others recommend instead the use of a retired minister or even offer to lead the funeral themselves. The group most often called upon, however, to conduct funerals for strangers are ministers from the Church of Scotland.

Today, such ministers usually expect that the bereaved will be involved in planning the content of the funeral service, even if they are not going to participate in the service in some way, although some families choose to leave all decisions about the funeral content to the minister. Mainland funerals typically include a tribute to the deceased which describes their life for mourners amidst judgements of 'honor and worthiness,'[25] and music will often be played that is reminiscent of the deceased. Whether the minister knows the family or not, he or she is likely to have little idea of the view that each family member takes on issues of the afterlife, the purpose of the funeral and the existence of God. Thus each interview with a bereaved family during which the minister begins to plan the funeral can be a delicate negotiation. Elias's game model can help to clarify the nature of this encounter between minister or celebrant and bereaved, but before applying it to the specific situation it is necessary to describe and discuss the theory briefly.[26]

5.   Elias' Game Model
Sociologist, Norbert Elias, suggests that the study of human beings in society presents difficulties which are founded upon the complexity of the relationships and inter-dependencies to be found there. One way around this is to make use of models, so that a particular situation or interaction is temporarily frozen in time and is brought into closer focus so that it can be understood more easily. One model he makes use of is that of the game or contest. In its simplest form this involves two players, one of whom is weak at the game and the other stronger, so that the stronger player has a clear advantage over the weaker player. However, in most situations the power in the game is more evenly divided, and it can also ebb and flow between players, for power is not something which an individual either does or does not possess, it is a process. It is also the case that the game is often played between groups rather than individuals, and this is something that inevitably affects the power balance.[27]

There are a number of aspects to game theory which need to be considered in order to make it a valuable tool. One basic notion is that the players in any particular game must be in a position where they have to make decisions, and these decisions must affect the other players.[28] In the planning of a funeral it is perhaps obvious to say that any decisions the funeral leader makes will have an effect on the bereaved family members; they may feel hurt if he or she refuses to include a particular piece of music, or if the officiant omits certain pieces of information from the funeral tribute the bereaved may find that they do not recognise the deceased in what they are hearing. Conversely, decisions made by the bereaved can also affect the funeral leader; a decision by the bereaved to include non-religious elements may cause an ordained minister to think hard about where his or her personal religious boundaries are, or a reading or piece of music requested may seem inappropriate to the funeral leader. In this model the wider group of mourners at the funeral, because they are not decision makers, are not taken into account. But what about the deceased?

Some individuals make choices about their funerals before they die, and this can vary in extent from telling their close relatives what music they wish to be played to planning the service in detail with whoever is going to be leading it. Most of the time, however, this is not the case, and the funeral planning is left to the survivors. The bereaved and the funeral leader often express a wish to plan a funeral that is coherent with the beliefs and wishes of the deceased, however little known those may be. In a practical sense the deceased is not affected by decisions made and is unable to participate in the decision making process although, for some bereaved individuals as will be discussed further below, there is a sense that the deceased has a presence during the planning and conduct of the funeral. The main decision makers for our application of the model, then, are the bereaved family and the person who is going to conduct the funeral.

Unlike games such as chess or football where, if one individual or team wins then the other inevitably loses, in a games model of a social interaction this is not necessarily the case. A funeral may be planned, for example, in which the minister feels that the service is compatible with his or her religious integrity and which the bereaved feel does justice to their sense of who the deceased was. In such a situation the game played out during the funeral planning may not have been confrontational, but built on a sense of mutual agreement. Games such as football and chess have rules that are rigorously applied, sometimes by the players themselves and sometimes by an outside referee. Social interactions, however, between individuals and groups have rules, but these are not invariable and they are not necessarily understood in the same way by all participants in an interaction.[29] The stricter Scottish Presbyterian denominations, for example, have invariable rules governing what may be included during a service of worship in their churches, and this applies to funerals as well as to other services. A bereaved family approaching the minister of such a church may not be aware of these rules, and may, therefore, offend the minister's susceptibilities by making requests deemed inappropriate by the minister. These aspects, the possibly non-confrontational nature of the game and the varied understandings of the game's rules, must be held in mind whilst applying the theory to practical situations.

Once the players in the game have been identified it is necessary to consider other aspects, particularly what are the possible choices that can be made; what are the likely outcomes of those choices; and what preferences do the players have about the elements that make up the funeral?[30] When players make the same choices as each other the game will be straightforward and the likely outcome is a funeral which meets the expectations of both bereaved and officiant. When players make different choices and their preferences differ then the game will be more complex, and the most straightforward way in which to consider these factors is by applying the model to real situations, and this is what the next section will do.

6.   Game Model in Action

The players in the game have been identified, and they are the minister or celebrant who is going to conduct the funeral service and the bereaved family, of whom there may be several members involved or just one or two individuals. There may also be a sense that the deceased has a part in this process and, while it might be expected that it would be the bereaved who would feel this, sometimes it comes from the minister. One Church of Scotland minister said:

> The day she died I was away, they (the family) got onto the funeral director and said get us a minister immediately, and they couldn't get me on the phone, so they organised someone else to do a service in the crematorium.[31]

In this case the deceased was an elderly woman who regularly attended the church of which the informant was minister. Her family all lived in another part of the country, and the deceased had indicated previously to her minister that she wished for her funeral to be a church service, followed by a burial. The minister was shocked that the wishes of the deceased had been overridden in this manner, but the fact that this could happen illustrates the way in which the deceased is powerless in this situation; while the family and the minister may express a desire to honour the wishes and beliefs of the deceased there is no compulsion under Scottish law for them to do so.[32]

The following sections will examine the process during which the minister and the bereaved make decisions in relation to the funeral content and identify and describe the different models of game that can be entered into. The term minister is used in the following sections in recognition of the fact that ministers of religion conduct most Scottish funerals, but the games described may also apply to encounters between bereaved and non-religious celebrants.

A.   The Non-Confrontational Game

In some cases a family will approach the minister of the church of which they are members, or an atheist will approach a secular humanist celebrant and the funeral will be planned with a sense of mutual agreement.

Each will know what to expect from the other and the bereaved know the boundaries outside which their chosen funeral officiants will not venture; an atheist, for example, will know that a secular humanist will not agree to the inclusion of a prayer in the funeral ceremony. A widow asked her minister to conduct her husband's funeral service because, she said, 'It seemed sensible to have him conduct the service because he knows us ... we both felt very happy with him, and that's important.'[33] The widow and the minister together planned a funeral which met her wishes and needs, but she also had the sense of her husband's presence during and after the funeral. While terminally ill her husband had not wished to speak about his funeral, but she made choices which she believed were compatible with his life and beliefs. During the research interview, which took place three years after he had died, the widow spoke of her husband in the present tense and she said of his funeral that, 'I knew for instance that I did not want his dead body in the coffin in church ... the flowers were in the church, but his dead shell was not and his spirit was above.'[34] This widow knew that her husband was dead, but he had an enduring presence in her life, so that she thought about him in the present and not the past tense.[35]

Sometimes the funeral planning process will also be consensual even when the bereaved do not share the belief system of the funeral officiant. A hospice chaplain, for example, takes the following approach to the process of funeral organisation:

> I would still encourage them (the bereaved) to tell their
> story, and I see that as very much part of the ritual...once
> you've done that you begin to co-construct a funeral ritual
> that emerges out of the story...I don't tell them what
> they've to do, but let them come to their own conclusion.[36]

His approach, which is not unusual among chaplains, is that the bereaved should take control of the process and that as officiant he should act as a facilitator even if this results in a funeral that is without religious content. The funerals he conducts are for individuals who die in the hospice where he works and sometimes the bereaved relatives will ask him to make all the decisions, but in most cases they work with him to plan an appropriate funeral.

In many cases, however, the minister and the bereaved do not share a belief system, or they lack an awareness of each other's beliefs and this means that different factors will come into play in the planning process.

B.   Rules of the Game
All social encounters have rules governing their progress, and the individuals involved must choose whether or not to follow the rules.

Sometimes actors in an encounter will interpret the rules differently to each other, and sometimes they will wish to convey a particular impression to others in the encounter so that they manage their behaviour and speech accordingly.[37] The usual rules on polite interactions are intensified in the process of funeral planning, however, by two factors. The first of these is that there is a general expectation that the bereaved will be treated with sensitivity by all those with whom they come into contact, and this expectation is particularly high with regard to the conduct of the professionals whom they employ in the course of organising and conducting a funeral. The second factor follows on from this, and relates to the high expectations that Scottish society has of the behaviour of a minister of religion under normal circumstances, and these expectations become even higher in a bereavement situation. The minister is expected to listen to what the bereaved say with an appropriate sensitivity and sympathy towards their situation of loss; he or she is not expected to challenge or distress the bereaved.[38] What, then, are the implications of this for the decision making process?

The invariable practice expressed by research informants was to meet with the bereaved in order to talk about the deceased and the requirements for the funeral, and the only time when this would not happen would be if the bereaved live a long distance away, and in this situation the arrangements would be made by telephone. Most informants said that they prefer to visit the bereaved in their own homes, for as one minister expressed it, 'I make an arrangement to see the next of kin, almost always I go round to the house that they're in, rather than them coming here, so they're comfortable.'[39] If the bereaved are comfortable because they are in their own home and surrounded by familiar people and things, they are more likely to feel able to express their wishes with regard to the funeral; having a pile of compact discs in view which the deceased played regularly may not only help the bereaved to recall what the deceased's favourite music was, but may also help them feel sufficiently confident to request that it be played during the funeral.

The bereaved have power in this situation conferred upon them by their loss and the intensified social rules governing the encounter with the minister. Bereaved individuals in Scotland are expected to be able to manage their grief in such a way that they weep quietly, for example, rather than wailing loudly. However, given that normal every day social rules do not permit public weeping without good reason, this is a special dispensation based upon their bereavement.[40] The minister is not expected to exacerbate the situation and provoke greater shows of emotion. Consequently, one can see that the minister is constrained to a greater extent than usual in what he or she can say or do, while the bereaved are less constrained in their behaviour than usual. While this appears to confer upon the bereaved a measure of power in the situation this may be limited by their lack of knowledge about what is expected and considered acceptable in a funeral.

C.   Holders of Expert Knowledge Game
          Most deaths in Scotland today are of elderly people: in 2007 for example 79 per cent of deaths were of people over the age of 65, while 28 per cent of deaths were of people over the age of 85.[41] This results in many individuals not encountering the need to organise a funeral until they are no longer young themselves, and they may find themselves unsure what to do. A Church of Scotland minister said of this situation:

> I get people of 50 come to see me, and they've never had to deal with a funeral, that's the first time they've ever been in this situation. One of the things that can happen with that is that they're dependent on the undertakers, they're dependent on the minister just to guide them about the practicalities.[42]

Even when the bereaved have needed to organise a funeral previously, they are not likely to be doing so frequently, and they may find that they cannot remember much about their previous experience; it is not unusual for the bereaved to retain only hazy memories about the funeral.[43]
          The minister conducting a funeral will, on the other hand, have a wealth of experience to draw on. Although the number of funerals any individual minister is involved with will vary according to the individual's particular professional circumstances, the planning and leading of funerals is part of the ministerial job. Church of Scotland ministers in particular regularly conduct funerals, and this leads to them knowing what makes a good funeral, what works and what does not, as well as the kinds of choices that other families have made. Ministers, that is, have expert knowledge and while this can be put to the use of the bereaved family, it is also the case that such expertise can leave those without it feeling bereft of power.[44] The owner of a specialist set of skills and knowledge begins a negotiation with an advantage over the game player who does not have such a set of skills. In this specific situation, because the minister has planned and participated in many funerals and is thus an expert, the bereaved may feel that he or she knows better than they do, and this may lead them to accept his or her suggestions rather than to put forward their own ideas and wishes. Linked with the notion of the minister as expert is the idea that a minister of religion or a humanist celebrant will have a clear set of beliefs regarding death and what the funeral should set out to achieve, while the bereaved family may not.

D.   Clarity of Belief Game

One clear advantage which the minister or celebrant has over the bereaved family is that the professionals will have a focused view of their beliefs, and they will know what is necessary for them to maintain a sense of their own integrity. Members of the bereaved family, on the other hand, may have ideas with regard to religion, death and the afterlife which are hazy and indistinct, or it may be that different members of the family hold different ideas. Possessing a clarity of belief makes it straightforward for a minister to maintain his or her position when it is challenged by the bereaved. One minister from the Free Presbyterian Church of Scotland, for example, said: 'One family, the son wouldn't even shake hands with me the day of the funeral, because I wouldn't agree to any of their demands.'[45] This minister is from a small denomination which holds to its principles of neither referencing the deceased during funeral worship nor playing any music at all, and its very strictness puts its ministers in a strong position vis-à-vis the bereaved in the planning process. Free Presbyterian Church ministers possess clarity of belief about what is acceptable, and their denomination has firm rules to which they must adhere.

Secular humanist celebrants from the Humanist Society of Scotland also maintain a strict position with regard to the content of funerals, in that nothing may be included which makes a religious reference, whether in words, music or symbols.[46] The strictness of the position again makes it simple for the celebrants, as for the ministers above, to maintain their integrity. One celebrant spoke of a planning session in which:

> The daughter was very keen on a humanist one, and the son
> said my wife has told me the only thing I have to make sure
> is that this hymn and that hymn are included, and I said I
> think there's some misunderstanding here because we don't
> do hymns, and he actually said to me why not...so I said
> well I can give you some ministers that you might want to
> contact.[47]

The bereaved family, when faced with such trenchant positions, have to decide whether they wish to accommodate themselves to the deeply held beliefs of the minister or celebrant, or whether they wish to go elsewhere.

Most ministers, however, take a more flexible approach. While maintaining their own clarity of belief, they also feel able to uphold their personal religious integrity, whilst simultaneously allowing the bereaved to impose something of their own stamp upon the funeral service. Such ministers enter into the planning process as a negotiation, seeking ways in which they can both remain faithful to their own core beliefs and provide a funeral that is meaningful for the bereaved.

E.   Choice of Officiant Game

All those involved in the conduct of funerals wish to do their best for the bereaved, and to produce a funeral that will meet their needs and wishes, but inevitably ideas about what is the best for bereaved families vary. The timescale within which funerals in Scotland are organised varies in different parts of the country, but the funeral usually takes place within a week of the death. As already mentioned, most families employ the services of a funeral director, and when the family has no religious affiliation the funeral director is often the first professional they call upon, and he or she will be keen to begin making arrangements. Church of Scotland ministers often receive a call from the funeral director to introduce them to a bereaved family and ask if they can take the particular funeral. Under the Church's Declaratory Acts, ministers need to have a good reason to refuse to conduct a funeral for someone who lives within their parish boundary.[48] Ministers will not be in a hurry to turn down requests made by families, and indeed for some ministers funerals represent the only point of contact they have with many of their parishioners and give them the only opportunity they are likely to get to present the church to those who do not attend worship. One minister described his intention of leaving mourners with 'a wee bit more of a sense of otherness to help them cope, not to be evangelical, but maybe in time to enable folk to think beyond themselves.'[49] This is a contact with the wider society that the church would be reluctant to lose, particularly at a time of low church attendances when the Church of Scotland has been described as in need of making itself more available and relevant to the unaffiliated public.[50]

The bereaved family in this situation may have less invested in having this minister from this particular denomination conduct their funeral than he or she has in conducting it. The bereaved, therefore, have the power to go elsewhere if they do not like the suggestions one minister makes or if they feel uncomfortable with the way in which he or she relates to them. In practice, few do, but the option is open to them.

F.   Numbers Game

Sometimes when a minister or celebrant meets with the bereaved to plan a funeral there will only be one member of the family present, but more often there will be a number of family members in attendance. At first sight this should tip the balance of power firmly in the favour of the family, for the minister's superior knowledge of funerals and clarity of belief should be outweighed by the numbers of the bereaved coupled with their occupation of the bereaved status. Sometimes this will be the case, but the situation is not necessarily as clear cut as it seems at first. If the members of the bereaved family are in agreement about the funeral and support each other, then it will be easier for them to prevail against the minister. However, should the family disagree with each other and either not support each other or even actively try to sabotage each others' ideas, then the minister may find that he or she is playing several games against different individuals, rather than one game against a group of people. Assuming the officiant does not find him or herself overwhelmed by the numbers involved the advantage here is with the professional.[51]

7.   Discussion

As the preceding section has illustrated, the process of planning the content of a funeral is a complex one, in which the balance of power can shift backwards and forwards between the minister or celebrant and the bereaved family, depending upon the particular circumstances and individuals involved. Officiants have clear beliefs and they also have expert knowledge and specialist skills which appear to give them a powerful advantage over the bereaved family. However, they are constrained to a greater extent than the bereaved by the social rules, and they will often be the single player against the many players of the family and this can offset their advantages. The advantages that the bereaved hold are counterpoint to the disadvantages of the officiants, in that they are less constrained than usual by social custom and there may be several of them in an encounter with a single minister or celebrant. Where the bereaved lack most power, however, is that they may be baffled by their grief in combination with the need to make decisions swiftly, for Scottish funerals take place quickly, usually within the week and often within three or four days. Sometimes, also, the bereaved may be vague about the nature of their beliefs about death and the existence of an afterlife, and one family group may have very different belief systems amongst its members, making it hard for them to agree upon a suitable funeral context.

When meeting to plan a funeral, the minister or celebrant will be calm and businesslike, at a time when the family may be in emotional turmoil for they are making what has been described as a 'distress purchase.'[52] How the process plays out in any given encounter depends in part on the dispositions of the individuals involved, but the game model can help to untangle the complex process that is at work in the planning of a funeral, and one way in which to illustrate this is through the examination of one specific encounter, as described by a minister from Stornoway.[53]

Funerals in Stornoway follow a similar format to each other in which there is little or no referencing of the deceased individual. Encounters between the bereaved and the minister who will be conducting the funeral do not usually present much difficulty, as the local traditions are well known and generally adhered to. Until 2007 all funerals taking place in Stornoway were religious.[54] One Church of Scotland Minister in the town is regarded locally as more flexible than most, in that he includes a tribute to the deceased in the funeral worship, which is contrary to traditional island practice. The playing of secular music is virtually unknown in Stornoway funerals, and it is seldom requested.

Like his colleagues, this Church of Scotland Minister will always 'Go and see the family as soon as possible.' On one occasion he was warned that he was going to be facing a potentially difficult situation, in that the bereaved family wanted secular music played during the funeral. He knew that he would be confronted by several family members, so he took steps to increase his own power base: 'I'd been told they were going to ask for something a wee bit different … I took an elder with me.' By taking an elder with him to meet with the family this minister was able to strengthen his own power in terms of numbers. Although there were several family members present during the course of the encounter, so that the minister and elder were outnumbered, it was not as difficult as it might have been, because although:

> His (the deceased's) only child felt very, very strongly she wanted this played…but in the way they (family) asked there was clearly an awkwardness, a nervousness and so that was actually helpful to me as I could see that they're struggling with this, although the daughter isn't, she just made it so clear, I really, really want this.[55]

Although the minister and elder were outnumbered by the members of the bereaved family, there was a discrepancy or doubt in the wishes of family members, and the minister consciously made use of this. The minister made it clear to the family that, '[i]n relation to worship it's my call on what happens, that's one of the things in the Church of Scotland, the minister has domain over worship.'[56]

The minister refused to play secular music as people were gathering in the church before the service, as he considered that this came under the domain of worship. However, he was aware of how strongly the daughter felt and that the family as a group were feeling grief, so a process of negotiation resulted in a funeral that met the family's wishes without offending the minister's tenets of faith. The requested secular music was played at the end of the service, which was a time the minister deemed more appropriate, and it was played by a professional keyboard player in a classical arrangement.[57] Another minister who had attended as a mourner said: 'We all know the tune, but it was gently done, not too syncopated.'[58] The number of family members present had the potential to present a challenge to the minister, but he met the challenge by taking one of the church's elders with him to support him in his decision making. He had, furthermore, consciously made use of the fact that the family, apart from one member, were unsure about the appropriateness of their request in order to make clear his ultimate authority over what happens in his church.[59] The family in this encounter did not have the power conferred by the ability to walk away. If this minister, the most flexible on the Isle of Lewis, had turned down their request there was no one else they could turn to.

Through consideration of this specific encounter between officiant and bereaved it is possible to see that it can be a complex social negotiation, in which the balance of power is shifting. Four different game models were in operation here. The rules of the game model came into play as the minister was reluctant to give an outright refusal to the family's wishes, although he would have done so if he had perceived this as necessary, but because the family were bereaved and the daughter in particular felt strongly he was prepared to negotiate. The minister here was a holder of expert knowledge, although in a setting like Stornoway this is less of an advantage than it might be elsewhere because funerals vary little from each other and those who live in the town attend funerals regularly and are familiar with the usual funeral format. The clarity of belief game was also in operation, as the minister knew what he believed and what he would permit in his church, but the daughter of the bereaved family was equally clear about what she wanted. Finally, the numbers game was in use, as there were several family members present and the minister took an elder with him because he knew that this would be the case. The choice of officiant game was not available to the family because this minister was the most flexible on the island. Ultimately, this minister had the power to say yes or no to the family's requests, and unlike in Inverness or Edinburgh on the mainland, there was no one else to whom they could turn.

8. Conclusion

When the funeral planning process works well it can produce a service or ceremony with which the minister or celebrant is comfortable, while at the same time honouring the wishes of the deceased and also meeting the needs of the bereaved. This is what happened in the following funeral, conducted by a hospital chaplain:

> One occasion when the person who died did not want any religious ceremony at all and the family did, and the compromise that we reached was to cut the service in half, and I took the whole service up to the committal non-religiously. After the committal I said the … family have asked for readings at this point, so I think the family were happy with that … they wanted to honour their mum's wishes, but they still wanted the comfort of prayers.[60]

The chaplain was keen to facilitate the family in planning a funeral that was appropriate for them, and the family were keen to acknowledge their own religious faith whilst also respecting their mother's lack of belief. In the planning process there was clarity about the beliefs and needs of the chaplain, the family and the deceased.

Often there is no such clarity, and the funeral planning becomes a complex negotiation. Elias's game model permits analysis of the power balance between players in this negotiation and allows us to see that sometimes the officiant has control of the situation, sometimes the bereaved have control, and sometimes neither has overall control, so that a negotiated settlement must be reached.

Notes

[1] N. Elias, *What is Sociology*, S. Mennell and G. Morrisey (trans), Columbia University Press, New York, 1970, pp. 71-103.

[2] C. G. Brown, *Religion and Society in Scotland since 1707*, Edinburgh University Press, Edinburgh, 1997, p. 17.

[3] The term officiant is used in this paper to refer to both religious and non-religious funeral leaders.

[4] K. Denison, 'The Theology and Liturgy of Funerals: A View from the Church in Wales', *Mortality*, Vol. 4, No. 1, 1999, p. 63.

[5] E. Durkheim, *The Elementary Forms of the Religious Life*, J. W. Swain (trans), 2nd Edition, George Allen and Unwin, London, 1976, pp. 396-403.

[6] A. Van Gennep, *The Rites of Passage*, M. B. Vizedom and G. L. Caffee (trans), University of Chicago Press, Chicago, 1960.

[7] Denison, op. cit., p. 63.

[8] P. C. Jupp, *From Dust to Ashes: Cremation and the British Way of Death*, Palgrave Macmillan, Basingstoke, 2006, pp. 1-18.

[9] H. James, *A Fitting End*, Canterbury Press, Norwich, 2004, pp. 25-43.

[10] D. J. Davies, *A Brief History of Death*, Blackwell Publishing, Oxford, 2005, p. 52.

[11] H. Suzuki, *The Price of Death*, Stanford University Press, Stanford, 2000, p. 40.

[12] R. Kastenbaum, 'Why Funerals?', *Generations*, Vol. 28, No. 2, 2004, p. 7.

[13] Jupp, p. 1.

[14] T. Walter, *Funerals and How To Improve Them*, Hodder and Stoughton, London, 1990, pp. 107-114.

[15] E. McFarland, 'Researching Death, Mourning and Commemoration in Modern Scotland', *Journal of Scottish Historical Studies*, Vol. 24, No. 1, 2004, pp. 20-44.

[16] E. McFarland, 'Working with Death: An Oral History of Funeral Directing in Later Twentieth-century Scotland', *Oral History*, 2008, pp. 69-80.

[17] E. McFarland, 'Passing Time: Death and Mourning in Twentieth Century Scotland', in *A History of Everyday Life in Twentieth-Century Scotland*, L. Abrams and C. G. Brown (eds), Edinburgh University Press, Edinburgh, 2010..

[18] British Sociological Association, *Statement of Ethical Practice for the British Sociological Association*, 2002, viewed on 1st September 2006, <http://www.britsoc.co.uk/equality/63.htm>.

[19] R. M. Lee and C. M. Renzetti, *Researching Sensitive Topics*, Sage, London, 1993, pp. 3-11.

[20] C. G. Brown, *The Death of Christian Britain*, Routledge, London, 2001, p. 166.

[21] A. G. McGillivray, *Introduction to Practice and Procedure in the Church of Scotland*, 2nd Edition, Church of Scotland, Edinburgh, 2001.

[22] Humanist Society of Scotland, *2007 Funeral Figures*, 2008, received in email on 21st February 2008.

[23] K. Garces-Foley, 'Funerals of the Unaffiliated', *Omega*, Vol. 46, No. 4, 2002-2003, p. 299.

[24] Free Church of Scotland Minister, Stornoway. When reference is made to what research informants have said, they will be referred to by their role in the research and their location.

[25] A. D. Kunkel and M. R. Dennis, 'Grief Consolation in Eulogy Rhetoric: An Integrative Framework', *Death Studies*, Vol. 27, No. 1, 2008, p. 2.

[26] Elias, op. cit., pp. 71-76.

[27] Ibid., pp. 76-103.

[28] H. Hamburger, *Games as Models of Social Phenomen*, W. H. Freeman and Company, San Francisco, 1979, pp. 1-2.

[29] Hamburger, op. cit., pp. 2-9.

[30] Ibid.

[31] Church of Scotland Minister, Inverness.

[32] Funeral Director, Inverness.

[33] Widow, Edinburgh.

[34] Ibid.

[35] G. Bennett and K. M. Bennett, 'The Presence of the Dead: An Empirical Study', *Mortality*, Vol. 5, No. 2, 2000, p. 139.

[36] Hospice Chaplain, Edinburgh.

[37] E. Goffman, *The Presentation of Self in Everyday Life*, Penguin Books, London, 1959, pp. 13-27.

[38] E. Goffman, *Behavior in Public Places*, The Free Press, New York, 1963, pp. 166-178.

[39] Church of Scotland Minister, Edinburgh.
[40] A. R. Hochschild, *The Managed Heart*, University of California Press, Berkeley, 1983, pp. 35-55.
[41] General Register Office for Scotland, *Deaths by Age, Sex and Administrative Area, Scotland 2007*, 2008, viewed on 2nd February 2008, <http://www.gro-scotland.gov.uk/files/05t5-2.xls>.
[42] Church of Scotland Minister, Inverness.
[43] J. Hockey, *Making the Most of a Funeral*, Cruse Bereavement Care, Richmond upon Thames, 1992, pp. 33-34.
[44] A. Giddens, *Modernity and Self-Identity*, Stanford University Press, Stanford, 1991, p. 192.
[45] Free Presbyterian Church of Scotland Minister, Inverness.
[46] Humanist Society of Scotland, Funeral Celebrant, Inverness.
[47] Humanist Society of Scotland, Funeral Celebrant, Edinburgh.
[48] McGillivray, op. cit., p. 66.
[49] Church of Scotland Minister, Edinburgh.
[50] Cf. McFarland, 'Passing Time', forthcoming, 2009.
[51] Elias, op. cit., pp. 82-84.
[52] B. Parsons, 'Conflict in the Context of Care: An Examination of Role Conflict between the Bereaved and the Funeral Director in the UK', *Mortality*, Vol. 8, No. 1, 2003, p. 71.
[53] Church of Scotland Minister, Stornoway.
[54] Funeral Director, Stornoway.
[55] Church of Scotland Minister, Stornoway
[56] Ibid.
[57] Ibid.
[58] Episcopal Church of Scotland Minister, Stornoway.
[59] Church of Scotland Minister, Stornoway.
[60] Hospital Chaplain, Inverness.

Bibliography

Bennett, G., and Bennett, K. M., 'The Presence of the Dead: An Empirical Study'. *Mortality*, Vol. 5, No. 2, 2000, pp. 139-157.

British Sociological Association, *Statement of Ethical Practice for the British Sociological Association*. 2002, viewed on 1st September 2006, <http://www.britsoc.co.uk/equality/63.htm>.

Brown, C. G., *Religion and Society in Scotland since 1707*. Edinburgh University Press, Edinburgh, 1997.

——, *The Death of Christian Britain*. Routledge, London, 2001.

Davies, D. J., *A Brief History of Death*. Blackwell Publishing, Oxford, 2005.

Denison, K., 'The Theology and Liturgy of Funerals: A View from the Church in Wales'. *Mortality*, Vol. 4, No. 1, 1999, pp. 63-74.

Durkheim, E., *The Elementary Forms of the Religious Life*. J. W. Swain (trans), 2nd Edition, George Allen and Unwin, London, 1976.

Elias, N., *What is Sociology?*. S. Mennell and G. Morrissey (trans), Columbia University Press, New York, 1970.

Garces-Foley, K., 'Funerals of the Unaffiliated'. *Omega*, Vol. 46, No. 4, 2002-2003, pp. 287-302.

General Register Office for Scotland, *Deaths by Sex, Age, and Administrative Area, Scotland, 2007*. 2008, viewed on 2nd February 2008, <http://www.gro-scotland.gov.uk/files/05t5-2xls>.

Giddens, A., *Modernity and Self-Identity*. Stanford University Press, Stanford, 1991.

Goffman, E., *The Presentation of Self in Everyday Life*. Penguin Books, London, 1959.

——, *Behavior in Public Places*. The Free Press, New York, 1963.

Hamburger, H., *Games as Models of Social Phenomena*. W. H. Freeman and Company, San Francisco, 1979.

Hochschild, A. R., *The Managed Heart*. University of California Press, Berkeley, 1983.

Hockey, J., *Making the Most of a Funeral*. Cruse Bereavement Care, Richmond upon Thames, 1992.

James, H., *A Fitting End*. Canterbury Press, Norwich, 2004.

Jupp, P. C., *From Dust to Ashes: Cremation and the British Way of Death*. Palgrave Macmillan, Basingstoke, 2006.

Kastenbaum, R., 'Why Funerals?'. *Generations*, Vol. 28, No. 2, 2004, pp. 5-10.

Kunkel, A. D. and Dennis, M. R., 'Grief Consolation in Eulogy Rhetoric: An Integrative Framework'. *Death Studies*, Vol. 27, No. 1, 2008, pp. 1-38.

Lee, R. M. and Renzetti, C. M., *Researching Sensitive Topics*. Sage, London, 1993.

McFarland, E., 'Researching Death, Mourning and Commemoration in Modern Scotland'. *Journal of Scottish Historical Studies*, Vol. 24, No. 1, 2004, pp. 20-44.

——, 'Working with Death: An Oral History of Funeral Directing in Later Twentieth-Century Scotland'. *Oral History*, Spring, 2008, pp. 69-80.

——, 'Passing Time: Death and Mourning in Twentieth Century Scotland', in *A History of Everyday Life in Twentieth-Century Scotland*. L. Abrams and C. G. Brown (eds), Edinburgh University Press, Edinburgh, 2010.

McGillivray, A. G., *Introduction to Practice and Procedure in the Church of Scotland*. 2nd Edition, Church of Scotland, Edinburgh, 2001.

Parsons, B., 'Conflict in the Context of Care: An Examination of Role Conflict between the Bereaved and the Funeral Director in the UK'. *Mortality*, Vol. 8, No. 1, 200, pp. 67-87.

Suzuki, H., *The Price of Death*. Stanford University Press, Stanford, 2000.

Van Gennep, A., *The Rites of Passage*. M. B. Vizedom and G. L. Caffee (trans), University of Chicago Press, Chicago, 1960.

Walter, T., *Funerals and How to Improve Them*. Hodder and Stoughton, London, 1990.

Glenys Caswell has been working at the University of Nottingham as a Research Fellow on a study entitled: 'Dying in Hospital: Care of the Patient with Dementia and the Family Carers' since June 2010. Between 2006 and 2009 she was working on her PhD at the University of Aberdeen. The social context of death and dying remains her main area of research.

Living with the Dead: Cremating and Reburying the Dead in a Megalopolis

Marcel Reyes-Cortez

Abstract
Mexico City, a saturated and heavily populated megalopolis, has a growing population that exceeds 22.9 million inhabitants, with deaths estimated at almost 3,000 per day - more than a million each year.[1] Rural spaces have been engulfed by the city's growth resulting in overcrowding of both cemeteries and spaces dedicated to housing the dead. This paper will examine why, although cremation has for many years offered a solution as a method of disposal of the dead, it still meets with resistance. It will also discuss and analyse the common experiences of various interest groups that include religious and cemetery officials, gravediggers, visitors and mourners of Panteón San Rafael and Panteón Jardín De Mexico in the borough of Álvaro Obregón, and the well-known cemetery Panteón Civil de Dolores. In doing so it takes particular interest in the social and cultural tools the communities of Álvaro Obregón have embraced to enable them to maintain the dead as active participants in the lives and spirituality of the living and the kinds of negotiations involved in adding new bodies to cemeteries.[2]

Key Words: Cemeteries, cremation, exhumation, gravediggers, memory, Mexico City, presence/absence, the dead.

*****

Photograph 1: Gravedigger Mrs Isabel Ramo Mora exhuming a grave in Panteón San Rafael, 2006.

1.   Introduction

Cremation and reburial are problematic processes that Mexico City is constantly reassessing. The importance the dead have to the living have practically facilitated and developed dynamic relationships that have direct impact on this problem. This paper addresses how the communities of a saturated megalopolis and multi-faceted, changing society have developed multiple layers of meaning and dynamic relationships with the dead through examples from interviews with research participants. Results of numerous interviews with families in Álvaro Obregón and Mexico City suggest that the dead act as an expression of social identity and heritage. Spaces dedicated to them, such as cemeteries, are spiritual and memory-making sites, where the presence of the dead helps recall and maintain memory and family unity through social processes found in these special spaces.[3] Thus dead persons are transformed into active social participants in the lives of the living as a result of the dialogue created with the dead as a social body; a social dead person and not as a corpse devoid of its spirit, agency or personhood.[4]

This examination includes a brief ethnographic overview and life experiences of the various daily activities, decisions and labour dynamics of working and managing the dead in an urban cemetery. It looks at the tensions existing between the choices people have to make when having to choose between cremating or burying their dead and with the mechanics of exhuming and reburying loved ones in Panteón San Rafael (fig. 1). The paper also shows the technical specialisation, professionalism and logistical management involved in the exhumation of graves, balanced with rural family traditions taken into an urban cemetery.

2.   Housing the Dead in a Megalopolis

Death could be seen as disruptive to the living, yet in Mexico it has turned into a multi million-dollar business (The recorded sale of coffins has risen to an estimated $43 million US dollars per year), with a highly complex lucrative and developed economy.[5] There are about 400 established businesses dedicated to the management of the dead in Mexico D.F. (Federal District). In 2007 the funeral industry provided the capital city with an estimated 16,000 jobs. At the same time it constructed new and different ways of permanently living with or beside the dead.[6] Rapid population growth has placed greater stress on the capital's burial capacity; many burial sites were closed to make way for the new roads and higher residential and commercial buildings of the expanding megalopolis. For example the 'Mexico City National Cemetery' in the borough of San Rafael; established for soldiers fallen in war on the 16th June 1851, was halved in size in 1976 from two acre to one acre to make way for the expansion of a highway.[7]

Panteón Jardín De Mexico was established in the early 1930s.[8] Approximately 11.5 times bigger than Panteón San Rafael with a capacity of

85,000 graves and 75 years since its inauguration, most of its graves have been reused 4 to 6 times. Mr Rodríguez Álvarez (retired cemetery official) suggested that exhuming and reusing graves has become part of a cultural norm for many new and established families. Now Mexico D.F's 108 cemeteries (103 government-run civil cemeteries) have exhausted their 2.5 million graves to bury the dead.[9] Cemetery officials interviewed over a 5-year period explained that because the sale of graves with perpetual rights came to an end in the 1970s, new spaces are rarely available in Álvaro Obregón or the rest of Mexico City. Population growth, expanding villages and towns engulf cemeteries on the outskirts of towns. Expansion is restricted and logistically complicated as Mexico City either lies over water canals or volcanic rock such as occurs in the graves found in Panteón San Rafael where it obstructs further digging down. Alternative solutions to the cemetery being tried out in Álvaro Obregón include Memorial San Ángel. This linen mill turned into a privately run multi-faith Mausoleum in 2006 has its own crematorium, columbaria and multi-faith chapels with wall niches can host at least 5,000 bodies, a capacity to triple its size and; according to its sales manager, no limit to how high it can be extended. Memorial San Ángel, boasts that it is the only space dedicated to the dead in the capital that has a Heliport, in case its VIP mourners wish to arrive undisturbed and in style.[10]

Father Vincent C. Schwahn, Dean of the Anglican Church in Mexico City and an expert on Mexican contemporary funerary practices, explains that Mexico City's sudden expansion and population growth is predominantly due to 2 to 3 generations of migration from rural areas. This reached its peak between the 1960s and 1970s but continues as a steady flow into the city.[11] Mrs Cecilia who arrived into Álvaro Obregón in the early 1960s suggested: 'We did not have housing, sanitation, schools for our children, paved roads, running water or electricity and many of my neighbours lived in tents while they built their existing houses.' Many neighbourhoods in Álvaro Obregón grew from the collective commitment of families migrating from various parts of rural Mexico. Local cemetery officials explain that this sudden influx of families making the capital their permanent home placed pressure not only on the spaces of the living but also filled the existing cemeteries that would have been available for long established local residents requiring a re-evaluation of customs and traditions dedicated to the dead. Newly established families reaffirmed their permanence in the city by placing their dead in established cemeteries. As suggested by Hirsh the 'landscape should be conceptualized as a cultural process';[12] in such a process I suggest that it is not only the land or its landscapes such as the cemetery that evoke heritage or memory or become spaces of social ritual ceremonies. I suggest that it is also the experiences and traces made and left by the living that give the space meaning. Religious officials interviewed during my time in Mexico City explain that people's inter-relationships and connections to the cemetery are used as a way to preserve heritage and became a crucial social and cultural platform for the majority of both rural and urban Mexicans. Great pressure has been placed on the capital's families and authorities to redevelop funerary practices, secondary mortuary methods and ritual performance in order to manage the capital's growing population of 'dead persons' in a way that helps people forge new and direct relationships with the dead and with each other.[13]

Photograph 2: 'I do not want to be cremated' 'Why?' 'Because it will hurt.'

What has been neglected in academic literature is the importance the dead hold in their own right in this process of reaffirming heritage, social identity and permanence. I suggest that for my research participants the dead are used as a social, political and cultural tool to assert social stability, recognition and heritage.[14] Father Vincent explains, 'These communities have brought rural funerary practices and customs into the urban space and many of its cemeteries (families) are still functioning as semi-rural sites in an urban setting' (fig. 2). As suggested by Cannon the spatial landscapes and shared ritual experience maintained by the living in the cemetery and alternative spaces to house the dead become 'the basis for collective memory that transcends personal memory.'[15] I suggest that the collective still provides the possibility for personal experiences to be practiced and shared.

3.   Resisting Cremation as a Form of Disposing of the Dead
        Cremation was practised by pre-Hispanic communities and is now the preferred choice for many contemporary middle and upper class urban families.[16] It was not until 1909 that Dr. Eduardo Liceaga inaugurated the first crematorium in Panteón Civil de Dolores, although it would seem

valuable for an over-populated megalopolis to use cremation to cope with ever-expanding populations of living communities and dead persons (fig. 3). Ramos de Viesca explains the three main reasons why cremation did not take on greater popularity: religious beliefs and practices, the retention of legal evidence and the growing science of anthropology in Mexico - anthropologists felt they might lose material for their laboratories. Father Vincent and cemetery officials explain that even though cremation is practised across Mexico, it was not until the 1970s that it was formally accepted by the Catholic Church. Yet today the choice of cremation or burial is still not as straightforward as it seems. Many family members of new city communities find it hard to readjust to urban social systems and have told Father Vincent that their village's local religious officials still do not accept or promote cremation. Many still want reassurance as to whether it is religiously acceptable and whether their cremated dead will go to heaven. These families maintain customs and rituals rooted in their rural life and found in communities in remote villages or small towns.

Religious officials interviewed, particularly those who work and serve middle and upper class families, find it hard to accept that cremation might not be a preferred option more widely practised by contemporary urban Mexicans (fig. 4), particularly when they have seen it grow in popularity in the communities they serve. What they have overlooked in their reflections is about the following: The Catholic Church is now diplomatically recovering a form of management and income that was taken away from them in 1859 through the Reform Laws (*Leyes de Reforma*).[17] Religious temples across the capital are capitalising by refurbishing their basements and hiring out wall niches. New funeral parlours, mausoleums and columbarias have been constructed and established all around Mexico City to manage cremation and host their cinerary urns. The wall niches under the Basilica of Guadalupe are full and prompted the newest and largest mausoleum development in 2007 being constructed opposite the Basilica of Guadalupe, boasting enough room to host 80,000 Guadalupeños (devotees of the Virgin of Guadalupe). This has a direct impact on the 50-60% of Mexico's population that lives on or below the poverty line.[18]

Photograph 3: A dead person being cremated in Panteón Civil de Dolores.
First cinerary oven built in Mexico City in 1909.

*Photograph 4: Mass given at Panteón San Rafael in memory of Mr José
González Niño who died on the 4th Nov 2007 at the age of 85.*

Mr Gabriel is around 80 years old and has worked for the capital's
cemetery head office before it was decentralised over 40 years ago
(cemeteries are now managed by local boroughs). Mr Gabriel provides
secular reasons including many unresolved practical issues that prevent
cremation being accepted more fully. 'At the moment, Mexico City has 5
functioning crematoriums with one or two ovens in each … . The city has
officially been cremating ever since I can remember. The most famous
cemetery and largest in Mexico and in Latin American is Panteón Civil de
Dolores established in 1875 in which no new graves have been created since
1975.'[19] Mr Garcias, from Funerarias Garcias argues that the original and
new ovens have not been able to cope with the growing demand; with a
turnaround of 5 to 6 bodies per day that is only 60 cremations daily across the
capital. 'We are trying to encourage a culture of cremation,' explains
Veronica Hernandez Guadarrama, head of Panteón Civil de Dolores. Even
though the crematoriums have been refurbished and they now have 4
crematoriums, Panteón Civil de Dolores cannot cope with more than 6 to 7
bodies per day. In comparison, they bury at least 10 dead persons a day in
reused graves.[20] 'Most of the ovens are breaking down,' says Mr Marco
Antonio, office manager of Álvaro Obregón's cemetery head office. In
Panteón San Rafael the cinerary urns taken into the cemetery either to be
stored into wall niches or buried into family graves is minimal in comparison
to the preferred practice of earth burial. Mr Gabriel said,

> We only have to look at the figures and realise that even
> though cremation exists and is actively practised, the civil
> crematoriums in the capital could never cope with the high
> number of dead persons the capital produces … and due to
> new pollution laws introduced in Mexico City, many new

crematoriums have to be established and run from outside
the capital.

This decreases accessibility and increase costs, putting the option of
commuting beyond the reach of many residents who live on or below
Mexico's poverty threshold.

Newly established private crematoriums such as Memorial San
Ángel may provide an answer. The sales manager of Memorial San Ángel
explains, 'This is a new business venture for many and very costly to run and
manage. We have one oven and it often breaks down and can be out of action
for several weeks.' Even when the oven is functioning, lower-earning
families are not able to afford their services. He adds that there is no room in
the capital's morgues to store thousands of dead bodies that might be
awaiting cremation. However, he explains,

> even though there might be no room left in the capital, the
> existing system of reburial, as chaotic as it might seem, still
> manages to organise itself and just about copes with the
> high level of dead persons the capital produces per year.

I met a small but growing number of residents in the capital, who do
not feel the need to connect to their dead or traditions of burial and cannot see
how to relate to what Seale (1998) describes as a decomposed 'bio-body'
buried in a grave.[21] They argued that the process of bonding with one's dead
can still be achieved spiritually irrespective of whether they are cremated or
buried.[22] Many research participants who choose cremation as a solution to
either the problem of space, finances or as a personal choice still placed the
cinerary urn in a special space where kinship ties and daily rituals could be
maintained. These took the form of a shrine, altar or wall niche at home or in
the garden, inside a flowerpot, cemetery niches, or in family graves or
mausoleums inter alia. The list of spaces observed that are dedicated to
hosting the dead is endless. I would argue that even if the connection for
many research participants and their families is through the soul at the same
time they insist in maintaining and developing active social bonds and daily
rituals with a person's ashes and the spaces that host them (fig. 5).

Photograph 5: Wall niche of Mr Leopoldo Navarrete Rubio who died in 2007. Memorial San Ángel, Álvaro Obregón, 2007.

Other than economic reasons, religious practices and social class, there is also a new wave of groups migrating from ethnic communities outside the country. Those who have different religious practices such as Hindus and Buddhists cremate their dead as part of their own religious practices (fig. 6). Mr Wong from Malaysia explains that the choice of cremation or burial is something already decided by his religion and associated customs (figs. 7 and 8).

The practice of cremation and exhumation also makes dead persons mobile, enabling a family to take dead relatives with them when they move out of the city, thereby it reunites parents, siblings or extended family members. It is interesting to see a family moving home and taking their furniture, fridge, microwave and their dead relatives in their car. Some upper class Mexicans and first and second generation Mexican European communities regard the practice of cremation as a refined and practical modern Euro-Mexican funerary practice.[23] Many young urban Mexicans in the capital see cremation as a fashionable choice. The ashes of Ms Mónica Martínez's dead, such as her late parrot and dogs are buried in a flowerpot she keeps in her bathroom and carries with her every time she moves. She adds and will keep adding the ashes of any other pet she has or will have in the future.[24] Monica reminds me that the spirits of her animals look after her and are part of her extended family. The plant that grew from the pot is for Monica a form of regeneration that, she argues, brings life from death. She suggests that 'death is not the end of her existence' but a simultaneity, although some might argue that life ends in death. I suggest that for many of my research participants it is important to see their perceived relationship between life and death as a reciprocal process. Monica does not have to wait till she dies before she can communicate or interact with her dead, but can be assisted by their presence and the material culture that has been developed, embraced and practiced by the living.[25]

*Photographs 6, 7, and 8: Wall niche of Mr Nakamura Katagiri in Memorial
San Ángel and Mr and Mrs Wong in their grocery store, Mexico D.F.*

However, even with a growing number of urban persons using
cremation, inhumation is still the first choice for many families in Álvaro
Obregón and Mexico City. This means that great pressure and importance are
placed on developing the rituals and practices surrounding the exhumation
and reburial of dead persons, together with the relationship that exists with
the dead and the spaces dedicated to host them. Having to reuse a grave or
dig up and re-locate a person's remains back into the family grave or into
family wall niches serves a multitude of social meanings, such as collective
and personal preservation, family kinship, local and national heritage, and,
importantly, preservation of the fragility of memory (figs. 9 and 10).[26]

*Photographs 9 and 10: Gravediggers building wall niches in order to provide
space for the dead of exhumed graves, Álvaro Obregón, 2005.*

4.   The Cemetery and the Reburial of the Dead

For a grave to be reused, exhumation becomes a vital process undertaken by gravediggers. Every exhumation and inhumation is unique in its own way. However, there are patterns shared across the variations in the procedures of exhumations. Research participants generally describe an exhumation in the following way: exhumation includes the digging up of the earth, removal of its contents, such as an old coffin, and reintroducing the remains of the dead. Finally, a new coffin is laid in the grave before it is refilled with earth and is then covered with flower arrangements. This explanation does not recognise the complex set of decisions and rituals carried out in the process of an exhumation, which makes each one unique. It also ignores the workers' logistical processes and the decisions and feelings faced by the mourners as they organise to exhume and inhume a family grave.

As the purpose of the shared family grave is to maintain genealogy in the family it would not be appropriate to remove family members but each is added to the space. I suggest that family unity is paramount for my research participants as death is seen as a unifying process and the grave a space in which the family in time of death can be reunited. Exhumations have their own peculiarity in the methods and practices used and the transformations are too drastic to disregard as they transform the inner space and its contents which include the remains of the dead body plus the relations with the living. For my research participants they do not necessarily mean changing the identity of their dead or the space. I suggest that the dead are still considered human beings even while being transformed by the various stages of decomposition. Even if some participants related to the dead as a spiritual being, the social element was not taken from it and the social and the spiritual coexisted.[27] The dead did not lose their humanity and dignity through the lack of what we could understand as active socialisation associated only with the living. For many of my research participants these tensions did not have an easy solution; but it was through their daily activities and practices that I was able to reflect on these fundamental phenomena.

An exhumation is a complex, ritualised process and is considered by my research participants in Panteón San Rafael as an emotionally difficult process which people outside the environment of the cemetery have limited opportunities to witness. Although in some sense cemeteries like Panteón San Rafael and Panteón Jardín De Mexico are public spaces, there are mechanisms in place to render some parts within the cemetery more private and hidden from 'public view.' Gravediggers in Panteón San Rafael explain that many visitors and mourners only experience the public spaces of the cemetery site or its commemorative rituals and are unaware of what is happening in the private space of the dead and even less inside the grave. There is, therefore, a general lack of awareness of what is required in order to keep a cemetery operational. Many of my urban research participants are unaware of the problematic and logistical decisions required in reusing and exhuming a grave and the treatment of a dead person's decomposed (decomposing) body. Religious officials, like Father Vincent, suggest that in many instances families do not face these issues until they have to manage a new death of their own, and even then the work is delegated to religious officials, funeral parlours and gravediggers.

Mrs Guadalupe Contreras Morales, gravedigger of Panteón San Rafael, explains that it is a combination of dealing with the death of a relative and the exhumation of a grave in which several other relatives' dead bodies become disrupted and exposed. It becomes a cocktail of emotions that amalgamate on the same day. Gravediggers in Panteón San Rafael explain that today it is very rare to find a family member taking part or performing an exhumation. In 2007 only about 00.5% of the exhumations in Panteón San Rafael were witnessed by family members, even though the cyclical maintenance, management of graves and its monuments is the responsibility of titleholders, both perpetual owners and leaseholders. Ángel Pérez Rafael, manager of Panteón San Rafael, explains, 'This was not the case about 30 years ago. A higher percentage of families used to manage their own exhumations and inhumations. The inhumation of a dead person was predominantly carried out by the male members of the family assisted by the gravediggers.'[28]

If a gravedigger's family member dies they themselves do not take part in the exhumation of their family grave. In Panteón San Rafael most of the gravediggers have been exhuming graves for over 25 years and they have family graves in Panteón San Rafael. Both Emelia and her sister, Guadalupe, explain that it is a difficult and a painful process to have to exhume their own family.[29] When Emelia and Guadalupe's mother died in 2004 they both helped remove the family ornaments, monuments and grave decorations but did not participate in the exhumation, leaving the cemetery to manage the funeral ceremonies and grieve their loss. Emelia explained that it is a shocking and traumatic process to see or experience - 'To have to add to the pain and trauma of our loss, the exhumation of a father or mother would only add to the pain we are already feeling. To have to exhume a relative who is still decomposing is too much to have to experience,' - even though it is her profession and she has been witnessing and partaking in these processes almost daily for many years. To see a relative being taken out of the grave in a high level of decomposition is a process very few family members in Álvaro Obregón wish to witness. Many research participants do not wish to have their last image of a relative to be that of a decomposed body.[30]

The work of exhumation and treatment of the body is not always a solemn process. It is treated with practicality, professionalism, speed and emotional detachment and sensitivity. The only occasion that I did not see them joke and laugh was when they had to exhume the grave of someone they knew personally; the former cemetery night watchman (figs. 11, 12 and 13). In this instance it was difficult for them to detach their emotions about the 'decomposed body' from the social person they all knew so well.

Photographs 11, 12, and13. Mrs Isabel Ramo Mora exhuming the body of Panteón San Rafael's ex-night watchman. Waste dump in the cemetery: 'Organic waste' and the wall niche of Elvira Espinosa, Panteón San Rafael, 2006/7.

It is not common practice to mix dead persons outside the family kinship, unless in pressurised circumstances. When a family finds he or she is unable to locate a usable grave there may be the option of borrowing one from a friend. Then when the 7-year legal limit for exhumation has elapsed they can be exhumed and reunited with their own family. A friend's mother died and her family had no access to a grave and could not afford to purchase a used exhumed grave in the capital so a family friend lent their grave until a purchase was possible. However, the lending family had a death within the first 3 years and urgently required the use of their family grave so my friend had to obtain a court order to exhume her mother and relocate the body. A legal official, a police officer and two others, at least one of whom had to be a direct family member, had to attend and witness the exhumation.

She explained that the procedure and experience of exhuming a recent grave of the grieving mourner and seeing her mother in full state of decomposition has remained a painful memory.[31] 'Flash-backs of that day are constantly in my mind,' and she explains she cannot separate her memory of the exhumation and her ability to imagine her mother as a social presence. Experiencing the exhumation of her mother greatly complicated this process.

The greater popularity of exhumations in Mexico's cemeteries has developed greater need to elaborate commemorative rituals and embrace tools such as material objects and photographs.[32] I suggest that these have assisted urban mourners to remember and visualise the dead not as 'corpses' or 'cadavers' but as 'social persons,' thereby reinforcing the meanings that exist between the living with the dead and its spirit.[33]

5.   The Logistics of Exhuming and Reusing Family Graves

Ownership of graves is divided into two main sections; an owner with a lease or in perpetuity. A titleholder either owns a grave in perpetuity or leases one from the cemetery head office. One family member will hold the certificate with perpetual and full rights to the space. The ownership of the grave can be transferred to other family members or sold to other persons outside the family. The reason for preventing the sale of new graves in perpetuity was that there was no land left for everyone in the capital for this to be possible for everyone. Cemetery officials argue that now new cemetery spaces are issued strictly on a rental basis. If in future these cemeteries are needed for urban redevelopment the local authority could ask for the land to be returned and families would have to disinter and relocate their dead.

Ángel Pérez Rafael and Jose Luis Yañez explain that the greatest problem is that many families or titleholders forget to pay their renewal fees.[34] If the cemetery management notices that a grave has not been paid for, after a predetermined period the grave can be exhumed and the space taken over and leased to a different family. The exhumed person/s will be placed at the bottom of the grave, until the family returns to claim their dead. If left for too long then the dead bodies of the new family will be placed on top of the bones of the exhumed family. If a cemetery has spare wall niches then the body remains will be stored until reclaimed This is a tricky situation, not uncommon in other cemeteries of Mexico City, Mr Gabriel explains: 'managers are often bending the rules and at times agreeing to bury a person in a grave without seeing the title deeds or without the permission of its owner.' Other managers sell very old 'historic' graves for underhand cash payments, hoping that the graves are too old and their owners will not return to use them. Some managers have also taken it for granted that because the dead person belongs to the same kinship group, it is acceptable to bury a relative into the family grave. Underhand payments of large sums help the mangers to overlook this important detail.[35] An example of such irregularity was witnessed in 2007, when a family turned up at the office of Panteón San Rafael for advice. They had the perpetual title deeds to their family grave and a recent death in the family (their father). On the day of burial the family realised the ceremony could not be carried out as the cemetery had recently buried a different person in the same grave. The person buried was a relative of their father, who was not on talking terms with the family of the titleholder. Even though they were from the same family kinship, their families had split (they were aware of the death but not that the burial was in their grave).

Whoever holds the deeds has a final say in what happens to the grave and who is buried there. The above case emphasises that the spaces of the dead can and do reflect the problems faced by the living.[36] Shondell and Rivera suggest that 'burial sites are centrally significant to a community's sense of well being' and is a social site that 'reflects the conditions and social realities of the surrounding community both past and present.'[37] Social and political issues are taken to the cemeteries in which the sacredness of the grave is not sacrosanct but relative to unforeseen circumstances.[38]

6.   Exhuming and Reusing Graves

In March 2007, after 20 years of burial a cemented tanked grave was exhumed. A female body was removed from a high quality metallic coffin. The outside of the coffin was well-preserved and as good as new. The female's clothing had not deteriorated and her body had been very well-preserved, yet still covered in the carcasses of the worms that had consumed the inside and the top of her body. When she was undressed we could see that her back still had her leathered skin attached to her bones, with minimal decomposition. Her clothing was intact, almost new, her hair and nails well-preserved. The coffin had a very tight seal and it stopped the body liquids from evaporating and being released. The further the description of an exhumation, the more unpleasant and emotional it becomes and the harder it is to deal with. It is not surprising that this practice would not have been a pleasant or healthy way for a family to see a relative. Experiencing this enabled me to understand why so many families in urban settings do not wish to partake in exhumations; it was a traumatic and disturbing experience even as a relatively new member of the space with some developed level of familiarisation to exhumations. Many research participants I spoke to in Álvaro Obregón and elsewhere in the capital said they did not wish to witness or partake in exhumations since it means seeing parents, grandparents and even children decomposing in the manner described above, wishing instead to remember their dead as social persons even after death and not as a decomposed bodies (figs. 14, 15 and 16).[39] Marco Antonio explains that '[l]ife in urban spaces has changed our ability to deal with such painful experiences and, even more, prevent us from partaking in them.'

Photographs 14, 15, and 16: Mrs Emelia Contreras Morales cooking lunch
for workers while Mr Fernando Rosas Ceron, Mrs Isabel Ramo Mora and Mr
Jose Antonio Falcon Espition finish the exhumation of an elderly female,
Panteón San Rafael, 2007.

I have found from pilot research projects in rural areas that many
rural families still actively participate in the exhumations of members of their
family. Grave digging is not a profession in remote villages, such as San Juan
de Yaeé, Oaxaca, and taking part in an exhumation is part of daily life, a
social funerary custom and more accepted than in urban areas. In rural areas
cemeteries are not as saturated and it is unlikely that a family would have to
exhume a grave within its first 7 years. This familiarity to the cemetery and
visualising their dead as social members of their community enables a more
active participation in exhumations by families and their friends. I have found
that the dead in Panteón San Rafael are still recognised, maintained and
assisted through various contemporary funerary rituals and customs, together
with material culture in which the dead are assisted in being kept in the realm
of the living and, most importantly, as 'social persons' and not just bio-
bodies (fig. 17).[40]

In 2007, Mr Ramirez came to Panteón San Rafael to oversee the
exhumation of one of the family graves he inherited from his grandparents in
order to reuse it and bury his sister-in-law that same afternoon. His family did
not have their own grave and it would have been too expensive to purchase
one outside the capital. While we exchanged a few beers and shots of tequila
that Mr Ramirez had bought for the gravediggers, I asked him whether his
preferred choice would be cremation or earth burial. This turned out to be a
problematic question, especially when the exhumed coffin of his grandfather
was being removed with a sledgehammer and large handcrafted crowbars.
The gravediggers stopped for a short while to rest and find shade from the hot
sun to join us for cold beers before Mr Ramirez's grandfather was removed.

We all stopped to listen to Mr Ramirez's reply: 'Well, if I had a choice, it would be cremation,' explained Mr Ramirez who already had inherited three graves in the cemetery. 'I want to be cremated because I do not want to end up in a grave, no one visits you and you might end up like my grandfather, forgotten or exhumed, being turned upside down if my grave is reused.' This I found was not an unusual reply from families who have migrated. For these families returning regularly to visit their dead relatives is complicated.

I followed by asking what he would like to be done with his ashes? 'I love Acapulco,' he replied. 'As a child we went on holidays there as a family. It would be fantastic to be scattered over the ocean waves. I would lie under the sun appreciating all the pretty girls sunbathing on the seashore. What better way to spend your days when dead.' We all laughed and more tequila was served while the gravediggers took the exhumed body of his grandfather from the broken coffin. Mr Ramirez did not really speak of death as a process in which as a dead person he could no longer perform the social functions that he enjoyed as a member of the living human community. He did not at any stage suggest that death meant an outward journey to a celestial space. Instead he envisaged remaining as a social dead person/spirit in the spaces of the living, enjoying what living people enjoy, 'sociability.' Soon after this the gravediggers continued removing the second coffin from the grave. At this stage Mr Ramirez left the cemetery and shortly returned with more beers and a second bottle of tequila where after things became more intense and interesting. We had the exhumed scattered body parts of his family on one side of the grave. Mr Ramirez poured me another tequila and sang a Ranchera[41] for all of us. He said: 'You know I have not been asked that question before, but I have been thinking about it all morning and in reality, seriously now' [pointing to the grave and the exhumed bodies of his relatives]

> if I did die I would not like to be cremated, I want to be buried just like them. I know that we live far from the cemetery and we do not really have the time to visit our relatives as often as we might have wanted, but if I was to die, I want to be buried because then if ever someone wanted to find me and visit me, they could. If I was scattered over the waves of the ocean, then where would my friends, children and family find me. They could not bring me flowers, talk to me and sing me a Mariachi.

This example illustrates the importance of family and of belonging to a community, even after death. Even when Mr Ramirez did consider cremation, his ashes had to be placed in a special place. Cost was not an issue to him, lack of space was not a problem, as he had access to various family graves in the cemetery. What did become crucial to Mr Ramirez was that he be placed in a space that could allow for family unity and for him as a dead person to remain socially integrated in the lives of the living and his family and friends.

Through my research I have found that the spaces of the dead and their exhumations are unseen, highly dynamic, laborious and logistically challenging extensions of a ritualised social experience. The cemetery space combines all the elements located in the spaces of the living with its personalities, labour force, tensions, politics, and ritualised socio-cultural tools required in the maintenance of the dead, the land and its relationships with the living. My research has found it critical to record these processes and the social ritual currents as richly as possible, as there is always a danger that past and current generations could be forgotten and lost forever under the increasingly expanding megalopolis.

Photograph 17: Exhumations in Panteón San Rafael, 2007.

7.   Concluding Remarks

This paper illustrates the complexity and importance of the reuse of graves in a saturated and over-populated megalopolis. Managing thousands of dead people per week has become a complicated task in a capital that has all its cemeteries full, especially when the dead and the presence of its body (or ashes) plays a dynamic and important role in the lives of my research participants. Cremation and reburial are not free from their contradictions and difficulties. When choices are being made the dead remain at all times at the centre of the decision making process. There is a clear reflection of research participants, exemplified by Mr Ramirez, in which they collectively realise they themselves will soon be members of the community of dead persons. This has facilitated their choices and the funerary and social practices that are followed and maintained. Crucial in these decisions is the social and spiritual reciprocity developed between the dead and the living, both needing each other in the processes of memory-making.

When I interviewed Mr Gabriel he laughed as he told me that he does not wish to be buried and he wants to be cremated and his ashes placed between his wife and his lover. He laughed as I opened my eyes in amazement and confusion. Although he has a higher than normal level of familiarity with the dead and funerary customs in the capital's cemeteries, his humour and attitude towards the dead is no different from that of other research participants that I have met in Mexico City. Mr Gabriel explains that he outlived his wife who died many years ago and he had her cremated and placed in an altar at home. He then fell in love again and once again outlived his new partner (whom he refers to as his lover). When she died she too was cremated. He tells me that he now has his wife and his lover sitting next to each other in an altar at home. Mr Gabriel explains that when he dies he too wishes to be cremated and placed in between both his partners, so they can keep him company in the afterlife. This example shows how my research participants have shifted the bonding to alternative and domestic spaces from that which they might have built with the land.

The growing practice of cremation is giving access to a new generation of communities to create and bond with new types of spaces, shifting away from existing practices and developing new funerary methods and relationships to accommodate these changes. Cremation and burial, with their difficulties and contradictions, both play a crucial role in the memory-making practices of my research participants. The choices available to Mr Ramirez and Mr Gabriel are facilitated by their desire to remain part of a social system, of a community and most importantly, being present in the lives of their loved ones even after death. For many the 'social dead person' is still treated as a dynamic entity in the lives of the living and the daily ritual is crucial for this maintenance of bonds, identity and history whether the person was cremated or buried (fig. 18).

Photograph 18: Gravediggers exhuming a grave in Panteón San Rafael. Mrs Isabel Ramo Mora, Mr Jose Luis Yañez and Mr Fernando Rosas Ceron, 2004.

I am grateful to the Department of Anthropology at Goldsmiths, University of London. My supervisors Dr Victoria Goddard and Prof. Stephen Nugent for their critical insights. I am also grateful to the participants of the 6th Global Conference: Making Sense of Dying and Death, Salzburg, 2008. Thanks for comments on earlier drafts to: Carole Edrich, Maggie and John Paterson. Importantly, I would like to thank the workers, visitors/mourners and gravediggers of Panteón San Rafael for sharing their knowledge and friendship together with Mónica Martínez's for her support and hospitality during my time in México.

Notes

[1] T. Brinkhoff, *City Population*, The Principal Agglomerations of the World, viewed in July 2009, <http://www.citypopulation.de/World.html>; Central Intelligence Agency, 'Death rate calculated at 4.8 deaths per 1,000 persons (July 2009 est.)', January 15, 2009, viewed in August 2009, <https://www.cia.gov/library/publications/the-world-factbook/geos/mx.html>.
[2] E. Hallam, J. Hockey, G. Howarth, *Beyond the Body: Death and Social Identity*, Routledge, London, 1999; E. Hallam and J. Hockey, *Death, Memory and Material Culture*, Berg, Oxford, 2001; J. Hockey, J. Katz, N. Small, *Grief Mourning and Death Ritual*, Open University Press, 2001, H. Kwon, *Ghost of War in Vietnam*, Cambridge University Press, Cambridge, 2008.

[3] A. Cannon, 'Spatial Narratives of Death, Memory, and Transcendence', in *The Space and Place of Death*, H. Silverman and D. Small (eds), *Archaeological Papers of the AAA*, No. 11, 2002, p. 193; M. Halbwachs, *On Collective Memory*, in *Heritage of Sociology Series*, L. A. Coser (ed), University of Chicago Press, Chicago, 1992; P. Nora, 'Between Memory and History: Les Lieux de Mémoire [1984]', *Representations*, Vol. 26, Spring, 1989, pp. 7-25.

[4] P. Connerton, *How Societies Remember*, Cambridge University Press, Cambridge, 1989; A. Gell, *Art and Agency, An Anthropological Theory*, Clarendon Press, Oxford, 1998. M. Reyes-Cortez, 'Communicating with the Dead: Social Visibility in the Cemeteries of Mexico City', in *Die Realität des Todes. Zum Gegenwärtigen Wandeln von Totenbildern und Erinnerungskulturen*, D. Groß and C. Schweikardt (eds), Campus Verlag GmbH, Frankfurt am Main, 2010, pp. 33-62; C. Seale, *Constructing Death, The Sociology of Dying and Bereavement*, Cambridge University Press, Cambridge, 1998.

[5] 'Metro', 31th October 2007, p. 3.

[6] S. Brandes, 'Is there a Mexican View of Death?', *Ethos*, Vol. 31, No. 1, 2003, pp. 127-144, *AAA*, 2003; W. Sebald, *Austerlitz*, Penguin Books, London, 2001.

[7] The 'Mexico City National Cemetery' was founded four years after the USA-Mexican war. The remains of 750 Irish-American soldiers, who sided with the Mexican plight, were recovered from their shallow battlefield graves and buried in a common plot. The space was also set-aside for the growing community of US citizens and ex-patriots. The cemetery was closed down in 1924.

[8] Cemeteries in urban and rural areas are officially and unofficially known as 'Panteón' (Pantheon).

[9] Out of 2.5 million graves 1.8 have perpetuity and the remainder are on a 7 or 21year lease. Mexico D. F. cemetery census, 2000 and 2001.

[10] Modern mausoleums in Mexico City contain wall niches and act as a contemporary columbaria (a public space for the storage of cinerary urns).

[11] This time span relates to dates given in interviews with families that settled in the borough of Álvaro Obregón, establishing new colonies like San Ángel and Copilco.

[12] E. Hirsh and M. O'Hanlon, *The Anthropology of Landscape: Perspectives on Place and Space*, Clarendon Press, Oxford, 1995.

[13] M. Chesson, 'Embodied Memories of Place and People: Death and Society in an Early Urban Community', in *Social Memory, Identity and Death: Ethnographic and Archaeological Perspectives on Mortuary Rituals*, M. Chesson (ed), *AAA*, Vol. 10, Arlington, 2001, pp. 100-113; L. Young, 'Death

and Civil Society', *The ANNALS of the American Academy of Political and Social Science*, No. 565, 1999, p. 193. I use the concept of 'dead person' rather than the 'deceased', 'corpse' or 'cadaver' as I hope to expand the interpretation of the 'dead person.' I argue that people do not stop being part of a social system because they have died or when their biological body ceases to exist.

[14] M. Herzfeld, *A Place in History: Social and Monumental Time in a Cretan Town*, Princeton University Press, New Jersey, 1991. Hirsh and Michael, op. cit.; K. Verdery, *The Political Lives of Dead Bodies, 'Reburial and Postsocialist Change'*, Columbia Press, New York, 1999.

[15] A. Cannon, 'Spatial Narratives of Death, Memory, and Transcendence', in *The Space and Place of Death*, H. Silverman and D. Small (eds), *Archaeological Papers of the AAA*, No. 11., 2002, p. 192.

[16] X. Balderas, *Rituales Funerarios en el Templo Mayor de Tenochtitlan*, INAH, Mexico, 2007; S. Gillespie, 'Body and Soul among the Maya: Keeping the Spirits in Place', in *The Space and Place of Death*, H. Silverman and D. Small (eds), *Archeological Papers of the AAA*, No. 11, 2002, pp. 67-78; L. Manzanilla, 'Houses and Ancestors, Altars and Relics: Mortuary Patterns and Teotihuacan, Central México', *Instituto de Investigaciones Antropológicas*, UNAM, AAA, 2002, p. 57; M. Ramos, 'La Cremación, Un Capítulo en la Salud Pública de México', in *Gaceta Médica de México, Academia Nacional de Medicina de México, A.C*, M. E. Ávila-R, G. Miriam, Chiapas-C, M. Avila, Le Pérez-D (eds), Vol. 138, No. 6, December, 2002, p. 581. Pre-Hispanic communities practiced cremation as part of their funerary ceremonies which was prohibited by the arrival of the Spanish conquest and Christianity. It was re-established in 1877 for the incineration of animals by the Uppu Health Council (el Consejo Superior de Salubridad).

[17] Benito Juárez's laws of reform nationalised church property and took away from the Catholic Church their right to manage the dead and its burial grounds.

[18] *New York Times*: Free-Market Upheaval Grinds Mexico's Middle Class, by Ginder Thompson, Published: Wednesday, September 4, 2002.

[19] Mr Gabriel worked for 40 years as an office coordinator and sub-manager for the cemeteries of the capital, when they were centrally managed from Panteón Civil de Dolores over 20 years ago. The cemetery has almost 700,000 graves.

[20] S. Tegel, 'Crowd Control - Trade Talk - Panteon Civil de Dolores Cemetery Runs out of Space, Mexico City, Mexico - Brief Article', in *Latin Trade*, Business Services Industry, Freedom Magazines Inc, December, 2002, viewed on 13th July 2009, <http://findarticles.com/p/articles/mi_m0BEK/is_12_10/ai_95355248/>.

[21] Bio-body meaning the biological body, the human flesh.

[22] H. Kwon, *Ghost of War in Vietnam*, Cambridge University Press, Cambridge, 2008.

[23] These persons tend to follow the trends practiced in Europe and the USA.

[24] She has yet to place ashes of a person into her plant pot as she has not yet had any deaths from close relatives.

[25] E. Hallam and J. Hockey, *Death, Memory and Material Culture*, 2001. Reyes-Cortez, *Communicating with the Dead*, forthcoming, 2010.

[26] M. Halbwachs, *On Collective Memory*, Berg, Oxford, 1992.

[27] Reyes-Cortez, op. cit.

[28] Through pilot projects in rural spaces of Mexico, I experienced and witnessed a greater percentage of family and friends taking part in exhumations and inhumations, like in the town of San Juan de Yaeé in Oaxaca.

[29] Emelia and Guadalupe Contreras Morales are sisters and female gravediggers in Panteón San Rafael.

[30] Religious officials explain that about 30-40 years ago, exhumations or reburials were not as frequent. Wooden coffins were the norm, so when a family took part in an exhumation it was very little of the coffin or the body that was actually seen. Exhuming the dead was less visibly traumatic experience than now.

[31] The metal coffin placed in a cemented grave preserves the body for a longer period of time and it decomposes at a slower rate.

[32] G. Batchen, *Forget Me Not: Photography and Remembrance*, Architectural Press, Princeton, 2006; C. Lomnitz, *Death and the Idea of Mexico*, Zone Books, Cambridge, MA, 2005; Reyes-Cortez, op. cit.

[33] Reyes-Cortez, op. cit.; Hallam and Hockey, op. cit.; P. Metcalf and R. Huntington, 'Celebrations of Death', in *The Anthropology of Mortuary Ritual*, Cambridge University Press, Cambridge, 1979.

[34] Ángel Perez Rafael is the administrator and Jose Luis Yañez is the site manager of Panteón San Rafael.

[35] The sums involved depend on individual cases, an information the cemetery managers do not provide.

[36] E. Hallam, J. Hockey, G. Howarth, *Beyond the Body: Death and Social Identity*, Routledge, New York, 1999: Hallam and Hockey, op. cit.; H. Silverman, 'Mortuary Narratives of Identity and History in Modern Cemeteries of Lima, Peru', in *The Space and Place of Death*, H. Silverman and D. B. Small (eds), *Archaeological Papers of the AAA*, No. 11, Washington, DC, 2007, pp. 167-190.

[37] M. Shondell DeMond and J. David Rivera, 'Hallowed Ground, Place, and Culture: The Cemetery and the Creation of Place', *Space and Culture*, No. 9, 2006, p. 348.
[38] Silverman, op. cit.
[39] Seale, op. cit.
[40] Hallam, Hockey, Howarth, op. cit.; Hallam and Hockey, op. cit.; Seale, op. cit.
[41] Music played by Mexican Mariachis.

Bibliography

Balderas, X. C., *Rituales Funerarios en el Templo Mayor de Tenochtitlan*. INAH, Mexico, 2007.

Batchen, G., *Forget Me Not: Photography and Remembrance*. Princeton Architectural Press, 2006.

Brandes, S., 'Is there a Mexican View of Death?'. *Ethos*, Vol. 31, No. 1, 2003, pp. 127-144, *American Anthropological Association*, 2003.

Cannon, A., 'Spatial Narratives of Death, Memory, and Transcendence', in *The Space and Place of Death*. H. Silverman and D. Small (eds), *Archaeological Papers of the AAA*, No. 11. 2002, pp. 191-199.

Chesson, M., 'Embodied Memories of Place and People: Death and Society in an Early Urban Community', in *Social Memory, Identity and Death: Ethnographic and Archaeological Perspectives on Mortuary Rituals*. M. Chesson (ed), *Archaeological Publications of the AAA Publication Series*, Vol. 10, Arlington, 2001, pp. 100-113,

Connerton, P., *How Societies Remember*. Cambridge University Press, 1989.

Gell, A., *Art and Agency, An Anthropological Theory*. Clarendon Press, Oxford, 1998.

Gillespie, S., 'Body and Soul among the Maya: Keeping the Spirits in Place', in *The Space and Place of Death*. H. Silverman and D. Small (eds), *Archeological Papers of the AAA*, No. 11, 2002, pp. 67-78.

Halbwachs, M., *On Collective Memory, Maurice Halbwachs 1877-1945*. L. A. Coser (ed and trans), *Heritage of Sociology Series*, University of Chicago Press, 1992.

Hallam, E., Hockey, J., Howarth G., *Beyond the Body: Death and Social Identity*. Routledge, London, 1999.

Hallam, E. and Hockey J., *Death, Memory & Material Culture*. Berg, Oxford, 2001.

Herzfeld, M., *A Place in History: Social and Monumental Time in a Cretan Town*. Princeton University Press, New Jersey, 1991.

Hirsh, E. and O'Hanlon, M., *The Anthropology of Landscape: Perspectives on Place and Space*. Clarendon Press, Oxford, 1995.

Hockey, J., Katz, J., Small, N., *Grief Mourning and Death Rituals*. Open University Press, Buckingham, 2001.

Kwon, H., *Ghost of War in Vietnam*. Cambridge University Press, Cambridge, 2008.

Lomnitz, C., *Death and the Idea of Mexico*. Zone Books, Cambridge, MA, 2005.

Manzanilla, L., 'Houses and Ancestors, Altars and Relics: Mortuary Patterns and Teotihuacan, Central México'. *Instituto de Investigaciones Antropológicas*, UNAM, Arlington, VA, 2002, pp. 55-65.

Metcalf, P., and Huntington, R., 'Celebrations of Death', *The Anthropology of Mortuary Ritual*. Cambridge University Press, Cambridge, 1979.

Nora, P., 'Between Memory and History: Les Lieux de Mémoire [1984]'. *Representations*, No. 26, Spring, 1989, pp. 7-25.

Ramos de Viesca, M. y cols, 'La Cremación. Un Capítulo en la Salud Pública de México', in *Gaceta Médica de México, Academia Nacional de Medicina de México. AC*. M. Ramos de Viesca, M. Ávila-R, M. Chiapas-C, M. de los Ángeles González A, L. Pérez-D (eds), Vol. 138, No. 6, December, 2002.

Reyes-Cortez, M., 'Communicating with the Dead: Social Visibility in the Cemeteries of Mexico City', in *Die Realität des Todes. Zum Gegenwärtigen Wandeln von Totenbildern und Erinnerungskulturen.* D. Groß and C. Schweikardt (eds), Campus Verlag GmbH, Frankfurt am Main, 2010, pp. 33-62.

Seale, C., *Constructing Death, The Sociology of Dying and Bereavement.* Cambridge University Press, Cambridge, 1998.

Sebald, W. G., *Austerlitz.* Penguin Books, London, 2001.

Shondell DeMond, M., and David Rivera, J., 'Hallowed Ground, Place, and Culture: The Cemetery and the Creation of Place'. *Space and Culture*, No. 9, 2006, pp. 334-351.

Silverman, H., 'Mortuary Narratives of Identity and History in Modern Cemeteries of Lima, Peru', in *The Space and Place of Death.* H. Silverman and D. Small (eds), *Archaeological Papers of the AAA*, No. 11, Washington, DC, 2007, pp. 167-190.

Tegel, S., 'Crowd Control - Trade Talk - Panteon Civil de Dolores Cemetery Runs out of Space, Mexico City, Mexico - Brief Article'. *Latin Trade.* FindArticles.com. Freedom Magazines Inc, December, 2002, viewed on 13th July 2009;
<http://findarticles.com/p/articles/mi_m0BEK/is_12_10/ai_95355248/>.

Verdery, K., *The Political Lives of Dead Bodies, 'Reburial and Postsocialist Change'.* Columbia Press, New York, 1999.

Young Otero, M., L., 'Death and Civil Society'. *The ANNALS of the American Academy of Political and Social Science*, No. 565, 1999, p. 193.

Marcel Reyes-Cortez lives and works in London. In 1993 he graduated with a BA (Hons) in photography from the London College of Printing in 1995 he gained his MA in Social Anthropology from SOAS, School of Oriental and African Studies and in 2010 he completed his PhD in Visual Anthropology from Goldsmiths, University of London. In his doctoral research he developed the use and practice of photography as a research methodology. In his research he explored the spaces, socio-cultural currents and the contemporary phenomenon of the dead in Mexico City focusing on photography, anthropology, visual ethnography, material and visual culture, memory, cemeteries, memoralisation and the contemporary funerary rituals in Mexico.

Heroic Death and Selective Memory: The US's WWII Memorial and the USSR's Monument to the Heroic Defenders of Leningrad

Susan M. Behuniak

Abstract
Just as war is a struggle to the death over conflicting values, so are war memorials a struggle over death and its meaning. This paper focuses on two parallel efforts to memorialise those who served during World War II (called the Great Patriotic War in Russia): the US's World War II Memorial in Washington, D.C. and the USSR's Monument to the Heroic Defenders of Leningrad (now St. Petersburg, Russia). What I will argue is that both of these memorials, rather than simply honouring the sacrifices of the dead, convey a deliberate political message: that those who died were heroes, and that a heroic death is one in which the sacrifice is worth it. Such a politicised agenda requires not only that collective memory be formed and preserved by an architectural structure, but that these mnemonic spaces also promote a forgetfulness of memories to the contrary. In this, these two memorials, one originating within democracy and the other within communism, demonstrate Harvey Weinstein's point that 'memorials represent a complex nexus between politics, trauma, collective memory, and public art.' The paper begins with a brief discussion of heroic versus tragic death as archetypes. Next, I examine and compare the American and Soviet monuments with attention to how the elements of timing, geography, architecture/art, and flow determine what is remembered, what is repressed, and in what form the Presence of the dead is invited to these spaces. I suggest that despite their significantly different wartime experiences and politics, both countries built triumphant renderings of the war - memorials that celebrated heroic death while denying tragic death - to promote not only national unity but also a patriotism based on militarism.

Key Words: Heroic death, Siege of Leningrad, tragic death, war memorials, war monuments, WWII.

*****

1. Introduction

War memorials stir more than the heart and the head to remember; they also rouse the public to react politically. Their construction, then, comes not just from the shaping of granite but from a desire to shape the public's perception of this 'form of socially sanctioned death.'[1] Yet, just as war is a struggle to the death over conflicting values,[2] so are war memorials a struggle over death and its meaning. In this, memorials have 'unique symbolic power because they invoke a sense of timelessness, awe, fear, and uncertainty.'[3] They recall the 'ultimate sacrifice' made by others, and so like graveyards, they are sites where the living and the dead meet. Memorials, then, serve not only to commemorate or mourn; they are also a 'means for a community to stabilize an event [by making] the past consequential for the present.'[4]

Given their intent and impact, it is no surprise that war memorials can be highly politicised and contested sites. They are structures that demand answers to charged questions: Who should be remembered and how? Which events should be highlighted - or disregarded? Should the message be clear, ambiguous, or even absent? When should the memorial be built and where? What, indeed, is its purpose - to mourn, warn, consol, celebrate, instruct, propagandise, or several of these at once?

One way to uncover the narratives contained within memorials has been to categorise them. 'Monuments,' those structures built in celebration of victory have been distinguished from grief-laden 'memorials' that primarily reference 'the life or lives sacrificed for a particular set of values.'[5] Another distinction has been drawn between 'traditional memorials,' i.e., physical structures built of stone, and 'living' memorials, an ironic word choice that erases 'war' and 'death' altogether. These living remembrances include such things as memorial highways, street names, social programs, and housing projects.[6] Memorials and monuments have also been classified according to whether they glorify, contest, or disavow an historical event or person.[7] The meaning of these structures have also been analysed in terms of whether their messages are intentional or unintentional, rendered as narrative or as symbolism, and conveying the event or its abstraction.[8]

What I explore here, however, is whether war memorials stylise death as heroic or as tragic. Tragic death is the more socially disturbing view because it is death without a clear purpose or meaning. Its associative grief comes from this understanding of death as disastrous - a life wasted or a loss that was preventable. Those who die tragically are characterised as having died too young, mistakenly, or without a justifiable cause. These dead (and even those who survive the horror[9]) are victims, innocents or unfortunates, but not heroes. In contrast, heroic death presumes the dead had both agency and courage; the dead hero freely gives up life for a cause, and so dies for others;[10] a trope that is Christ-like. In this way, death itself is transcended through participation in something of lasting worth.[11] This depiction of death as heroic is personally consoling, but also culturally meaningful as it 'displace(s) awareness of what is terrible' with a dis-remembering so complete that it may at first seem impossible.[12] To successfully depict heroic death, then, memorial designs must choose from among competing war memories those victorious images that reinforce the greatness and the rightness of the war and, by implication, the associated deaths. Such memorials trumpet military might rather than toll for the lives lost.

2.   The American and Soviet Memorials

To explore this theme, this paper focuses on two parallel efforts to memorialise those who served during World War II (called the Great Patriotic War in Russia): the World War II Memorial in Washington, D.C. and the Monument to the Heroic Defenders of Leningrad, (now, St. Petersburg, Russia). These two memorials, one originating within democracy and the other within communism, demonstrate Harvey Weinstein's point that 'memorials represent a complex nexus between politics, trauma, collective memory, and public art.'[13] Despite their significantly different wartime experiences and politics, both the US and USSR built triumphant renderings of the war - memorials that celebrate heroic death while denying tragic death. To do so, these physical narratives drew on four elements: the timing of construction, the geographic location, the mnemonic features of the designs that incorporated some wartime memories while 'forgetting' others, and 'flow,' i.e., the interaction between the structures and the people who move through it. In this way each of the memorials created a setting for a specific sense of Presence to emerge so that the living could connect with the dead.

A.   Timing

Although the Great War ended in 1945 it was not until thirty years later that the Leningrad Monument was completed. The delay can be attributed to at least two things: the all-consuming effort to rebuild the USSR, and Stalin's concerted effort to curtail further discussions about the war, (e.g., by demoting Victory Day from a national holiday to a working holiday in 1947).[14] Eventually, a tidal shift came from a mix of changing politics that distanced and re-examined the Stalinist regime, and the approaching 30th anniversary of Victory Day. As a result, the 'cult of World War II' was born.[15]

The period between war and memorial was even longer in the US. Built in 2004, the memorial followed not only the Korean and Vietnam Wars but also the building of their memorials; the Vietnam Veterans Memorial (VVM) in 1982 and the Korean War Memorial in 1995. The delay in commemorating WWII can be explained both by a post-war preference in favour of 'living' monuments (e.g., memorial highways, arenas, and scholarships) over traditional stone monuments,[16] and by a public questioning of war in reaction to the Korean and Vietnam conflicts, neither viewed as triumphant nor heroic. In fact, between 1970 and 1998, WWII 'virtually disappeared in US popular culture.'[17] But as in the USSR, a cult of WWII eventually did arise in the US, this time heralded by the 50th anniversary of D-Day in 1995 and reflected by pop culture events such as Stephen Spielberg's film, *Saving Private Ryan*, Tom Brokaw's book, *The Greatest Generation*, and the HBO series, *Band of Brothers*. The urgency for building the memorial only increased with the growing awareness that the WWII generation was dying off.[18]

If, as the geographer Yi-Fu Tuan reminds, '[t]he cult of the past calls for illusion rather than authenticity,'[19] in arising from the cult of the 'Great' war, the timing was right for American and Soviet memorials that would reflect heroic death.

B.   Geography

Where, then, to place these memorials? It was only natural that Leningrad, the city that withstood a 900-day siege, would memorialise its own, but the specific location of the memorial was viewed from the start as a critical decision because it would determine whose experience would be set into stone.[20] To build the memorial on the battlefront would pay homage to the soldiers; locating it within the historic district of the city would honour the civilians. The final decision was to build on the southern extreme of Moskovskii Prospekt, at a site dubbed Victory Square; an ellipse of land at the centre of a traffic circle that had been a part of a line of defence that ringed the city (i.e., where front and city met,) and where a Triumphal Arch had been temporarily erected in 1945 to greet the returning troops.[21]

Choosing a location for the WWII memorial in Washington was perhaps an even more contentious issue since one of the proposed sites was that of the 'sacred' space of the National Mall; a two-mile promenade spanning from the Lincoln Memorial to the Washington Monument to the US Capitol. To situate the memorial on the Mall was understood by both proponents and opponents as establishing a 'specific vision of the war and its meaning in American history.'[22] A public service advertisement featuring Tom Hanks, the star of *Saving Private Ryan*, fused fiction, myth, facts, and politics in the campaign to promote this site by quoting from the actor: 'It's the right time. It's the right place. Please help build [the memorial] here on the Mall... .'[23] Eventually, the advocates for this prime location won. The announcement stone to the monument left no doubt as to the symbolic meaning of its chosen location:

> Here in the presence of Washington and Lincoln, one the eighteenth-century father and the other the nineteenth-century preserver of our nation, we honor those twentieth century Americans who took up the struggle during the Second World War and made the sacrifices to perpetuate the gift our forefathers entrusted to us: a nation conceived in liberty and justice.'[24]

Situating the WWII monument between these icons, then, deliberately constructed this 'victorious' war, rather than the more problematic Vietnam or Korean conflicts, as the most significant event of the 20th century.[25]

Therefore, merely the choice of location foreshadowed the symbolic meanings of the memorials yet to be built. Both the US and USSR memorials were strategically located for the telling of a heroic narrative: the Leningrad monument positioned at the site where civilians and soldiers met to successfully defend their city from invasion, and the American WWII memorial situated between the Washington Monument, the symbol of democracy, and the Lincoln Memorial, the symbol of unity. Given this, it would no longer seem possible to construct these tributes to the war in tragic terms - indeed the ground had literally been laid to erect structures that affirmed a national identity built on military superiority.

C.   Mnemonic Architecture and Forgetfulness

Shanken summarises the challenge of designing the US memorial in this way: 'How would America commemorate a war that included genocide, mass killings, and nuclear death...?'[26] The construction of the heroic narrative of WWII was also threatened by other problematic memories: the government's failure to foresee the attack on Pearl Harbor, the internment of Japanese-American citizens, the military's discriminatory policies based on race and gender, and the country's original resistance to entering the war. A similarly daunting challenge also confronted the choice of a heroic Soviet design: how to deal with Stalin's pact with Hitler, the lack of preparedness for Germany's Operation Barbarossa, the Kremlin's policy that accepted the starvation of Leningraders over surrender, and the cannibalism and crime that occurred in Leningrad during the siege.[27] In order that the memorials be constructed according to national narratives of heroic death in victorious war,[28] memories such as these had to be omitted by both the American and Soviet designs.

The use of numbers serves as a revealing example of what was to be remembered versus forgotten. The US memorial, designed by Friedrich St. Florian includes a Freedom Wall containing 4,000 gold stars that pays homage to the 400,000 dead American troops with the inscription: 'HERE WE MARK THE PRICE OF FREEDOM.' The memorial is silent, however, concerning the millions of dead among allied troops and the civilians of all the involved nations - failing even to note those who died in the Holocaust, Hiroshima, and Nagasaki. In contrast, the numbers cited in the Soviet design are not employed to count the fallen but instead to mark the duration of the siege: 900 days, 900 nights. In emphasising the longevity of the siege the focus of the memorial is on the heroism of Leningraders rather than on the tragic deaths of an estimated one million of them. Indeed, the Soviet monument names Leningraders as the 'heroic defenders' of the city[29] and not as the victims of the war or of government policy.[30] This shift in terminology has been viewed as symbolically important; it is embraced by some scholars as acknowledgment of the sacrifices made by the mostly female population,[31] while rejected by others as romanticising the wretched struggle of children, women, and the elderly to survive in the midst of unspeakable conditions caused by political decisions.[32]

Both memorials adopt typical heroic stylistic elements on a grand scale. The American memorial spans 7.4 acres and incorporates the pre-existing Rainbow Pool. Its classical design includes: two pavilions with 43-foot triumphal arches that honour the Pacific and Atlantic fronts; bronze eagles and wreaths; and a circular plaza with walls engraved with battle names and inspirational quotations. Emphasising unity on the home front, there is a ring of fifty-six 17-foot-high pillars representing the states, territories, and District of Columbia, and a tiered ceremonial entrance lined by twenty-four bas-relief sculptures depicting scenes of America at war.

That this triumphant monument was erected following the construction of the austere Vietnam Veterans Memorial (VVM) speaks to the deliberate message of the design. Whereas the competition rules for designing the VVM required that the design make no statement about the war,[33] the WWII memorial was erected with a clear message of military victory. This triumphant narrative has been both lauded as 'simple, solemn and dignified,'[34] and disparaged as an 'excessively busy design.'[35] One critic charged that the memorial embodied the architecture of the Third Reich and faulted it as 'gigantic and grandiose, bombastic and authoritarian, faceless and monolithic.'[36] To this others added the observations: 'imperial and triumphant,'[37] 'Federalist Stalinist,'[38] a 'tasteless monstrosity,'[39] and 'a shrine to not knowing or, more precisely, of forgetting.'[40] Its proponents argued that the 'elegiac memorial'[41] emphasises national unity, undaunted courage, and the effort 'to liberate a world fast falling to forces of tyranny.'[42]

The Monument to the Heroic Defenders of Leningrad designed by Valentin Kamensky and Sergei Speransky is equally as busy and triumphal a memorial. There is a 48-meter obelisk, a classical design element that connotes 'imperial trophy,'[43] that bears the dates of Soviet involvement in the war, 1941 to 1945. At its base stand larger than life sculptures of a male soldier and a male worker, unabashedly titled 'The Victors.' Six sculptural groups by Mikhail Anikushin, a witness to the siege, line the sides of the staircase, giving human faces to the 'defenders' of Leningrad: soldiers, sailors, pilots, snipe-shooters, a female medic, foundry workers, a mother saying farewell to her son, and civilians with shovels poised to dig trenches. Following a stairway downward through a ring of granite, the lower level contains the sculpture, 'The Blockade,' that features the women of Leningrad: one woman whose breasts can be seen beneath a thin fabric stands holding a sagging child in her arms, another kneeling and cradling a younger woman, and a third limp and shrouded being supported by a male soldier. It is here that visitors leave red and white carnations. This sculpture documents the suffering that is noticeably absent from its American counterpart. (It is, therefore, ironic that the American structure is labelled a 'memorial' although it clearly elevates the celebration of militarism over mourning, while the Soviet structure is termed a 'monument,' a label indicative of victory remembered). Yet, as Kirchenbaum notes of 'The Blockade' sculpture, with the exception of the shrouded woman, this depiction of the women of Leningrad sanitises starvation and suffering: their faces are stoic, they are unbowed, and their bodies are ample, even voluptuous.[44]

During the debate over what the design of this Soviet monument should say, polarising urges emerged - that victory be celebrated or that tragedy be documented.[45] During the public discussion of the proposed designs, one architect suggested, '[t]he need for a site specific narrative that did not try to redeem trauma with overblown images of victory.'[46] The resulting design, instead, wedded heroism to military victory, a decision chastised by historian Nina Tumarkin as a 'massive effort to obliterate collective memory of the most horrific war in the history of humankind.'[47]

To focus on the design details of the US and USSR monuments is to see them as quite different. Although there is an information booth near the American memorial, there is no museum attached to the site. In contrast, the Leningrad monument includes a subterranean museum that contains: artefacts from the siege; an electronic map of the front; a documentary film; two enormous mosaics, one depicting the start of the War and the other Victory; and 900 electric torches. How to memorialise the dead also distinguishes them. The American honours the war dead through the symbolism of stars on a wall while the Soviet pays homage to both the dead and the survivors by depicting them in eight clusters of larger than life sculptures. There are also structural differences with the American memorial dominated by the Rainbow pool, a circular water feature ringed by pillars, and the Soviet design marked by a towering obelisk that is balanced by a sunken area that creates an outdoor room.

Yet, when the focus is shifted from the details to the footprints of the two monuments, they can be seen in remarkably similar terms. If the US monument is approached from the Lincoln Memorial, the obelisk that is the nearby Washington Monument becomes a part of its profile. Given this wider view, the addition of an obelisk to this design would have been redundant. The US and USSR monuments also employ similar design elements including a descending staircase at one end, a sunken circular structure (a fountain or a 'room') at the centre, the elevation of an obelisk, and definition provided by traffic patterns that 'contain' the monuments. The Leningrad monument is an island of land ringed by a traffic circle, and the D.C.

monument is confined by 17th Street, the reflecting pool, and the sidewalks on either side of the mall.

Both monuments also page homage to important events of the war, although arguably unintentionally. Viewed from the height of the Washington Monument, the WWII memorial suggests the outline of a mushroom cloud;[48] a reference to the nuclear bombs that the US dropped on the Japanese cities of Hiroshima and Nagasaki in an effort to end the war. The stem of the cloud is formed by the wide ceremonial staircase, the cloud itself is outlined by the ring of pillars, and the animation of detonation is suggested by the spray of the fountains in the Rainbow pool (see photograph 1).

Photograph 1: View from the Washington Monument of the WW II Memorial. Source: © Richard Latoff/Latoff.com.

Thus, even though the memorial does not overtly address this military action, there is an abstract and most likely unintentional reminder of this particular horror of WW II. The design of the Soviet monument also embodies a wartime experience as it is itself a blockade. Like Leningrad itself, the monument is surrounded and cannot be broached except by way of a tunnel that leads beneath the traffic circle (see photograph 2).

Photograph 2: The Monument to the Heroic Defenders of Leningrad.
© 2004 Behuniak, printed with permission from Susan M. Behuniak

This traffic circle, then, forms a barrier, a literal roadblock that recalls the line that stopped the Germans and ultimately forced retreat. So too do viewers of the monument have to turn back once they have reached its edge.

And, although both the American and Soviet WWII experiences are complex stories of defeat and victory, death and survival, and complicity and courage, the memorials erected to these experiences embellish their heroic elements. This point is emphasised by official statements about the monuments themselves; statements that strike the theme of heroism by both governments. The Leningrad monument brochure published by the State Museum of the History of St. Petersburg describes the Great Patriotic War as 'the time of great trial and great heroism for Leningrad-St. Petersburg' and the city itself as a 'great symbol of the Soviet peoples' unprecedented courage.' The WWII monument brochure published by the National Park Service of the US Department of Interior contains a photo of one of the monument's engravings; a quote by President Harry S. Truman that reads: 'Our debt to the heroic men and valiant women in the service of our country can never be repaid. They have earned our undying gratitude. America will never forget their sacrifices.' In this elevation of heroism over tragedy and myth over memory, the two memorials illustrate how catastrophic events can be suppressed so they might be canonised into victories.

D.   Flow and Movement
        The timing, geography, and design of monuments become meaningful only with the interaction of the human beings who view them, walk through them, and use their senses to fully experience them.

> The path of our movement can be conceived as the perceptual thread that links the spaces of a building, or any series of interior or exterior space, together. Since we move in Time, through a Sequence of Spaces, we experience a space in relation to where we've been and where we anticipate going.[49]

Therefore, any analysis of monuments must include the interplay between these structures and people; i.e., how people approach, enter, move through, interact with, and exit these spaces. This analysis also sets the foundation for discussion of Presence: what relationship does the monument, whether intentionally or not, foster between the living and the dead?
        The approach and entry to the monuments quite literally set into motion human interaction with the structures. That there is only one way into the Defenders monument sets all visitors on the same path; through an underground tunnel beneath the traffic circle, up the staircase to the entrance of the monument, and downward again into the circular centre of the structure where the Blockade sculpture awaits. In contrast, the DC monument can be accessed from numerous directions although it has a formal ceremonial entrance denoted by the tiered staircase that leads from 17th Street to the fountain area. These access differences define the Leningrad monument as a destination, a place where one intentionally goes, while making it possible for the DC monument to be circumvented or passed through en route to other sites such as the Lincoln Memorial.
        Both monuments are designed with a depressed base plane to isolate the spaces from the larger contexts that surround them.[50] The walls surrounding the Blockade sculpture of the Leningrad monument are high enough to suggest a room and deep enough to silence the traffic. The pathway out of this space is on the opposite side where the circle is broken. The walker has the choice to go further underground to the museum or take the staircase that leads upward toward the obelisk and the seven other groupings of sculptures. Likewise, the centre of the WWII monument is approached by stepping down stairs and is ringed by a higher level marked by the pillars and pavilions. This use of different planes defines the boundaries of both of the monuments, but the technique is used differently as the Soviet

design separates the monument from its surroundings while the lowered plane of the US is more subtle so that the monument remains visually joined to the landscape of the other monuments of the Mall.

The sequence of spaces through the Leningrad monument follows a clear flow: through the underground tunnel, up stairs, down stairs, up stairs, around the border, and then a return to the underground tunnel again. In contrast, the DC monument lacks a discernible pattern of flow because there are multiple points of entrance, exit, and direction possible. One can enter the monument from one of five walkways, can walk around the pillars going clockwise or counter-clockwise, or can enter the lower fountain area and turn either right or left. While the Leningrad sculptures give the viewer specific destinations in the form of the sculptural groups, the repetitive design of the DC memorial (i.e., the twin arches and the 58 pillars) make it unclear as to where viewers should go next. In terms of interacting with the monuments, then, this means that there is more of a shared experience among viewers of the Leningrad monument than is possible at the DC monument.

E.   Setting the Stage for Presence

Although it may seem that war memorials would almost by definition encourage a sense of Presence - that sense of awareness that the living have for the dead - this is not always the case, or at least, the strength and form of Presence can vary greatly among memorials. The concept of Presence is an integral part of most memorials, yet it is also a subjective matter dependent on the sensibilities and sensitivity of individuals who respond to these structures. Presence is an intangible component of monuments; it is a sense, a feeling, a perception. And this sentiment will vary by degree on a very individualised basis in that some individuals perceive a powerful Presence of the dead while others remain oblivious.

Yet while it is true that Presence is influenced by individual sensitivity, the architectural features of memorials are also influential, enhancing or impeding perceptiveness. As previously discussed, the timing, geography, design, and flow of monuments form an experience for people and it is this interaction that determines the degree that the Presence of the dead is felt. Because both the US and USSR memorials primarily embrace literal renderings of the war over abstract representations, and a heroic sense of death rather than a tragic rendering, it may be tempting to suggest that memorials that are literal and heroic uniformly discourage a sense of Presence. But this does not seem to be true because there are differences not only in how these memorials invite Presence into these spaces but the kind of Presence they contain.

Presence, in the form of remembering the Leningrad dead, is given a place at the Defenders monument. While the city bustles around it, the monument it is cut off from these ordinary sounds and activities through the use of the sunken, torch lit room that contains the heartbreaking Blockade sculpture. Even the street noise fades when the recording of a ticking metronome is played, emphasising the slow passage of time through 900 days and 900 nights. While the heroic elements of the monument are still in place, the suffering that took place on this ground is palpable. This, then, is clearly a solemn place of mourning, a sort of sacred ground where the living feel the Presence of the dead.

In contrast, Presence is quite different at the WWII memorial, a place of commemoration and not the site of an actual battleground. The festive atmosphere, the ease with which viewers can misinterpret the water feature as a recreational fountain, and the movement of tourists this way and that give this place energy. One can pass by the wall of stars without remembering that they represent 400,000 lives lost. This, then, is a place of celebration, not of mourning. Given this, Presence is noted not by death but by a legacy of accomplishment - a war won. It is at a site further down the Mall that Presence in its more meditative form is felt - at the Vietnam Veterans Memorial (VVM), an abstract V-shaped memorial that projects a stylised sense of tragic death. It is not only the VVM's engraved list of the names of the dead and the missing that serves as a reminder of the lives lost, but also the way the structure invites solemn interaction between viewers and the monument. These connections take several forms: in the way the black granite reflects the faces of the viewers, joining the names of the dead with the faces of the living; in the flow of the walkway that leads all viewers into its sunken centre and back out again; in the tactile experience of touching the names and taking rubbings from the wall; and in how visitors add to the memorial by leaving behind flowers, notes, and artwork. The VVM may be an abstract monument that invites interpretation as to the meaning of the war but it is also a memorial that honours the dead as real people rather than as abstract heroes. And although no body is buried at the VVM, there is a sense of those named as being present.

Presence, then, is an ephemeral concept that seems to be shaped by several aspects of monuments even as it works to define those monuments. As part of a heroic rendering of death, it is not so much the dead themselves as individuals who are remembered but their collective actions and ultimate successes that are recalled. Presence, then, can evoke a sense of celebratory gratitude. But Presence can also find a home in sites of mourning, and these seem to require space for meditation. Such monuments create stillness, focal points to concentrate on, and opportunities to interact with the memorial or with other people through shared experience. So while both the WWII Memorial and the Defenders Monument elevate the heroic over the tragic, and adopt literal over abstract narratives of the war, the American structure invites Presence in the name of celebration while its Soviet counterpart invites Presence in the form of mourning.

3.   Discussion and Conclusion

The connection between heroic death and successful warfare may seem inevitable, but I want to argue that they are not. Instead, the linkage between the two is one that is deliberately constructed to advance a particular political agenda.

For example, the US experience in WWI could also have been told using a heroic and victorious narrative, but the commemorative memorials told a different story. Rather than triumph, these memorials struck the theme of healing and of lessons learned. WWI was memorialised as 'the war to end all wars' and as a promise of 'never again.'[51] The cultural discomfort with the notion of celebrating the victory explains the popularity of useful, living memorials over the building of symbols in stone.[52]

And although '[i]mperial countries do not usually erect monuments that memorialize their guilt,'[53] there are counterexamples of this as well. The VVM[54] in the US and the Solovki Stone[55] (a gulag memorial) in Russia were built with the therapeutic objective of healing and so neither serves as a 'tool of state power.'[56] Both these memorials illustrate how the tragic view of death rejects a singular and coherent narrative of war, instead recognising that great loss implicitly asks us to weigh whether the cost in human life was worthwhile.[57] Whereas heroic death uses epic terms, clichés, and partial stories to fix a narrative to which contrary facts and memories must conform, tragic death employs a richer and multifaceted view of warfare that encourages public mourning and reflection. These memorials show a reverence for life and for death by inviting citizens to question the meanings of the killings and/or the war, and how, then, to heal in order to move forward.[58]

For example, Maya Lin, who designed the abstract VVM, said that her work was influenced by a sharp awareness of death as loss.[59] Interestingly, the open-ended design that invited such reflection proved too disturbing to some, and so additions were later added to the site that were more in line with heroic symbolism: a flagpole and a realistic sculpture of three male soldiers in 1984; and in response to this gendered image of the war dead,[60] a sculpture of women nurses in 1993.

Whereas tragic death accommodates complicated and even contradictory memories, heroic death depends on selective memory. Barbara Biesecker states that consciousness is reorganised 'not by way of explicit propaganda, but by replacing and simplifying memories people actually have with image traces of political experience about which people can have political feelings that link them to other citizens and to patriotism.'[61] The heroic narrative is well suited to this task since the hero's world is a one-dimensional pairing of polar opposites: us versus them; victory versus defeat; good versus evil.[62] The hero, then, emerges as an uncomplicated and 'untainted' figure.[63] This rendering even makes death denial possible since heroes do not die;[64] a sentiment encoded in eternal flames, granite structures, and larger-than-life statues.

Because war memorials are indeed 'self conscious attempts to solicit public participation in the politics of the day,'[65] the choice of whether to depict death as tragic or as heroic not only determines interpretations of past wars but also instructs present day politics on both the national and individual levels. Again, memorials that embrace the tragedy of death not only encourage healing but also a weighing of the price of victory. In this rendering, neither national identity nor individual notions of citizenship are dependent on militarism alone for meaning. In contrast, the heroic renderings of war deaths discourage a questioning of war and instead pose an explicit threat of future warfare by showcasing military superiority.

Both the American and Soviet WWII memorials illustrate this point. In that each nation claimed for itself the pivotal role of having saved the world from fascism,[66] each memorial links heroic death to military success by cultivating the belief that the greatness of a generation, a city, or a country is due to victory in war. Such a message sanctions future warfare and constructs citizenship as a duty to fight to the death in the next patriotic war, or at minimum, to offer unified support at home. This distilling of wartime deaths into the archetype of heroic death not only shapes an account about the past, but sets expectations about the present and the future. How, then, 'to create authentic memory and how to preserve it,' remain important political questions.[67]

Notes

[1] C. A. Corr, C. M. Nabe, D. M. Corr, *Death & Dying, Life & Living*, Wadsworth, Belmont, CA, 2009, p. 79.

[2] C. L. Griswold and S. Griswold, 'The Vietnam Veterans Memorial and the Washington Mall: Philosophical Thoughts on Political Iconography', *Critical Inquiry*, Vol. 12, 1986, p. 689.

[3] K. Verdery as quoted in B. Forest and J. Johnson, 'Unraveling the Threads of History: Soviet Era Monuments and Post-Soviet National Identity in Moscow', *Annals of the Association of American Geographers*, Vol. 92, 2002, p. 526.

[4] E. Reimers, 'Public Memorials as Communicative Tools to Construct, Deconstruct, and Negotiate History and the Present', Paper Presented at the 'Death, Dying and Disposal', 8th Conference, Bath, UK, 2007, p. 1.

[5] M. Sturken, 'The Wall, the Screen, and the Image: The Vietnam Veterans Memorial', *Representations*, Vol. 35, 1991, p. 120.

[6] A. M. Shanken, 'Planning Memory: Living Memorials in the United States during World War II', *The Art Bulletin*, Vol. 84, 2002.

[7] Forest and Johnson, op. cit.

[8] S. Whiting, 'Monument', in *The Question of Memory: The WTC Memorial Design*, School of Pratt Architecture, International 2002 Summer Seminar and Conference on Architecture and Urban Design, pp. 5-6.

[9] See T. Des Pres, *The Survivor: An Anatomy of Life in the Death Camps*, Oxford University Press, New York, 1976, p. 4; T. Todorov, *Facing the Extreme: Moral Life in the Concentration Camps*, A. Denner and A. Pollack (trans), Henry Holt and Company, New York, 1996, p. 10.

[10] Todorov, op. cit.

[11] E. Becker, *The Denial of Death*, Free Press, New York, 1997 [1973].

[12] Des Pres, op. cit., p. 5.

[13] Quoted in J. Barsalou and V. Baxter, 'The Urge to Remember: The Role of Memorials in Social Reconstruction and Transitional Justice', *Stabilization and Reconstruction Series No. 5*, United States Institute of Peace, Washington, DC, 2007, p. 4.

[14] N. Tumarkin, *The Living & The Dead: The Rise and Fall of the Cult of World War II in Russia*, Basic Books, New York, 1994, p. 104.

[15] Tumarkin, op. cit.

[16] Shanken, op. cit., p. 130.

[17] B. A. Biesecker, 'Remembering World War II: The Rhetoric and Politics of National Commemoration at the Turn of the 21st Century', *Quarterly Journal of Speech*, Vol. 88, 2002, p. 405.

[18] L. Benton-Short, 'Politics, Public Space, and Memorials: The Brawl on the Mall', *Urban Geography*, Vol. 27, 2006, p. 305.

[19] Y. F. Tuan, *Space and Place: The Perspective of Experience*, University of Minnesota Press, Minneapolis, 1977, p. 194.

[20] L. A. Kirschenbaum, *The Legacy of the Siege of Leningrad, 1941-1995*, Cambridge University Press, New York, 2006, p. 211.

[21] The State Museum of the History of St. Petersburg, 'Monument to the Heroic Defenders of Leningrad' Brochure, Leetsey Publishing House, St. Petersburg, 1999.

[22] Benton-Short, op. cit., p. 297.

[23] Mills, op. cit.

[24] Mills, op. cit., p. 209.

[25] Benton-Short, op. cit., p. 323; see also Mills, op. cit., p. 217.

[26] Shanken, op. cit., p. 134.

[27] Forest and Johnson, op. cit., p. 432; Shanken, op. cit., p. 145.

[28] Kirschenbaum, op. cit., p. 283.

[29] see C. Simmons and N. Perlina, *Writing the Siege of Leningrad: Women's Diaries, Memoirs, and Documentary Prose*, University of Pittsburgh Press, Pittsburgh, PA, 2002.

[30] See Tumarkin, op. cit.

[31] See Simmons and Perlina, op. cit.

[32] See Tumarkin, op cit.

[33] Griswold and Griswold, op. cit., at footnote 21, p. 718.

[34] M. Fisher, 'A Memorial, Yes, But What About Its Message?', *The Washington Post*, July 22, 2000, p. B-1.

[35] Ibid.

[36] S. Kalson, 'World War II Memorial a Classic Example of Excess', *Pittsburgh Post-Gazette*, May 30, 2001, p. B-1.

[37] J. S. Felderman as quoted by I. Molotsky, 'Panel Backs World War II Memorial on Mall in Washington', *New York Times*, July 21, 2000, p. 13.

[38] P. Greenberg, 'Monumental Mistake', *Arkansas Democrat-Gazette*, May 30, 2001, p. B-8.

[39] R. Ebert, 'Bad Idea, Bad Spot for WWII Memorial', *Chicago Sun-Times*, May 31, 2001, p. 41.

[40] H. Muschamp, 'New War Memorial Is Shrine to Sentiment', *The New York Times*, June 7, 2001, p. 1.

[41] Mills, p. 216.

[42] National Park Service, US Department of Interior, 'World War II Memorial' Brochure, Washington, DC, 2007.

[43] Sturken, op. cit., p. 121.

[44] Kirschenbaum, op. cit., p. 225.

[45] Ibid, p. 214.

[46] Ibid, pp. 214-215.

[47] Tumarkin, op. cit., p. 51.

[48] This observation was pointed out to me by Courtney Coyne-Jensen at the 6th Global Conference of 'Making Sense of Dying and Death', Salzburg, Austria, November 2008.

[49] F. D. K. Ching, *Architecture: Form, Space, & Order*, 3rd Edition, John Wiley & Sons, Hoboken, New York, p. 240.

[50] Ching, op. cit., p. 112.

[51] Sturken, op. cit., p. 122.

[52] Shanken, op. cit., p. 130.

[53] Etkind, op. cit., p. 40.

[54] J. C. Scruggs and J. L. Swerdlow, *To Heal a Nation: The Vietnam Veterans Memorial*, Harper & Row, New York, 1986; R. Wagner-Pacifici and B. Schwartz, 'The Vietnam Veterans Memorial: Commemorating a Difficult Past', *The American Journal of Sociology*, Vol. 97, 1991, pp. 376-420; Griswold and Griswold, op. cit.

[55] Etkind, op. cit., pp. 51-55; B. Forest and J. Johnson, 'Unraveling the Threads of History: Soviet Era Monuments and Post-Soviet National Identity

in Moscow', *Annals of the Association of American Geographers*, Vol. 92, 2002, p. 541.

[56] Wagner-Pacifici and Schwartz, op. cit., p. 407.

[57] Griswold and Griswold, op. cit., p. 711.

[58] J. C. Scruggs and J. L. Swerdlow, *To Heal a Nation: The Vietnam Veterans Memorial*, Harper & Row, New York, 1986; Griswold and Griswold, op. cit., p. 712.

[59] Griswold and Griswold, op. cit., at footnotes 17 and 21, p. 718.

[60] Sturken, op. cit., p. 131.

[61] Biesecker, op. cit., p. 397.

[62] Todorov, op. cit., p. 12.

[63] Wagner-Pacifici and Schwartz, op. cit., p. 379.

[64] Tumarkin, op. cit., p. 128.

[65] S. Cooke, 'Negotiating Memory and Identity: The Hyde Park Holocaust Memorial, London', *Journal of Historical Geography*, Vol. 26, 2000, p. 450.

[66] See the statements by the National Park Service, US Department of Interior, and The State Museum of the History of St. Petersburg.

[67] J. Mayo, *War Memorials as Political Landscapes: The American Experience & Beyond*, Praeger, New York, 1988, p. 250.

Bibliography

Barsalou, J. and Baxter, V., 'The Urge to Remember: The Role of Memorials in Social Reconstruction and Transitional Justice'. *Stabilization and Reconstruction Series No. 5*, United States Institute of Peace, Washington, DC, January 2007.

Becker, E., *The Denial of Death*. Free Press, New York, 1997 [1973].

Benton-Short, L., 'Politics, Public Space, and Memorials: The Brawl on the Mall'. *Urban Geography*, Vol. 27, 2006, pp. 297-329.

Biesecker, B. A., 'Remembering World War II: The Rhetoric and Politics of National Commemoration at the Turn of the 21st Century'. *Quarterly Journal of Speech*, Vol. 88, 2002, pp. 393-409.

Ching, F., *Architecture: Form, Space, and Order*. 3rd Edition, John Wiley & Sons, Inc., Hoboken, New York, 2007.

Cooke, S., 'Negotiating Memory and Identity: The Hyde Park Holocaust Memorial, London'. *Journal of Historical Geography*, Vol. 26, 2000, pp. 449-465.

Corr, C. A., Nabe, C. M., Corr, D. M., *Death & Dying, Life & Living*. 6th Edition, Wadsworth, Belmont, CA, 2009.

Des Pres, T., *The Survivor: An Anatomy of Life in the Death Camps*. Oxford University Press, New York, 1976.

Ebert, R., 'Bad Idea, Bad Spot for WWII Memorial'. *Chicago Sun-Times*, May 31, 2001, p. 41.

Etkind, A., 'Hard and Soft in Cultural Memory: Political Mourning in Russia and Germany'. *Grey Room*, Vol. 16, 2004, pp. 36-59.

Fisher, M., 'A Memorial, Yes, But What About Its Message?'. *The Washington Post*, July 22, 2000, p. B-1.

Forest, B. and Johnson, J., 'Unraveling the Threads of History: Soviet Era Monuments and Post-Soviet National Identity in Moscow'. *Annals of the Association of American Geographers*, Vol. 92, 2002, pp. 524-547.

Greenberg, P., 'Monumental Mistake'. *Arkansas Democrat-Gazette*, May 30, 2001, p. B-8.

Griswold, C. L. and Giswold, S., 'The Vietnam Veterans Memorial and the Washington Mall: Philosophical Thoughts on Political Iconography'. *Critical Inquiry*, Vol. 12, 1986, pp. 688-719.

Kalson, S., 'World War II Memorial a Classic Example of Excess'. *Pittsburgh Post-Gazette*, May 30, 2001, p. B-1.

Kirschenbaum, L. A., *The Legacy of the Siege of Leningrad, 1941-1995*. Cambridge University Press, New York, 2006.

Mayo, J. M., *War Memorials as Political Landscapes: The American Experience & Beyond*. Praeger, New York, 1988.

Mills, N., *Their Last Battle: The Fight for the National World War II Memorial*. Basic Books, New York, 2004.

Molotsky, I., 'Panel Backs World War II Memorial on Mall in Washington'. *New York Times*, July 21, 2000, p. 13.

Muschamp, H., 'New War Memorial is Shrine to Sentiment'. *The New York Times*, June 7, 2001, p. 1.

National Park Service, US Department of Interior, 'World War II Memorial'. Brochure, Washington, DC, 2007.

Reimers, E., 'Public Memorials as Communicative Tools to Construct, Deconstruct, and Negotiate History and the Present'. Paper Presented at the 'Death, Dying and Disposal', 8th Conference, Bath, UK, 2007.

Scruggs, J. C. and Swerdlow, J. L., *To Heal a Nation: The Vietnam Veterans Memorial*. Harper & Row, New York, 1986.

Shanken, A. M., 'Planning Memory: Living Memorials in the United States during World War II'. *The Art Bulletin*, Vol. 84, 2002, pp. 130-147.

Simmons, C. and Perlina, N., *Writing the Siege of Leningrad: Women's Diaries, Memoirs, and Documentary Prose*. University of Pittsburgh Press, Pittsburgh, PA, 2002.

The State Museum of the History of St. Petersburg, 'Monument to the Heroic Defenders of Leningrad', in *Brochur*. Leetsey Publishing House, St. Petersburg, 1999.

Sturken, M., 'The Wall, the Screen, and the Image: The Vietnam Veterans Memorial'. *Representations*, Vol. 35, 1991, pp. 118-142.

Todorov, T., *Facing the Extreme: Moral Life in the Concentration Camps*. A. Denner and A. Pollack (trans), Henry Holt and Company, New York, 1996.

Tuan, Y-F., *Space and Place: The Perspective of Experience*. University of Minnesota Press, Minneapolis, 1977.

Tumarkin, N., *The Living & The Dead: The Rise and Fall of the Cult of World War II in Russia*. Basic Books, New York, 1994.

Wagner-Pacifici, R. and Schwartz, B., 'The Vietnam Veterans Memorial: Commemorating a Difficult Past'. *The American Journal of Sociology*, Vol. 97, 1991, pp. 376-420.

Whiting, S., 'Monument', in *The Question of Memory: The WTC Memorial Design*. School of Pratt Architecture, International 2002 Summer Seminar and Conference on Architecture and Urban Design, pp. 5-7.

Susan M. Behuniak is Professor of Political Science at Le Moyne College in Syracuse, New York, where she teaches constitutional law. Her publications include works on death and dying, physician-assisted suicide, and elder rights.

Preserving the Dead in the Lives of the Living

Nate Hinerman

Abstract
This paper examines how we might use personal grief archives (such as those constructed in a classroom, explained below) as a way to study community-wide outpourings of grief and the archives they produce following tragedies labelled as 'public' and/or 'national.' The theoretical nature of this paper considers personal grief archives as a way to reflect on death attitudes derived from various agents of socialisation. In this case, the personal archives discussed result from a series of in-class writing assignments that include death inventories, childhood loss/early thoughts about death diaries, questionnaires about life-threatening illness and death fears, advance directives, and ethical wills. The practical nature of this paper considers a pedagogical mechanism to approach the events of September 11th, 2001 in light of personally constructed grief archives. My research will elaborate how meaning-making on the individual level in times of loss provides a vital lens through which to consider, to critique, and ultimately to evaluate the meaning assigned to those same events vis-à-vis more 'national' or 'public' stages. Every death, like any archive, tells a story. Sharing these stories can provide emotional relief and promote a search for meaning. Grief archives can function as a means to bring people together in mutual support during a time of loss. Grief archives also assist individuals and communities to revise, reform, and continue relationships with the deceased over time. Bonds sustained through memories and linking objects serve as 'threads of connectedness' to those deceased whose deaths are grieved and remembered. They also form complex (and sometimes problematic) lineages through which individuals preserve, (re-)orient and (re-)frame their own histories/identities within the context of a larger societal matrix.

Key Words: Archive, death attitudes, grief, national, meaning, teaching end-of-life, writing.

*****

1. A Research Study Provides Unexpected Results

In 2004, I began teaching a course entitled, *Death and Dying*. Primarily designed for nursing students seeking to complete a core requirement in Theology and Religious Studies, I crafted a syllabus that addressed both the clinical and more 'metaphysical' aspects of dying in the US. On the first day of class, I passed out a survey. The survey was an adaptation of a famous assessment developed by Edwin Shneidman from the

Center of Advanced Study of Behavioral Sciences in consultation with other researchers at Stanford University during the early 1970s. Their survey, 'You and Death: A Questionnaire,' probes important terrain for any student (or professor, for that matter) studying death and dying. My purpose in passing out this questionnaire was to ascertain, in advance of any formal group research, the exposure to and experiences of death and dying by my students. My hope was that by reading these questionnaires at the start of our class, I could cultivate important sensitivities to any traumatic grief encounters potentially experienced by my students. In this way, I hoped to tailor my lectures and our group discussions in ways that might best honour and respect their difficult experiences of loss and bereavement. I also wanted a clue into the general exposure my students had with death and dying. The questionnaire results gave me this information, and much more.

Before covering some results of the survey, let me say that I have taught this class each semester since 2004, and I still use this questionnaire to gauge the students' experiences with death and to calibrate initial sensitivities to the material we must explore carefully together. Each time I give the questionnaire, the responses follow a typical pattern with respect to six questions in particular (discussed below). I originally developed these particular six questions as way to help me understand the individual perceptions of students to the events of September 11th, 2001. Although that material is always slated towards the end of the term, I am always concerned about how to cover this incredibly complex chapter of recent US history. So, I asked the students six specific questions to learn how they felt about these events. Overall, 201 students took the survey in 2004. Here are the six questions to which I am referring, and the responses I received in 2004:

75. Are you actively grieving the events of September 11th, 2001?

196 - No
  5 - Yes

76. Do you sometimes experience confusion, disbelief, anxiety or even depression concerning the events of September 11th, 2001?

11 - No
190 - Yes

77. Do you sometimes experience anger or outrage concerning the losses from the events of September 11th, 2001?

4 - No
197 - Yes

78. When reflecting on the events of September 11th, 2001, do you sometimes sigh, feel an emptiness in your abdomen, or experience shortness of breath?

32 - No
169 - Yes

79. When reflecting on the events of September 11th, 2001, do you sometimes cry, or avoid talking or thinking about those events, and those that died?

26 - No
175 - Yes

80. Since the events of September 11th, 2001, have you questioned or re-examined your religious or spiritual beliefs as a result of failed attempts to make meaning of the losses?

34 - No
167 - Yes

The research I present here is 'rough,' and so I will resist making any wide-sweeping generalisations due to the informal setting in which this information was gathered. However, given my original purposes, the exercise proved helpful (i.e., I simply wanted basic access into how my students were grieving and coming to terms with September 11th, 2001 so that I could teach the topic more effectively and most respectfully). And for those basic motives, these results proved both staggering and quite revealing. Notice question 75 in particular. Only 5 students were aware of their active grief response to the aforementioned events. Yet, if you look to questions 76-80, the overwhelming majority of students reported an experience of grief. *Grief is defined most simply as the reaction to loss*, and we can grieve in many different ways: mentally (question 76), affectively (question 77), physically (question 78), behaviourally (question 79), and even spiritually (question 80). Even though we must proceed cautiously when interpreting the survey data, the results of this informal survey still communicate a simple message: so often, we do not consciously realise we are grieving even when we are presenting classic signs of grief. For a professor who crafted a class syllabus where grief was a central theme, I realised (quickly) I needed a skilful mechanism that could be individually tailored to each student to assist his/her efforts to contact his/her experiences of grief. The rest of this paper elaborates that mechanism I developed, which I refer to as a *grief archive*. Before detailing my approach to creating grief archives, let us consider briefly some factors that often make it so difficult to acknowledge occasions of active grief in the US.

2.   Current Attitudes Toward Death and Dying in the US

Many behavioural psychologists assert that many contemporary attitudes toward death in the US serve an explicitly death-denying function.[1] First, there is no reason to be simple-minded: death is arguably the most challenging of all human experiences. When we face our own mortality, or when our loved ones die, we can be (and usually are) affected powerfully in every aspect of our personhood. However, given the magnitude of death's significance to living persons, it may seem odd to some that death and dying seldom gets discussed amongst friends, family, or even health care professionals in today's America.[2] Instead, death exists for many as a mysterious, anxiety-producing possibility looming on life's horizon. Given such a perception, it is no wonder that many avoid, repress, or deny altogether the reality of death.[3]

Second, in the US, life expectancy continues to increase, which obviously means Americans are living longer.[4] In part as a result of advances in life-sustaining technologies developed and perfected primarily during the late 1950s and early 1960s, many Americans have come to view death as something to be 'mastered' (or at least *controlled*) through continued technological advancements. In addition, the primary causes of death now are slow, progressive illnesses (cancer, heart disease, liver disease) rather than acute infectious diseases (diphtheria, syphilis, etc).[5] These epidemiological transitions have pushed end-of-life care from the home to the hospital, in part so that the dying can be proximate to important life-extending technologies. Resulting from these transitions, caregiving at the end-of-life largely has been (re-)assigned to medical professionals, rather than friends and family. The impact of this migration has caused the average person in the US to have an increasingly passive role in caring for the dying.[6] Even more, many chaplains assert that a serious challenge has arisen surrounding how to explore spiritual issues with the dying (i.e., questions of meaning, questions of value, and questions of relationship) when the context of care they are receiving is almost purely geared towards the biological dimension of their personhood.[7]

Third, infant mortality rates have decreased dramatically over this past century,[8] and given that many who are the end-of-life no longer live at home, the average American is unlikely to be confronted by death early on in the lifespan as has been true for every generation prior to 1950. Furthermore, consider the fact that one out of every six Americans changes residences annually.[9] Multi-generational homes, once the norm, are now the exception; cities have become the chosen locus for living instead of rural environments (many factors play into this migration). Odds are that many cannot actually provide care to their dying loved ones even when they would like to due to prohibitive geographic distances. On average, American families simply do not live as close to one another as they once did.

Each of these changes in our collective attitudes toward death has contributed to a 'cultural lag' in terms of our willingness and overall capacity to address directly issues of death and dying (including grief). For many in the US, death has become a 'medical failure' rather than a 'natural event.' While science tries to 'tame death' on the one hand, death continues to become increasingly more 'invisible' on the other.[10] The sum of these attitudes has contributed to a special form of death denial: a state in which death is not discussed, confronted, or directly experienced with an active and open orientation by most in society. Instead, most take an increasingly passive role in caring for the dying, and this trend further pushes dying into institutional settings (and more out of mainstream view). Augmenting 'American individualism' and a privileging of patient autonomy within our health care systems, our increasingly passive role in providing care to the dying leaves, for many, few opportunities to reflect on and consider carefully one's own mortality.

3.   The Rise of Death Anxiety
An unintended cost of this growing passivity in caregiving for and decreased exposure to the dying has been an increase in Americans' death anxiety (i.e. fear of death).[11] Certainly, the events of September 11th 2001 exacerbated such fears. Interesting research has emerged that studies the relationship between 'terror' and death anxiety. A burgeoning field within psychology addresses squarely the consequences of death anxiety, and hundreds of recently-conducted empirical research studies support many of its core tenants. Known as Terror Management Theory (TMT), the common thesis in these studies suggests that when people are confronted with or reminded about death, the test subjects tend to demonstrate aggressive behaviour towards those perceived as different and positively towards those perceived as similar. Test subjects also tend to exhibit both intolerant and aggressive behaviour towards those perceived to support immortality ideologies different from the test subject's own. One implication from this research posits that increases in our individual and collective death anxieties often render us more inclined to exhibit intolerant beliefs, attitudes, and actions towards those perceived or labelled as 'different.'[12] TMT researchers commonly cite such intolerance as advancing in four stages: accommodation, dismissal, assimilation, and if these fail, annihilation.

TMT also asserts that people have a deep need to sustain faith in a meaningful worldview.[13] A 'meaningful worldview' can be described as a need to feel valued, protected, and ultimately, significant. Psychologists generally might call this self esteem, but in this case the taproots extend deeper. These meaningful constructs function securely when they are met and unthreatened. When they are threatened, anxiety arises and the push to defend them occurs. Building from TMT, the 'mortality salience hypothesis' argues that if culture really does provide a death-denying capacity, then alerting people (or reminding them) about their impending mortality should induce a greater need for these death-denying constructs of their belief systems, and this need should be evidenced in their actions.[14]

Considered through the lens of these research findings, the attacks of September 11th 2001 serve as a compelling real life example of these impulses to act aggressively towards others labelled as 'different.'[15] The aftermath of the attacks in the media clearly posed the attacks as a clash of American (i.e., 'Christian') and Middle Eastern (i.e., 'Muslim') worldviews. At first, after the initial shock of the attacks, many felt strong feelings of anxiety and anger. Clearly, these events served as powerful reminders to all Americans of their mortality. Returning to the death questionnaire discussed in the first section, the student responses to the six questions I provided support the notion that feelings of grief continue to emerge, often from depths below the surface of conscious awareness. Furthermore, this is precisely the scenario in which TMT research claims the most potentially hazardous kinds of 'labelling of difference' occur (i.e., when personal anxieties about death and the grief that accompanies loss go unacknowledged and unexplored).

4.   The Presence of Death in Language and Multi-Cultural Societies
People that have first-hand experiences with others who have died know a different portrayal of death. Many people retain memories of their loved one's death rattles, or gurgling and gasping sounds as they enter the final stages of breathing. As people die, their pallor also changes from flesh tones to shades of blue. The skin of someone dying turns from warm and flexible to cold and flaccid. People often remark after experiencing the death of a friend or loved one, 'I was not prepared to deal with this; dying is nothing like I thought it would be.' Almost always, the 'real death' of someone you know feels very different from its mere portrayal on television or the news media amidst a host of competing stories.

One of the first questions asked by the bereaved is 'why did they die?' A question such as this, on a certain level, suggests that death occurs as the consequence of an unnatural act. Death as portrayed in media and on television usually gets depicted as resulting from the hands of another person, or some outside force. These depictions reinforce the idea that dying occurs as something that happens to us, instead of something we all do at some point. Whether death gets portrayed as an accident or the result of a violent act, it rarely gets portrayed in the media as natural process.

Another consequence of portraying death unrealistically lies in desensitising viewers to real violence and its victims. In addition, such depictions can create unwarranted anxiety about becoming a victim, as well as contribute to increased violent behaviour. Ironically, cinematic and television depictions of crime and violence usually neglect to cover the real and ongoing damage done to victims (i.e., exploring their suffering, confusion, and bereavement), nor do such depictions usually wrestle with appropriate punishment for perpetrators. Unrealistic portrayals of death can contribute unwittingly to a 'mean world' syndrome through which 'the symbolic use of death contributes to an irrational dread of dying and thus to diminished vitality and self-direction in life.'

The presentation of a 'mean world' results from not just sensationalised stories, but largely as a result of news media and other alleged 'fact-based' programming. 'Blue-collar' crimes like homicide and armed robbery provide more scintillating newscasts (think Quarterback Michael Vick and allegations of dog fighting) than discussing 'white-collar' crimes like insider trading and embezzlement (think of the collective energy level generated by discussing Enron at a dinner party). The overall sense often communicated is that most crime is of the former type, and that the criminal population in this country mostly reflects people committing these types of violent crimes. Not surprisingly, many viewers begin to see the television 'world' as the real world. As first hand experiences with dying and death continue to diminish in the modern age, such representations of dying and death by the media heighten the sensationalism of such events, and provide an image of death that people perceive as reality. These misrepresentations and sensationalised depictions of death conceal more accurate language about the realities of death.

Exploring a mature concept of death requires reflection on earlier experiences with death had by our ancestors and imagining our future in light of the life-extending technology currently possessed, we can identify prevailing attitudes toward death, the evaluation of which may lead to developmental shifts in attitudes more suited to the way people die today. Our attitudes concerning dying and death reveal themselves in the words people employ to address death, the humour they use to cope with death, and the myriad ways death and dying are portrayed by media outlets, as well as in visual arts, literature, and music. Even though people may experience death less directly and take a more passive role in the caretaking of dying individuals, death retains a vital role in our social fabric.

Many have suggested that in societies that treat every person as a unique, vital and irreplaceable part of society, death, in general, is marked by a community-wide outpouring of grief for what is a genuine social loss. In societies that treat people as expendable, replaceable, and competitors for limited resources, little damage is (perceived) done to the social fabric by the loss of an individual, outside perhaps that felt by direct friends and family of the deceased.

Depending on one's background, developing a mature understanding of dying and death depends on the larger development process of socialisation. Socialisation interrelates life long learning and the ongoing synthesising of values, rules, and norms of a particular society. Through the process of socialisation, young people in society learn certain behaviours, ideals, and knowledge from older adults (and vice versa to a degree). Socialisation, however, does not cease at any given point in one's childhood; rather, it continues throughout one's lifespan, as people experience new relationships, new values, and new social roles. Socialisation does not mean simply 'assimilation,' a process of conforming to a set of monolithic, accepted standards of conduct in order to 'fit' into a given society. Instead, socialisation involves a dynamic process whereby a society's values and norms become re-thought and modified as new members take on social roles and obligations.

Institutions and other communities and social systems provide a particular society with its own flavour, helping to make it different from other societies. Distinctiveness within society can be defined as culture, or the characteristic features of ordinary life shared in common by people in a particular time and place. A particular culture can share similar ways of acting, feeling, or thinking. Considering this definition of society in light of death, ponder this perspective:

> Like nearly every other aspect of our lives, our understandings and feelings about dying and death are derived form our involvement in the myriad of groups, organizations, and institutions that represent our communities and, ultimately, constitute our society. As these religious, economic, legal, and familial structures change over time, we also change. This is because, as social beings, all of the meanings we attach to personal and cultural concerns - including dying and death - are inexorably tied to our social worlds.... . If you were born a century earlier, would you feel the same way? Is the difference due to individual or social factors?

Often, people learn about death and dying on an 'ad hoc' basis; that is, in an unstructured, often chaotic, unexpected, or impromptu manner. Most people in the US do not learn about death in seminars or courses. Since death education for most people involves happenstance more than systematic instruction, locating the starting point of our ideas about death remains difficult for most. The differences in how individuals learn about death, and come to talk about and acknowledge death depend largely on their more particular social groups. Death in multicultural societies, such as those found in the US, demonstrates well how different groups possess particular lifestyles and customs related to death. Obviously, the US contains much cultural diversity. Social groups with distinctive lifestyles and identities within the larger society exist as subcultures. Subcultures can share a certain ethnic heritage, or subcultures can be said to occupy unique places in history due to the 'spirit of the times,' etc. Subcultures can share a distinctive accent and their own slang. Differences between subcultures can occasionally produce violence or tension within societies, although the existence of a 'cultural mosaic,' or ethnic and cultural diversity within society, allows for a wider range of meaning-making and experience for society's overall membership. Subcultures often sway mainstream culture through fashion, music, and forms of advertising.

Jessica Mittford's 'The American Way of Death' provides an exposé of the funeral industry circa 1963 in the US, as she fearlessly reveals ways in which funeral homes scandalised the bereaved through unnecessary procedures and price-gouging. However, the title of her book conceals an important truth that, in fact, there exist many 'ways of death' in the US. Many American subcultures maintain distinct attitudes and beliefs about death that reveal themselves in their respective customs and behaviours. Like any generalisation, the title of Mittford's work glosses over the tremendous diversity that exists among people 'artificially' grouped with one another. One might ask, is death interpreted, acknowledged, or even spoken about in the same ways by most Americans? Or does there exist a wide range of practices surrounding death, practices that correspond to particular subcultures within the larger American society?

The extent to which individuals self-identify within subcultures, and maintain distinctive attitudes and customs varies widely, among both ethnic groups and those who share a common heritage. Yet, cultural factors such as ethnicity often influence ways individuals within a subculture cope with life-threatening illness, perceive pain, give social support to those dying, express grief, experience mourning, and arrange funeral services. A study comparing bereavement and mourning rituals within particular ethnic and other social groups in the US reaffirmed that, 'while adapting partly to Western patterns, these groups also adhere to the bereavement procedures of their own cultures.'

One part of the study focused on African American funerals and mourning customs. The study confirmed that traditional customs can endure even with the passage of time and change of physical circumstances. Ronald Barrett observes that many elements of traditional West African practices remain important observances around death for many African Americans. Evidence of this can be found in customs like congregating around the gravesite to offer godspeed to the deceased, and calling funerals 'home-going' that pay tribute to the deceased's spirit. David Roediger argues that these customs emerged 'from deep African roots, gained a paradoxical strength and resilience from the horrors of mid-passage, and flowered in the slave funeral - a value laden and unifying social event which the slave community in the United States was able to preserve from both physical and ideological onslaughts of the master class.'

Another example, recuerdo, meaning 'remembrance,' continues on in Spanish-speaking communities in New Mexico. Recuerdo involves a traditional rite of paying tribute to the deceased and providing consolation to those grieving. Offered as a written story or ballad, recuerdo recounts the deceased's life in an epic and heroic way. This tribute to one's final departure, known as la despedida (meaning 'leave-taking'), memorialises the transitory dimension of existence, and affirms the idea that life is bestowed almost like a loan from God. The moral of this epic tribute? We should be thankful for the time we receive. A fascinating aspect of the recuerdo lies in the acknowledgement that life possesses meaning precisely because there is not a limitless supply of it - death comes to all living creatures, which makes our time here richer.

Diverse attitudes and customs surrounding death can contribute greatly to society at large by providing a wealth of different, specially nuanced cultural resources that assist people in their efforts to cope with death. Such diversity can also present challenges to society struggling to adapt to the demands of plurality. For some, participating in culturally sanctioned customs and beliefs surrounding death may feel inappropriate, or inauthentic. Some have argued that cultural diversity in acknowledging death may disrupt or conflict with other practices believed to be 'healthy.' For example, some cultural communities refuse to speak of death, for fear such talk with actually cause the death to occur. Some, although not most, discuss death with friends and family in order to ensure end-of-life wishes are honoured and to assist in the grieving process by allowing feelings an outlet to be shared. Uncertainty regarding which social norms to honour when confronting death can be a very complex situation. Contemporary funerals in the US demonstrate a varied struggle for how people attempt to deal with death.

Socialisation involves process. The process remains continual and thoroughly complex. A person's understanding of death evolves over the course of one's life. By experiencing death and loss, a person likely will modify previous beliefs to accommodate the realities of the new experience. The old understandings of death transform into more current understandings, ones that provide meaning to our ongoing lives. What counts as a 'mature' concept of death depends on one's society. Early ideas of death acquired as a child provide the foundation for understandings of death in adulthood. Furthermore, death and dying cannot be confined to tidy, prescriptive concepts. Socialisation with other subcultures may very well lead to an understanding of death significantly more 'fuzzy' and complex: concepts may evolve that acknowledge death's reality on one hand, and still allow for a variety of interpretations about its meaning on the other. Ideally, the binary thinking embedded in the 'either/or' logic children use to understand certain core components about death acts as a revisable precursor to the greater theoretical sophistication necessary to see a plurality of meanings for death later in life.

By increasing our own cultural radar to include cultural lenses other than our own, we can broaden our perspective and expand the range of choices and meaning-making capacities in our encounters with death. David Plath remarks:

> We are born alone and we die alone, each an organism genetically unique. But we mature or decline together. In the company of others we mutually domesticate the wild genetic pulse as we go about shaping ourselves into persons after the vision of our group's heritage. Perhaps the growth and aging of an organism can be described well enough in terms of stages and transitions within the individual as a monad entity. But in a social animal the life courses have to be described in terms of a collective fabricating of selves, a mutual building of biographies.[16]

Examining earnestly the customs, rituals, and ideas of another culture provides an antidote to ethnocentrism. Ethnocentrism includes the fallacy of judging others exclusively in terms of one's own cultural assumptions and biases. To counter and overcome ethnocentrism demands one become aware of how one is prone to use one's own cultural criteria as a benchmark standard to judge the values of other communities. By viewing ourselves as beings of culture, we can better grasp others as beings of culture. All of us receive early and ongoing socialisation. Part of being alive includes this continual process; no one is exempt from it. To become more mature and culturally competent, we must recognise the fallacy of stereotyping others. In truth, there often exist more differences within a cultural group than between cultural groups. The very essence of death education lies in the ability to see others as they see themselves, and share in some meaningful way their customs as well as their perceptions.

5.   Creating Grief Archives

In an attempt to reach these more subterranean death anxieties, and their corresponding grief responses, I began work on a collection of in-class assignments designed to explore in a personal way various aspects of dying. I initially wrote and refined one reflection for each class (so a total of 32). I coordinated each reflection with the topic of the unit we covered in class for that day. At the start of each class, I provide the reflection exercise to each member of the class and they then complete the exercise (time extensions are happily granted for students who want to think more deeply outside of class about a particular subject). After the class completes a reflection, I almost always notice a palpable change in the mood of the room. As we reflect individually on our fears, anxieties, and wishes for end of life care, and especially as we make contact with our grief, I sense a gradual 'opening up' in the overall orientation of the class to the topics of death and dying. These exercises create a special sense of reverence which often produces genuine, honest moments of discussion, ones that encourage compassionate responses to the experiences of their fellow students, and those of the authors we study. Students do not read each others work. They are free to share anything (or nothing) about their own experiences. I do read the reflections after class and return them at the start of the next class. I treat each reflection in each student's burgeoning 'grief archive' as I would a diary entry. I do not pressure students to complete them in any particular way; however, I do ask that they complete each reflection in a way that accords genuinely with their experiences. Here is a sample list of names from the 32 reflections I developed:

My Earliest Memories of Loss
My Losses: An Inventory
My Feelings Concerning Death
My Philosophy Concerning Death
Coping with a Life-Threatening Illness
My Fears About Death
My Values: A Worksheet
When the End is Near
Reflections on the Virginia Tech Shootings
Reflections on September 11th, 2001
My Ethical Will
My Funeral
My Wishes for Organ Donation

The very last reflection exercise we do is an advance directive. I feel that it is most appropriate to enter the terrain of advance planning only after each of us has meditated on these other areas first (I personally do each exercise anew along with the students each term). Once we complete the advance directive, I have the students create some type of 'vessel' in which to house their individual grief archive reflections. Commonly, students will design a folder with the names (and sometimes images) of those who have died in their life. Others have created more elaborate ways to preserve their archives. The goal with these exercises is for the students to investigate their narratives and to explore affectively, intellectually, physically, and spiritually their losses, and to make contact with certain aspects of grief that accompany each case.

6.   Conclusions

I review each archive at the end of the term. I then return them for the student to keep. Every archive, like every death, tells a unique story. I believe that sharing these stories can provide emotional relief and promote a search for meaning, both individually and collectively. TMT research posits that intolerant reactions in the face of death anxiety and grief are likely to emerge if such experiences and feelings go unacknowledged. Seen then in their best light, grief archives function as a means to bring people together in mutual support during a time of loss. Although I never force students to speak about their experiences of grief and loss, many do (and cite specific questions in a particular reflection as the launching point for their comment). In this way, grief archives can assist individuals and communities to revise, reform, and continue relationships with the deceased over time. As opposed to more Freudian notions of 'attachment theory' or 'grief-work models' that attempt to help a client break bonds with the deceased and re-invest them in something or someone else, my approach using these archives is more narrative-based. My work in using grief archives has, in my experience, demonstrated that bonds sustained through memories and linking objects can serve as valued 'threads of connectedness' to those deceased whose deaths are grieved and remembered. When we make contact with our own grief responses, we often are better active listeners to another's story of grief.

These grief archives also can reveal complex (and sometimes problematic) lineages through which individuals preserve, (re-)orient and (re-) frame their own histories/identities within the context of a larger societal matrix. Said differently, many students begin to notice half-way through the term the many ways in which their respective views about death have been shaped by agents of socialisation such as peers, family, religion, political ideology, and sometimes even the socio-economic circumstances in which grew up. Questions of ethno-cultural identity surface throughout the course, too, in relation to the construction of these archives. In the context of a course on religious studies and philosophical theology, these are precisely the topics I want to raise and address together with my students. Death, and our complex reactions to it, has the capacity to link all of these existential concerns together in powerfully significant ways. Grief archives not only provide a mechanism to initiate such meaning-making, but they also serve as an important lens through which to consider larger, more public tragedies such as the events of September 11th, 2001, and all those labelled 'public' or 'national.' Grief archives reveal the variety of reactions we have to death, and allow us to cultivate vital sensitivities to *differences*, broadly conceived, as well as refine our lenses of critique with regard to how certain memorials archive collective losses.

Notes

[1] See S. Solomon, J. Greenberg, T. Pyszczynski, 'A Terror Management Theory of Social Behavior: The Psychological Functions of Self-Esteem and Cultural Worldviews', *Advances in Experimental Social Psychology*, Vol. 24 Academic Press, San Diego, 1991, pp. 91-159.

[2] C. Shilling, 'Modernity, Self-Identity and the Sequestration of Death', *Sociology: The Journal of the British Sociological Association*, Vol. 27, No. 3, 1993, pp. 411-431.

[3] In an effort to avoid extremes, we must both accept and deny death. Talcott Parsons expressed the American attitude towards death well when he wrote, '[rather than deny death] modern societies bring to bear every possible resource to prolong active and healthful life, and come to accept death only when it is inevitable.' Cf. T. Parsons, 'Death in American Society: A Brief Working Paper', *American Behavioral Scientist 6*, No. 9, 1963, pp. 61-65.

[4] 'Deaths and Death Rates', *Historical Statistics of the United States, 2006*, p. 74.

[5] R. N. Anderson, 'Leading Causes for 2000', *National Vital Statistics Reports 50*, No.16, 2002, p. 8. Also, see 'Resident Population by Age', *Statistical Abstract of the United States: 1999*, p. 869; and 'Death and Death Rates by Leading Causes of Death and Age: 2000', *Statistical Abstract of the United States*, 2002, p. 82.

[6] J. J. Farrell, *Inventing the American Way of Death, 1830-1920*, Temple University Press, Philadelphia, 1980.

[7] T. E. Quill, 'Initiating End-of-Life Discussions with Seriously Ill Patients: Addressing the "Elephant in the Room"', *JAMA*, 2000, 284, pp. 2502-2507; and T. E. Quill, *Caring for Patients at the End of Life: Facing an Uncertain Future Together*, Oxford University Press, New York, 2001; Also see M. J. Silveira, A. DiPiero, M. S. Gerrity, C. Feudtner, 'Patients' Knowledge of Options at the End of Life: Ignorance in the Face of Death', *JAMA*, 284, 2000, pp. 2483-2488. Also see J. Lynn, 'Learning to Care for People with Chronic Illness Facing the End-of-Life', *JAMA*, 284, 2000, pp. 2508-2511.

[8] US Census Bureau, 'Expectation of Life at Birth', *Historical Statistics of the United States, Colonial Times to 1970*, Government Printing Office, 55, Washington, DC, 2006; and *Statistical Abstract of the United States: 2006*, 126th Edition, Government Printing Office, Washington, DC, 2006.

[9] Cf. 'Mobility Status of the Population', *Statistical Abstract of the United States*, 2006, p. 29.

[10] D. Callahan, 'Frustrated Mastery: the Cultural Context of Death in America - Caring for Patients at the End of Life', *Western Journal of Medicine 163*, No. 3, 1995, pp. 226-230.

[11] Cf. E. Becker, *Denial of Death*, Free Press, New York, 1973, pp. 1-75.

[12] See 'An Interview with Dr Sheldon Solomon and Dr Tom Pyszczynski: Symbols: Jumping the Spatio-Temporal Gap to Make the Unreal Real'. *ESI Special Topics*, 2005. The Interview transcript can be found here: <http://esi-topics.com/terrorism/interviews/SheldonSolomon.html>.

[13] Solomon, Greenberg, Pyszczynski, op. cit., pp. 91-159.

[14] J. Greenberg, S. Solomon, T. Pyszczynski, 'Fear of Death and Human Destructiveness', *The Psychoanalytic Review*, Vol. 90, Issue 4, 2003, pp. 457-474.

[15] J. Greenberg, T. Pyszczynski, S. Solomon, 'In the Wake of 9/11: The Psychology of Terror', *American Journal of Psychiatry*, Vol. 160, No. 5, 2003, pp. 1019-1023.

[16] D. W. Plath, 'Resistance at Forty-Eight: Old-Age Brinksmanship and Japanese Life Course Pathways', in *Aging and Life Course Transitions: An Interdisciplinary Perspective*, T. K. Hareven and K. J. Adams (eds), New York: Guildford Press, 1982, pp. 109-125.

Bibliography

Anderson, R. N., 'Leading Causes for 2000'. *National Vital Statistics Reports 50*, No.16. Hyattsville, MD: National Center for Health Statistics, 2002.

'An Interview with Dr Sheldon Solomon and Dr Tom Pyszczynski: Symbols: Jumping the Spatio-Temporal Gap to Make the Unreal Real'. *ESI Special Topics*, 2005,
<http://esi-topics.com/terrorism/interviews/SheldonSolomon.html>.

Becker, E., *Denial of Death*. Free Press, New York, 1973, pp. 1-75.

Callahan, D., 'Frustrated Mastery: the Cultural Context of Death in America - Caring for Patients at the End of Life'. *Western Journal of Medicine 163*, No. 3, 1995, pp. 226-230.

'Deaths and Death Rates'. *Historical Statistics of the United States*, 2006.

'Death and Death Rates by Leading Causes of Death and Age: 2000'. *Statistical Abstract of the United States*, 2002.

Farrell, J. J., *Inventing the American Way of Death, 1830-1920*. Temple University Press, Philadelphia, 1980.

Greenberg, J., Solomon, S., Pyszczynski, T., 'A Terror Management Theory of Social Behavior: The Psychological Functions of Self-Esteem and Cultural Worldviews', in *Advances in Experimental Social Psychology*. M. P. Zanna (ed), Vol. 24, San Diego, Academic Press, 1991, pp. 91-159.

——, 'Fear of Death and Human Destructivenessø'. *The Psychoanalytic Review*, Vol. 90, Issue 4, 2003, pp. 457-474.

——, 'In the Wake of 9/11: The Psychology of Terror'. *American Journal of Psychiatry*, Vol. 160, No. 5, 2003, pp. 1019-1023.

Lynn, J., 'Learning to Care for People with Chronic Illness Facing the End-of-Life'. *JAMA*, 284, 2000, pp. 2508-2511.

'Mobility Status of the Population'. *Statistical Abstract of the United States: 2006*, p. 29.

Parsons, T., 'Death in American Society: A Brief Working Paper'. *American Behavioral Scientist 6*, No. 9, 1963, pp. 61-65.

Plath, D. W., 'Resistance at Forty-Eight: Old-Age Brinksmanship and Japanese Life Course Pathways', in *Aging and Life Course Transitions: An Interdisciplinary Perspective*. T. K. Hareven and K. J. Adams (eds), New York: Guildford Press, 1982, pp. 109-125.

Quill, T. E., 'Initiating End-of-Life Discussions with Seriously Ill Patients: Addressing the "Elephant in the Room"'. *JAMA*, 284, 2000, pp. 2502-2507.

——, *Caring for Patients at the End of Life: Facing an Uncertain Future Together*. Oxford University Press, New York, 2001

'Resident Population by Age'. *Statistical Abstract of the United States*, 1999, p. 869.

Shilling, C., 'Modernity, Self-Identity and the Sequestration of Death'. *Sociology: The Journal of the British Sociological Association*, Vol. 27, No. 3, 1993, pp. 411-431.

Silveira, M. J., DiPiero, A., Gerrity, M. S., Feudtner, C., 'Patients' Knowledge of Options at the End of Life: Ignorance in the Face of Death'. *JAMA*, 284, 2000, pp. 2483-2488.

Solomon, S., Greenberg, J., Pyszczynski, T., 'A Terror Management Theory of Social Behavior: The Psychological Functions of Self-Esteem and Cultural Worldviews'. *Advances in Experimental Social Psychology*, Vol. 24 Academic Press, San Diego, 1991, pp. 91-159.

Statistical Abstract of the United States. 126th Edition, Washington, DC, Government Printing Office, 2006.

US Census Bureau, 'Expectation of Life at Birth'. *Historical Statistics of the United States, Colonial Times to 1970*, Washington, DC, Government Printing Office, p. 55.

Nate Hinerman is on the faculty at the University of San Francisco where he teaches courses in death and dying as well as religious studies. He serves as Chair of the San Francisco Bay Area End of Life Network. He is also a psychotherapist specialising in grief and loss, as well as a hospice volunteer.